Books are by People

Interviews with 104 Authors and
Illustrators of Books for Young Children

Lee Bennett Hopkins

Curriculum and Editorial Specialist
Scholastic Magazines, Inc.

Citation Press, New York • 1969

For reprint permission, grateful acknowledgment is made to: Norma Millay Ellis for "RENASCENCE" from *Collected Poems*, Harper & Row. Copyright 1912, 1940 by Edna St. Vincent Millay.

Photograph credits: Ann Oakes Studio, p. 1; Hilda Bijur, p. 17; Galen Williams, p. 37; Weston Woods, p. 41, 164; Charles Daugherty, p. 44; Paul Ferencz Galdone, p. 84; Ralph Paterline, p. 88; Nancy Levering, p. 94; Jerome Weidman, p. 121; Gertrude K. Lathrop, p. 125; J. L. Nodset, p. 144; Ray Huff Studios, p. 152; Harvard Alumni Bureau, p. 169; Peter Basch, p. 173; Hope Wurmfeld, p. 176; David Gahr, p. 226; Houghton Mifflin, p. 230; Bob Brooks, p. 250; Bernice Abbott, p. 259; Leon Kotofsky, p. 263; Henry W. Leichtner, p. 283; John Hemansander, p. 286; Self-portrait, p. 289; Baur Photographers, p. 303; Robert P. Brown, Jr., p. 316; Grace Rothstein, p. 326.

LIBRARY OF CONGRESS CATALOG CARD NUMBER: 70-96312

Designed by June Martin

Printed in the U.S.A.

Second printing, December 1972

To all of you
— from Adrienne to Charlotte —
who have made children's lives so much richer
and —
To Donna Lea, my sister, with all my love

Acknowledgments

I WOULD LIKE TO thank the following people for the generous assistance they gave me in the preparation of this volume:

Jean Karl, Atheneum House; Vicki Brooks; Marjorie Naughton, Thomas Y. Crowell; Sophie Silberberg, Thomas Y. Crowell; Diane Lewis Majer, Dial Press; Elsa Glauber; Mary Holdsworth; Joan Robins, Harper and Row; Ann Greenaway, Houghton Mifflin; Virginie Fowler, Alfred A. Knopf, Inc.; Gloria Morrow, J. B. Lippincott; Marjorie W. Rines, Little-Brown; Sally Grady, Lothrop, Lee and Shepard; Susan Sauerteig; Ellen Davidson, William Morrow; Walter Retan, Random House, Inc.; Kathleen Speer; Claudia Cohl, Franklin Watts, Inc.; Alexandra C. Whitney, Henry Z. Walck, Inc.

Special thanks also to Janet Schulman, Macmillan, and Arthur Bell, Random House, for their many extra efforts; to Mary L. Allison, my excellent editor who shared the many ups and downs in my writing of this volume; to Misha Arenstein for his constant encouragement and for his time-consuming and patient editorial assistance. — L. B. H.

Contents

Preface

EVERY TEACHER AND LIBRARIAN will thank Lee Bennett Hopkins for writing this book. Time after time teachers have asked me, "Where can we find out about the authors and illustrators of children's books?" "How can we make them come alive for boys and girls?" I have known conscientious teachers who have read all the Newbery and Caldecott acceptance speeches and many articles in various publications in order to make a card file of interesting anecdotes about authors to share with their students. Now Mr. Hopkins has provided within the covers of one book fresh human interest materials on some 104 authors and illustrators of books for young children.

This then is a book that we have long needed. It is also the book that I secretly wish I could have written. Imagine what fun it must have been to interview these wonderful people, to see where they live, learn how they work, and discover what they value most about their role in making books for boys and girls!

In these perceptively written interviews, Mr. Hopkins doesn't tell you about these persons, as much as he lets them reveal themselves. His selection of anecdotes shows much insight into what will intrigue young children. They will be delighted, for example, to learn that Don Freeman might have remained a trumpet player except that he lost his trumpet on the subway; that Feodor Rojankovsky had never heard Mother Goose rhymes until he was asked to illustrate them, that Else Minarik wrote the Little Bear stories for her own first-graders, and that the d'Aulaires pitched their tent along the trails that Abraham Lincoln walked while they were writing and illustrating his biography. These are just a few of the interesting stories that will convince children that books are indeed written by people.

Our sincere thanks to you, Lee Bennett Hopkins, for making these many authors and illustrators come alive through your vital and personal interviews. As we introduce them to our students, let us hope that we can reflect your contagious enthusiasm for books and the wonderful people who create them.

CHARLOTTE S. HUCK, Professor
Elementary Education, Ohio State University
Co-author, *Children's Literature in the Elementary School*

Reflections

ONCE UPON A SHORT time ago, a third-grader asked me, "Mr. Hopkins, are authors people?" I couldn't help but think what a provocative question this was, for many times I, myself, have wondered about the people who create books for young children. Who are they? What are they like? How do they live? How do they work? Why have they chosen to devote much, or all, of their adult lives to devising books for boys and girls? After a solid year of totally immersing myself in children's books and the people who write and illustrate them, I now have some of the answers.

Since the field of children's literature is a vast one, I had to consider many factors in deciding whom to include in this volume. I limited the scope to authors and illustrators who have produced books for the young child, from pre-kindergarten through grade three. To give a rounded picture, I included people who created books for children when children's book publishing was still in its beginning stages, promising newcomers to the field, people who have won awards, people who have written fiction, non-fiction, and poetry. Of course, in a single reference volume such as this, one could not possibly include all the people who are involved in making books for boys and girls. I have selected 104 living authors and illustrators; there are at least 104 more who deserve attention, perhaps in a future volume. I hope that after reading this book librarians, teachers, and parents will acquaint children with many of the interesting facts I have discovered about book people.

Yes, authors *are* people! Among the authors and illustrators I interviewed and corresponded with, I found young people, old people, short people, tall people, fat people, thin people, bald people, hairy people, married people, single people, black people, white people, brown people, yellow people. I found that in books for children there are no color barriers, no geographic barriers. Some book people come from the United States — their homes stretch across the continent from New York to California — some come from the Caribbean, some from all parts of Europe, some come from Asia, and others from Africa. All draw upon their wealth of experiences and talent with carefully chosen words and/or an abundance of pictures.

"Are all authors dead?" one second-grade girl asked me. I found out that they are very much alive and very much involved in all aspects of life — from politics and civil rights struggles, to the theatre, advertising, the war in Viet Nam, gardening, sailing, cooking, and camping! In fact, many remain alive even after they pass away. It is impossible to think of such greats as Dorothy Aldis, Ludwig Bemelmans, Margaret Wise Brown, Virginia Lee Burton, Robert Lawson, or Miska Petersham as being dead. And since youngsters do not think about death in the same way adults do, the following anecdote is easy to believe:

> One fall morning in a Connecticut library, a five-year-old youngster told the librarian he was going to write a letter "to the lady who wrote about the house that kept moving." The child was referring to Virginia Lee Burton's Caldecott Award winner, *The Little House* (Houghton, 1942). With some trepidation and hesitation, the librarian told the boy that the lady who wrote the book had died recently. "That's O.K.," he replied. "I'll mail the letter to God. He'll know where to get in touch with her!"

One morning a child asked me, "Do authors live in regular houses or publishing houses?" Well, I have been in all kinds of houses and found that authors live in huge houses, teeny houses, one-room studios, five-room duplexes, cellar apartments where one has to walk down to enter, walk-ups where one has to climb up and up and up to enter, brownstones, houses near the shore, ranches in Maine and Colorado, country houses, city houses, handmade houses, and even observation towers. But none of the people I met lived in a publishing house.

"Hey, Mr. Hopkins, do authors eat?" I was asked. To prove they do, I sipped sherry and ate fruitcake with Berta and Elmer Hader, shared pizza with Brinton Turkle, had hot tea and toast with Maurice Sendak, hamburgers with Marie Hall Ets, tomato soup with Ezra Jack Keats, corn pudding and fresh ham with Adrienne Adams and Lonzo Anderson, and consumed a host of other meals served by the gracious people I met. Perhaps the most curious delicacy was the nest of quails' eggs Else Holmelund Minarik sent me at Christmas time; they were pied and hard-boiled as could be!

"Can people who make books make any kids?" asked a fourth-grade boy. They certainly can! They have kids and kids of all kinds — newborn babies, newly adopted babies, young children, teenagers, hippies and yippies, pixies and protesters, professionals and tradesmen, very grown-up children, many grandchildren.

I found out a great deal about children's book people and had such a great time doing so that I want to share many of the fascinating facts about these authors and illustrators — some never before revealed. I have had a wonderful year sharing the information within these pages with children of every age level — from kindergarten classes I visited to college campuses — and with teachers, librarians, and parent groups. If nothing else, I've learned that books *are* by people. They are! They really are! And I want you to meet and know them too.

LEE BENNETT HOPKINS
January 1969

Adrienne Adams
(John) Lonzo Anderson

IT'S ABOUT A 65-mile drive from New York City to the forested area of New Jersey where Adrienne Adams and her husband-writer (John) Lonzo Anderson, live. As one drives along an old winding road to their house, he sees cows and horses grazing in pastures, dairy farms, cottages, and woodlands — all familiar sights to lovers of picturesque countrysides. When the Andersons "discovered" this area some 30 years ago, it was nothing but woodland. For several summers they camped in a tent while constructing a permanent home. Both Andersons worked with a two-handed saw, using some of the tall trees on their property for the raw materials, to build a comfortable log cabin. Today they live in a beautiful home that has developed from their efforts of earlier years.

Adrienne Adams was born in Fort Smith, Arkansas, and grew up in Okmulgee, Oklahoma. After her college years, she taught for a short time in Okmulgee and then left both the town and the profession for a career in New York City. There she became a fabric designer and served as an art director in a display house. Also in New York she met Mr. Anderson. She began illustrating books for children in her spare time and soon discovered that this was the work she enjoyed most.

She is an artist who has illustrated many types of books: several volumes of poetry by Aileen Fisher, a host of fairy tales by Hans Christian Andersen and the Brothers Grimm, the French carol *Bring a Torch, Jeanette Isabella* (Scribner, 1963), and informational books by Alice E. Goudey, two of which (*Houses from the Sea,* Scribner, 1959, and *The Day We Saw the Sun Come Up,* Scribner, 1961) were runners-up for the Caldecott Medal.

Miss Adams truly experiences each book. "I enjoy researching everything I can about a book," she told me. "I'm a designer at heart and begin at the bottom. When I begin a book, I do a thumbnail sketch, turn that into a miniature dummy about 4x5 inches in size, and then do a big dummy, each time revising and refining the artwork. When I illustrated *Butterfly Time* (Scribner, 1964) by Goudey, I had to make accurate color drawings of many varieties of butterflies. I found a copy of *National Geographic* that had illustrations of butterflies and was helpful. Then I bought some mounted ones and finally took to nature to watch live, fluttering examples. I did *The Ugly Duckling* (Scribner, 1965) after visiting Denmark. John went to Denmark to do research in the archives there for an adult novel he was planning, and *The Ugly Duckling* came about on a return trip from Europe. We took a Danish freighter from Copenhagen to Reykjavik by way of the Faeroes. Try it sometime! We went to the castle of Gisselfeld where Hans Christian Andersen was visiting when *he* wrote the story. The grounds were beautiful, with a large greenhouse filled with tropical plants and fruits. There were all kinds of ducks and swans on a system of lakes. The trip was an invaluable aid to me when I began re-creating the land of *The Ugly Duckling*."

It usually takes Miss Adams about three months to complete the illustrations for a book. "It takes me a long time to get started," she said, "and I need a deadline. I'd never do anything if I didn't have one. I simply procrastinate. The due date is a way of life for me. During the last three weeks of a book I work like a riveting machine filled with creative energy."

Only recently has Mr. Anderson written for children. He has authored *The Ponies of Mykillengi* (Scribner, 1966), a book that took the team to Iceland to actually see the ponies, and more recently *Two Hundred Rabbits* (Viking, 1968), a delightful retelling of an old French folktale. Both texts were illustrated by his wife. Although she enjoys working with her husband, Miss Adams remarked that she wouldn't want to collaborate on everything. In reply to this, he commented, "Dean (her nickname) loved the story of the rabbits, but while illustrating it, she rather plaintively wished it had fewer characters!"

"Two hundred rabbits *are* a lot of rabbits to draw," she laughed.

The Andersons own a cottage on St. Johns in the Virgin Islands where they spend their winters working and enjoying the comforts of the Caribbean climate. "To get around the

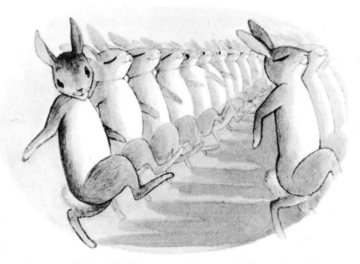

island we usually buy an old jeep when we get there and sell it when we leave," she stated. Stateside they use a Volkswagen camper to pick up and go — and they often do just that. If there's an interesting event occurring somewhere, a play they'd like to see, or whenever the whim occurs, they are off!

To end a perfect morning in the Hunterdon Hills, the Andersons served a scrumptious home-cooked lunch. While eating together, we discussed everything from Miss Adams's cooking to the dishes we ate from — they came from their travels to San Miguel de Allende in Mexico. "She loves to bake breads," Mr. Anderson exclaimed. "We get wheat grains from Texas. I grind the flour, and Dean does the rest!"

Together they work, they travel, they live, and together Adrienne Adams and (John) Lonzo Anderson are a charming, warm, and exuberant couple. Leaving them was like leaving old friends, and a standing invitation to return will one day soon be accepted!

OTHER BOOKS BY MISS ADAMS:

Aileen Fisher. *Going Barefoot* (T. Y. Crowell, 1960).
———. *In the Middle of the Night* (T. Y. Crowell, 1965).
Grimm. *Snow White and Rose Red* (Scribner, 1964).
———. *Jorinda and Joringel* (Scribner, 1968).

C. W. Anderson

THE FIRST THING one notices about Clarence William Anderson is his size! He is a walloping 6 feet 4 inches tall, weighs 220 pounds, has distinguished gray hair that was once very blond, and blue, blue eyes. Boys and girls may not know him by name, but they do know him as "the man who writes and draws Billy and Blaze books."

Mr. Anderson was born in Wahoo, Nebraska. He went to school there and later taught for two years to earn money to attend the Art Institute of Chicago. He always liked to draw, and his parents encouraged him. After art school he moved to New York where, early in his career, he developed an interest in horses. He drew horses for his own pleasure and soon became a specialist in this field. At about age 45, he produced his first pen-and-ink picture book, *Billy and Blaze* (Macmillan, 1936), at the suggestion of the art editor at Macmillan, publisher of all his books. This initiated a series of easy-to-read books, which include *Blaze and the Gypsies* (1937), and *Blaze and Thunderbolt* (1955). The series has become popular with young readers. Mr. Anderson receives about 500 letters a year from children about the Blaze books.

He confessed to me, "Both Billy and Blaze are imaginary, but they are slightly based on boys and ponies I have known." Be-

5

sides this series he has done other books for both young and older readers, including such studies of thoroughbred horses as

From BILLY AND BLAZE by C. W. Anderson, copyright 1936 by The Macmillan Co., renewed 1964 by C. W. Anderson. Permission of The Macmillan Co.

Deep Through the Heart (1940) and *A Touch of Greatness* (out of print). "*A Touch of Greatness* is my favorite book," he said, "for it gives my true feelings for horses."

Commenting on his work habits he remarked, "I usually make a rough dummy for my youngest picture books and try it out on children. On my older ones, I read the text to my wife (Madeline Paltenghi, a poet). From the evidence to date, her judgment has been one hundred per cent correct." He works in lithography; most of his books are made directly on the stone. "Outside of my horse activities I like to paint, not only horses but also landscapes and figures. Nature fascinates me. I have many sketchbooks full of careful drawings of wild flowers, grasses, mere weeds, and trees when their leaves are gone so you can see the twisting and rhythmic design of the branches."

Mr. Anderson's prints have been displayed in most of the important galleries and museums throughout the United States. He believes that landscape in a horse subject should contain both the character and the individuality of the place where the horses live.

The Andersons live in a country home in Mason, New Hampshire, a small village settled two hundred years ago. Mr. Anderson built a stone studio there out of native granite. "The area is full of abandoned wood roads over which my wife and I have ridden almost daily for 20 odd years. All the country settings for my books are drawn from this locale." The Andersons also maintain a studio apartment in Boston where they spend the winter months.

SOME OTHER BOOKS BY MR. ANDERSON (All Macmillan):

Blaze and the Indian Cave (1964).
Blaze and the Lost Quarry (1966).

Mr. Anderson died on March 26, 1971.

Pura Belpré (White)

In the 1920's a young, first-year university student left her home in Puerto Rico to come to the United States. "I came for the wedding of a sister," recalled Miss Belpré "and I never went back." Pura Belpré (*poo* rah *bell* pray), was one of five children born in Cidra, "the smallest town in Puerto Rico." Shortly after coming to New York, she enrolled in the New York Public Library School, where she studied for six months to become a trained librarian. The course included storytelling.

"I feel that I was *born* a storyteller," she remarked, "but I guess you always have to go through all these things, like studying and learning things you don't want to learn. One of our assignments in school was to read a story to the class. I wrote out one of my favorites, *Perez and Martina,* a Puerto Rican folktale handed down through generations by word of mouth and told to me by my grandmother." One of her fellow students who was doing free-lance work for Frederick Warne and Company told Mr. Warne about the tale. It wasn't too long before *Perez and Martina* came out in book form (1932) with colorful pictures by Carlos Sanchez, a young artist.

As part of the New York Public Library program, Miss Belpré conducted many, many story hours for children in nearly every nook and cranny of Manhattan. To enhance her story telling, she became interested in designing and making puppets. "I had never seen a puppet show until I was an adult," she commented. "I must have had a feeling for the art of puppetry even as a child, without knowing it. I remember taking long mangoes and using the silk from them for hair and putting on eyes with paint. When I first saw a puppet show I said to myself, 'Pura, this is it!'"

"I read every book I could get my hands on and made some puppets from clay. Señor Perez and Señorita Martina were originally made from clay, but they kept chipping. I had never heard of the thing called a kiln. But now, now I have graduated," she laughed. "I use papier mâché!" Miss Belpré showed me some of her exquisite puppets, which she keeps carefully wrapped in large plastic bags ready for their next performance. Their costumes are meticulously designed and sewn; one of the foxes she uses even has a real fox tail that she picked up in New York's garment center.

Increased exposure as a puppeteer-storyteller brought her greater recognition. Once when her work took her out of New York to read a paper at a national convention, she met Clarence Cameron White, a musician and composer, whom she later married. Mr. White died several years ago. Miss Belpré feels his loss greatly; she speaks fondly of her memories — his proposal in New York's Cloisters, their summers in the Berkshires, and their meetings with Aaron Copland, Jascha Heifetz, Langston Hughes, and Countee Cullen. Miss Belpré sighed as she relived her memories but added: "I had a beautiful, beautiful life."

One can tell instantly that she is a storyteller, for when she talks her hands move expressively, her dark eyes flash, and her brow rises and falls with her words. She is still actively involved in storytelling and puppetry and has a strong desire to acquaint all children with the cultural heritage of her native Puerto Rico through folk literature. She is, and has been, a tremendous asset to the many Spanish-speaking immigrants who arrive on the mainland, for she goes to them and tells them the stories of old, providing a link between their native country and their new home in America.

The pretty cockroach, Martina, and the gallant little mouse, Perez, will be around a long, long time; because of Pura Belpré's efforts they too have found a place in American folk culture.

SOME OTHER BOOKS BY MISS BELPRÉ:

Translator of Munro Leaf's *The Story of Ferdinand* (Viking, 1936): *El Cuento de Ferdinand* (Viking, 1962).
Adaptor. *Juan Bobo and the Queen's Necklace* (Warne, 1962).
Translator of Else Holmelund Minarik's *Little Bear* (Harper, 1957): *Osito* (Harper, 1969).
Oté (Pantheon, 1969).

Jeanne Bendick

KELLEMES KANYARÖT! was the first American children's book to be published in the Hungarian language. Its English title is *Have Happy Measles, Have Merry Mumps, and Have a Cheery Chickenpox* (McGraw-Hill, 1958). The book was written and illustrated by Jeanne Bendick, with the help of her two children, Karen (Candy) and Robert, Jr. This book is only one of more than one hundred titles she has created. Mrs. Bendick is especially known in the field of children's literature for her work in the area of science education. Prior to writing books of her own, she illustrated books relating to science and did free-lance artwork for the children's magazine, *Jack and Jill.* "I became interested in electronics one day," she said, "and could find absolutely nothing on it written in simple terms. Rather than complain about it, I decided to write a book and I did — *Electronics for Young People* (McGraw-Hill, 1945)." In 1955 this book went into its fourth revised edition.

Mrs. Bendick was not formally trained in science, though she does have an art background. She attended the New York City High School of Music and Art, Parsons School of Design, and the New York School of Fine and Applied Art. "A great many people in my family drew, and from my earliest memories I was writing stories and illustrating them. All I needed was a couple of minutes, a pencil, and nice, clean white paper. I always wanted to be an illustrator. I feel there is an advantage in *not* being trained in science. I can approach all of my work from a child's point of view. I love working with children for they have such wonderfully fresh ways of looking at things. I try out a lot of my work with boys and girls; they are a great help to me. Naturally I find drawing easier than writing, yet I have a good time writing. There are times when illustrating becomes frustrating to me."

Mrs. Bendick works primarily in black-and-white and two colors and describes her style as "relaxed representational." She generally uses pen or brush and ink for black-and-white, as in *A Fresh Look at Night* (Watts, 1963). "I like to design my own books. I pick the type, do the layout, and work with separations in doing my illustrations. I made up my mind as a child that pictures should be on the same pages where something is being explained." In 1959 she collaborated with her husband, Robert, on *Television Works Like This* (McGraw-Hill). "Bob is a free-lance television and film producer-director. He was one of the first TV cameramen in the country. This book stemmed from his interests." (Besides working in television, Mr. Bendick does a great deal of work on films. He was the co-producer of the first Cinerama film, *This Is Cinerama*.)

The Bendicks live in a modern house perched on one of Long Island Sound's picturesque inlets. It is located in the village of Rye, New York, and sits just below the eight-bedroom house in which their children grew up. The house is tastefully furnished and reflects the Bendicks' love of travel and nature. Artifacts are arranged everywhere. A garden in the living room contains varieties of potted plants that stand on a seashell collection; floor-to-ceiling windows provide a dramatic view of the Sound. For recreation Mrs. Bendick enjoys traveling. "Bob's work takes him all over," she commented, "and when I'm not meeting deadlines, I join him. We both like to sail. We have a sailboat and draft our friends to become crew members. I like to cook too. When I reach an impasse in my work, I go out to the kitchen and stir up something!"

As our interview ended, Jeanne Bendick said good-bye and returned to her drawing board. She had to continue work on her latest five books.

SOME OTHER BOOKS BY MRS. BENDICK:

All Around You (Whittlesey House, 1951).
First Book of Automobiles (Watts, 1955, 1966).
Archimedes and the Door of Science (Watts, 1962).
The First Book of Space Travel (Watts, 1963).
Shapes (Watts, 1968).
The Human Senses (Watts, 1968).
Why Can't I? (McGraw-Hill, 1969).

Claire Huchet Bishop

I HAVE USED *The Five Chinese Brothers* (Coward, 1938) time and time again with children on every grade level. Whether they are seven-year-olds or eleven-year-olds, who usually balk at picture books, it does to them what the Beatles do to teen-agers. Consequently, I was delighted when Claire Huchet Bishop related how the book came into being. "I never decided nor intended to do books for children. I opened the first French children's library in Paris many years ago. It was called *L'Heure Joyeuse* and was a gift to France from America. I told stories to the children there and I enjoyed it. I also told stories in the public gardens, which brought me front-page reviews and pictures in the leading French daily newspapers. My mother had inherited from her father the storytelling ability. My grandfather used to entertain the whole community of his Brittany island with legends, folktales, the great classic Celtic tales such as "The Holy Grail" and "Tristan and Isolde," and with poems. Without television or radio, the winter evenings were long, and a good storyteller was a boon. One of the stories I have always loved to tell is *The Five Chinese Brothers*."

After marrying the American pianist, Frank Bishop, she left her native France, came to the United States, and joined the staff of the New York Public Library.

"The New York Public Library asked me to tell *The Five Chinese Brothers* in English. I felt my way for adequate expressions. I knew the oral text was good because of the children's response. Then, in order not to forget the translation, I wrote it down for the first time, just for myself. My husband liked it so much he made me go to a publisher, something I had never dreamed of doing. And that was the beginning of it all." (At least for children. In France she had had adult poems published in a French avant-garde literary magazine.)

Mrs. Bishop lives in an apartment, with trees and gardens in the back, on Manhattan's East Side. She enjoys music and likes to practice her piano. She also likes to read, swim, and garden. Commenting on work habits she stated, "I am a morning writer, about five hours at a stretch, sometimes more, sometimes less. In the evening I do revising, never creative work. Ideas dawn suddenly; they do not refer to something happening at the time but go back to something that took place in the past and had been, so far, totally forgotten by me. It could be something seen, heard, or felt. Even one word, dropped into the subconscious, can eventually start a whole imaginative sequence. The past can be last year or years and years ago.

"I have tried some of my stories on children. It is not necessary to do this, however. When I write, I am both creator and listener. While I am writing a story, I have practically no social life whatsoever for months on end, except for making or hearing music. However, there are periods during the year when I am much in demand for lectures and storytelling, and that means traveling all over the United States. I give talks to adults and to young people. When it is far, I travel by plane; otherwise I prefer a train. A train always inspires me. Ideas come to me while I speed along."

Other books by Mrs. Bishop include such popular stories as *Pancakes-Paris* (Viking, 1947), a true story about a ten-year-old American boy who made pancakes for her, and *Twenty and Ten* (Viking, 1964), a book about Jewish children who were given refuge in a French Catholic orphanage. "Many of my stories take place in France and deal with present-day French boys and girls of the working class, with whom I have the opportunity to associate when I am in France. Some of my books published in America pleased some French publishers, and I have had to translate them from English into French. Though I was born and educated in France, I now write directly in English."

Her favorite book? "Always the last one!" she exclaimed. Mrs. Bishop has written and lectured extensively about various social movements in France and has been deeply involved for years ("long before Vatican Council II") in the movement for a better understanding of the Jews by Christians. She is the editor for the American edition of the works of Professor Jules Isaac. ("Hence my frequent travels to France.") Her books have remained modern classics, particularly *The Five Chinese Brothers*. Generations of children will continue to be enchanted by this charming tale because this tiny French lady, Claire Huchet Bishop, wrote it down.

SOME OTHER BOOKS BY MISS BISHOP:

Happy Christmas: Tales for Boys and Girls (Viking, 1956).
Tot's Triumph (Hale, 1957).

Franklyn M. Branley

Night falls, cloudless and serene.
A great domed room seemingly
becomes the sky. The universe
opens to view.

The Planetarium is the most
dramatic of theatres. Its stage is the
whole of creation; its actors the
stars in the sky; its plot the story
of nature itself, timeless but
modern, simple yet vast in scope.

From the 1968 program for the
American Museum Hayden Planetarium

FRANKLYN M. BRANLEY and his wife Margaret, an elementary schoolteacher, live in a house "which is too big" in Woodcliff Lake, New Jersey, a suburban town on the outskirts of New York. Their children, Sondra and Mary Jane, are both married. "I'm a three-time grandfather," their father chuckled. Dr. Branley loves gardening and water sports, particularly snorkeling in the salt waters of the Caribbean. And he likes to write books for young children!

"To me, writing is a way of relaxing," he commented. "To write is to accept a challenge. You have to find out what children really want to know, assess yourself, and determine what skills you have to give them. Each book should be important, interesting, contain an element of surprise for *every* reader, whether it is about the sonic boom or honeybees or how a baby is conceived. Actually, a good book for children is also a good book for adults."

As I sat in Dr. Branley's office in New York's Hayden Planetarium, he told me of his background. He trained to be an elementary schoolteacher. While teaching various grades in public schools, he noticed the tremendous lack of material in science education for children and began writing articles for professional magazines. He contributed an article a week to *Young America* (now out of print). While teaching and writing, he continued his education, receiving his master's degree and doctorate in science education from Columbia University. In the late 1940's, at the suggestion of Elizabeth Riley, editor at Thomas Y. Crowell, Dr. Branley collected his articles in the book *Experiments in Science,* which was written in collaboration with Nelson F. Beeler. The book's success encouraged him to write eight more, all published by Thomas Y. Crowell.

In 1954 Dr. Branley joined the teaching staff of Jersey City State Teachers College in New Jersey, where he served as an associate professor. Here he met Eleanor K. Vaughan with whom he coauthored *Mickey's Magnet* (1956), *Rusty Rings a Bell* (1957), and *Timmy and the Tin Can Telephone* (1958). "This series was a difficult one to do," he said. "The hardest thing in the world to do is weld fiction and fact. We had to develop a story line, yet present factual information that could be digested by the very young child. Eleanor and I were a perfect writing team — she knew children, I knew science, and we both had decided that good science books for young boys and girls should appear on the educational scene."

After two years at Jersey City State Teachers College, Dr. Branley was appointed associate astronomer and Director of Educational Services at the Hayden Planetarium. Today he is

Chairman of the Planetarium. In 1960, under his coeditorship, a new series of books was initiated by Crowell, "Let's-Read-and-Find-Out Science Books." Books in the series are written and illustrated by some of the top people in the field of children's literature, including Nonny Hogrogian, Clyde Robert Bulla, Ed Emberley, Ezra Jack Keats, Adrienne Adams, and Paul Galdone. Dr. Branley has also authored many titles in this series. Several of the titles have been translated into Spanish.

Dr. Branley is a man with a wide scientific background; he has tremendous foresight and thinks ahead of the times. His book *Exploring by Satellite* was published October 5, 1957, the day after the U.S.S.R.'s Sputnik was launched!

Our interview was interrupted by a mechanic who was having difficulty with one of the Planetarium's projectors. "Want to come with me?" he asked. "I must take a look at this." We entered a huge, dark room. It was blacker than any night I had ever seen. While I groped for the nearest seat, Dr. Branley made his way expertly through rows of chairs to the gigantic monsterlike machine that projects the various star shows. I sat there feeling strangely alone, yet I enjoyed a private show as the mechanic and Dr. Branley tinkered with slides for a forthcoming performance he was to narrate.

Franklyn M. Branley's work is varied, but whether he is lecturing, fixing complicated equipment, or writing about rain, snow, sky watching, satellites, or the north, south, east or west, he knows his material and willingly shares it.

Some Other Books Written by Dr. Branley (All T. Y. Crowell):

Snow Is Falling (1963).
Flash, Crash, Rumble, and Roll (1964).
The Milky Way: Galaxy Number One (1969).

Sara W. and John E. Brewton

SARA W. AND JOHN E. BREWTON are best known as compilers
of poetry anthologies for children. Dr. Brewton told me how this
came about. "When I was a graduate student at George Peabody
College, I wrote a thesis on animal themes in children's poems.
This began my continuing interest in collecting and publishing
anthologies of poetry for children and young people. Out of my
work on this thesis, my first book, *Under the Tent of the Sky*
(Macmillan, 1937), developed. Sara worked with me on this
volume. It is a collection of poems about animals large and
small." Mrs. Brewton recalled, "Yes, John and I began collaborating soon after we were married; my name did not appear,
however, on the first two anthologies."

The Brewtons have continued to compile volumes of poetry
for boys and girls and, of course, they have several personal
favorites. Dr. Brewton said, *"Under the Tent of the Sky* and
Gaily We Parade (Macmillan, 1940) rank high with us because
they gave us our start and because Robert Lawson illustrated
them. Then, there is *Bridled with Rainbows* (Macmillan, 1949),
a favorite because of the pleasure we had in selecting the highly
imaginative poems and because of the decorative designs of
Vera Bock. Of our more recent books, our favorite is *America*

Forever New (T. Y. Crowell, 1968), for here we tried to do what had not been done before — namely, to show the real America in all its diversity without sentimentality or chauvinism. We were fortunate in having an illustrator such as Ann Grifalconi, whose illustrations reflect the spirit of the book."

The Brewtons gather ideas for their subject anthologies from studying children's interests and needs. "Children are interested in animals, all kinds of people, make-believe, holidays, birthdays, humor, and America, so we have made anthologies to meet these interests and needs. We first thoroughly research a field, gathering all appropriate poems on the subject. Then we subject the poems to a distillation process, keeping only the best selections for the final book," said Dr. Brewton.

Another popular book of theirs is *Birthday Candles Burning Bright* (Macmillan, 1960). Mrs. Brewton explained, "After we had done a Christmas book (*Christmas Bells Are Ringing,* Macmillan, 1951), it occurred to us that *everybody* has a birthday, so why not a book devoted to birthdays. Strange as it may seem, this was not an easy book to do; few poets have written about children's birthdays."

In 1942 the Brewtons prepared *Index to Children's Poetry: A Title, Subject, Author, and First Line Index to Poetry in Collections for Children and Youth* (H. W. Wilson). If you think the title is long, take a look at this volume! The Brewtons worked with 130 collections, indexed more than 15,000 poems by over 2,500 authors, and classified them under more than 1,800 subjects. Dr. Brewton recalled this ambitious undertaking. "The idea of *The Index* originated when we were working on our first book. At first we had in mind a much smaller and simpler index — one that would give the sources for finding poems on a given subject, for example, dogs. When we approached the H. W. Wilson Company with the idea, it became an expansive and truly more useful reference tool. *The Index* took about seven years to complete. Each of the two supplements took about two years. We are now beginning work on the third supplement and expect to spend two years on it."

Dr. Brewton was born in a little settlement across the river from Brewton, Alabama, which was called Pollard. "Brewton, Alabama, was named for my family," he said. "Incidentally, Mark Twain crossed the river to Pollard. The river rose, and he was forced to spend the night there. Later he wrote of the experience and said that he would rather have lived in vain than to have lived in Pollard!"

The Brewtons live six months of the year on a farm outside Nashville, Tennessee; they spend the other six months in a cottage in the Carolina mountains. They have one daughter and three grandsons. Dr. Brewton's greatest pleasure in life is gardening, growing vegetables and flowers, particularly roses and chrysanthemums; his extraordinary green thumb has produced flowers that attract many tourists.

Commenting on their work together, he stated, "A husband-wife collaboration is a pleasure for you can always settle everything quickly and agreeably through first-hand communication, even when it involves argument and disagreement!"

SOME OTHER ANTHOLOGIES COMPILED BY DR. AND MRS. BREWTON:

Sing a Song of Seasons (Macmillan, 1955).
Laughable Limericks (T. Y. Crowell, 1965).
Shrieks at Midnight: Macabre Poems, Eerie and Humorous (T. Y. Crowell, 1969).

Raymond Briggs

EACH YEAR THE Library Association of Great Britain presents
the Kate Greenaway Medal for the most distinguished illustrated book for children published in the British Isles. In 1967
this award was given to Raymond Briggs for his book *The
Mother Goose Treasury* (Coward-McCann, 1966). I asked
Mr. Briggs, "Has winning the Kate Greenaway Medal affected
your life?" His answer was short and succinct — "Yes, it has.
My hat size is now *two* sizes larger!"

Mr. Briggs lives in Sussex, England. "I live in a small house
in the country, where I have a garden with cows and sheep. Very
good country and hills surround me. It is the second best town
in England, and Brighton is only 15 minutes away. I have no
particular favorite possessions except my house and my garden.
I'm not a sociable man. I'm a poor conversationalist and dislike
parties and small chat. I'd rather read, garden, grow fruit, or
listen to modern jazz, particularly the music of Charles Lloyd
and Charlie Mingus. I'm single and have one tortoise and one
cat. I have no children, naturally, but am quite interested in
them. I am also interested in pigs but do not want them around
the house for the same reasons I wouldn't want children around
the house; they're too much work, they make noise, they smell,

23

they cause dirt, and you're always cleaning up after them!" he told me emphatically.

Mr. Briggs was born in Wimbledon, London, in 1934. He recalled, "I had an uneventful but happy childhood and home life. My parents were happily married. Their faces turn up constantly in my illustrations but quite unconsciously. I hated school for there was too much emphasis on teamwork, competition, sports, science, and mathematics — all the opposite interests of an 'arty' type." At the age of 15, he went to the Wimbledon School of Art, where he studied painting for four years. He then went to the Slade School of Fine Art in London to further study painting. "The training I had at Wimbledon had nothing to do with painting in the modern sense at all. We were all trained in a nineteenth-century academic tradition—of still life, life, figure composition — a perfect training for an illustrator, no abstract stuff at all."

He has always been interested in books and had designed book jackets before Oxford University Press commissioned him to illustrate a book of Cornish fairy stories in 1957. His first book, a large full-color book of nursery rhymes, was titled *Ring-a Ring o' Roses.* "This was to be a one-rhyme book about Jack and Jill, similar to what Caldecott books were like. American publishers, however, suggested adding more rhymes. The book seems rather sentimental and old-world now. At the time I was keen on 'snob-junk' (antiques). I am now cured of that hobby!"

Many books followed, including *Fee Fi Fo Fum,* which was nominated for the Kate Greenaway Medal in 1964. Regarding his work, he commented, "All artwork of any kind has to be done by yourself for yourself. Anything else is merely market research. I depend heavily on text for inspiration and have no ideas outside the text. I cannot work for magazines or for advertising because the text is always dismal."

One day a week Mr. Briggs teaches at Brighton College of Art. "I wouldn't be without this," he said. "It breaks up the routine of work, which I find an insidious vice. In fact, I never seem to stop working unless I'm on a train to Brighton or facing a roomful of students. I teach mainly to learn *from* the students."

Early in 1964 his publisher suggested to him the idea of doing *The Mother Goose Treasury*. "It started out as an extra-large rhyme book of almost one hundred pages. Then the American publisher had the bright idea of making it a supercolossal type-book — the biggest and best ever, two hundred pages plus!" The finished book contains 224 pages — one of the largest color-illustrated Mother Goose books ever produced. "The book took me nearly two years to do. It was difficult keeping up with the schedule, churning the stuff out while trying to keep up the standard *and* getting it in on time. After I had made the original selection of something over 400 rhymes, I estimated a working arrangement of nine double-page spreads a month, half of them in black-and-white and half in color. Then I sorted the rhymes into those that were best treated in black and white and those that lent themselves to color treatment. I would then break down my month's selection, typing out the rhymes and sorting them out on the page, grouping them to form a satisfactory composition, although this required a good deal of shuffling around and a good many false starts. After sticking down the rhymes on the spread, I would stare at them for a good while and then begin to work over the drawings in pencil, following this with pen-and-ink finished drawings in the case of the black and white and gouache for the color. I might add that I had to go to the doctor for pills for nervous strain at the end!"

During the past several years he has done illustrations for a new series, "The Champion Books," which are adventure stories for older readers. They were an idea of Bruce Carter, the author and also the director of the children's book department at the Hamish Hamilton Publishing House in London. "It is a nice change to do the illustrations for this after the wee rhymes," he stated.

Raymond Briggs' illustrations are another example of the universality of children's books, for whether they are produced in the United States or abroad, youngsters everywhere enjoy them.

SOME OTHER BOOKS BY MR. BRIGGS (All Coward-McCann):

The White Land (1963).
Bruce Carter. *Jimmy Murphy and the White Duesenberg* (1968).
———. *Nuvolari and the Alfa Romeo* (1968).

Marcia Brown

I WONDERED WHAT IT WOULD BE like to meet Marcia Brown, the author, illustrator, storyteller, lecturer, critic, and the only woman to win the coveted Caldecott Award twice! I went to visit her on a lovely, wintry January day, a day that will remain memorable for me for Miss Brown was the last of the 104 book people about whom I was to write in this volume.

After several moments of conversation, Miss Brown and I clicked! I found her warm, personable, and brimming over with energy and enthusiasm for her work, despite a recent attack of the Hong Kong flu. Her studio is an interesting one. It overflows with books; many are contained within the bookcases and shelves she built herself, and others are scattered on tables, chairs, and, to borrow a word from Ruth Krauss, "everywheres!" Most of the volumes are art books, which she browses through time and time again. Her workroom is filled to capacity with papers, sketchbooks, files, and the various tools that she uses to prepare her illustrations. On a worktable I saw the woodcut blocks, made from pine planks, for her most recent book *How, Hippo!* (1969). Miss Brown showed me the cuts and then brought me the final dummy of the book, which she had just completed. Going into her files, she pulled out other dummies to show me —

the beginnings of *Felice* (1958), a story set in Venice, *Peter Piper's Alphabet* (1959), and her books for older readers, Hans Christian Andersen's *The Wild Swans* (1965) and *Backbone of the King* (1966), a Hawaiian folk legend. The dummies are intricate and closely suggest the way the completed book will look after it has traveled the long road to publication.

Miss Brown and I talked about many things — about her life, her work, and the field of children's literature in general, in which she is quite an expert. She was born in Rochester, New York. Because her father was a minister and lived in various places, she and her two sisters grew up in several towns. Miss Brown was an avid reader from the time she can remember. After each of the family's moves, she would seek out the nearest public library and obtain a library card before her parents had finished unpacking their belongings. Miss Brown attended Catskill and Kingston High Schools and went on to study at the State College for Teachers in Albany. She became interested in designing and painting stage sets and received a scholarship to study with Judson Smith at the Woodstock School of Painting. She taught English and drama on the high school level; however, art and the possibility of doing book illustrating haunted her.

"I decided to go to New York," she recalled. "I studied at the New School with Yasuo Kuniyoshi, Louis Schanker, and Stuart Davis. I also worked on exhibitions for five years at the New York Public Library, in the rare book collection, and telling stories. I would go to playgrounds and recreation areas all over the city and tell all kinds of tales to children. I left library work in 1948 to devote my time to doing books." Her first book for children, *The Little Carousel,* was published in 1946. Miss Brown related how this story developed. "I lived in the middle of a Sicilian neighborhood on Sullivan Street in Greenwich Village. From my apartment window I saw the little street carousel arrive, and the episode that makes the plot of the story happened before my delighted eyes."

This book, as are all her others, was published by Charles Scribner's Sons. I was curious to know how Miss Brown came to adopt Scribner as her publisher, and she told me the story. "I had to go somewhere. I had heard Alice Dalgliesh (*dal* gleesh) speak and admired the Scribner list, so I made my way to Alice's office. Alice, who later on became a very dear friend, was too busy to see me. There I was, armed with *The Little Carousel* in complete dummy form and at such a high pitch that I burst into tears. I left the office and walked around the corner to Viking. But there I found Viking tied up with an elevator strike, and Miss Massee's office was on a high floor! So, rather than climb, I decided to wait for Miss Dalgliesh, who took the book. I've been with Scribner ever since." Years later she told the story to May Massee, who was shocked to learn of the great loss that the elevator strike had caused Viking! Ah, publishing!

Miss Brown has contributed greatly to the field of children's literature. Versatility is a word that has often been used aptly to describe her artwork. Each of her books is quite different in style, and they vary in media. For Howard Pyle's *Dick Whittington and His Cat* (1950), she used linoleum cuts; for Hans Christian Andersen's *The Steadfast Soldier* (1953), four-color gouache and line drawings; for *Cinderella, or The Little Glass Slipper* (1955; winner of the 1956 Caldecott Award), which she translated from Charles Perrault's French version, casein gouache and crayon; for *Once a Mouse* (1961; winner of the 1962 Caldecott Award), a simple fable from India, woodcuts in two and three colors; *How, Hippo!* is done in four-color woodcuts. Commenting on this versatility she remarked: "The need for variety is a matter of temperament. I could no more stand using the same style art in book after book than I could eating the same food every day — and I love food and eat everything!"

Miss Brown's travels have been extensive; many of her books reflect her love of the places she has visited and lived — Italy, Hawaii, Jamaica, the Virgin Islands, and Mexico. The story

From HOW, HIPPO! by Marcia Brown, © 1969 by Marcia Brown. Permission of Charles Scribner's Sons.

and the setting often dictate the medium used in the book. Besides traveling, Miss Brown loves music and the dance. She often attends concerts, the opera, and the ballet. "I studied ballet when I was young, but I wasn't young enough to pursue it seriously," she commented. "I love to read, and I like jazz, although I'm too naive about it to follow all its developments. I think the times in which we're living are fascinating. Some of me is sympathetic toward the youth of today and their movements. I am, however, impatient with destructiveness."

Our conversation continued as we discussed children's literature at length and the importance placed on book awards. "There's too much emphasis on awards in our society. It has no effect on your work and how you do it!" she declared. The afternoon had turned to early evening. Miss Brown switched on a light above her chair, and we talked some more. She is an easy person to talk with; she is so fluent and knowledgeable about art and the publishing world. The January day was nearing an end. I left Miss Brown's studio, looking forward to the day when we would meet again. Going down 16 flights in the elevator, I felt relieved that I had finished my interviewing for *Books Are By People* and was overjoyed that it had ended on such a high note.

SOME OTHER BOOKS BY MISS BROWN (All Scribner):

Stone Soup (1947).
Henry-Fisherman (1949).
The Flying Carpet (1956).

Clyde Robert Bulla

CLYDE ROBERT BULLA lives in a big, old house on a wide street in the middle of Los Angeles, California. In it he has many books, including inscribed copies given to him by author friends, a few paintings acquired from different parts of the world, and a collection of recordings, most of them operas. "Sometimes I complain about Los Angeles' smog, traffic, and high taxes, but all in all I'm happy and contented here," he said. "The mountains, the ocean, and the desert are all nearby. There are theatres, museums, libraries, and concert halls. Many writers and illustrators of children's books live in the area, and some of them are among my best friends. I love the theatre — plays, operas, concerts — and I love to travel too. My idea of a good vacation is a long voyage on a freighter. I play the piano and write music. I paint in oils and watercolors, not very well but with enthusiasm! The longer I live, the more I value peace and quiet. I am not a person who is easily bored."

Mr. Bulla was born on a farm near King City, Missouri, and grew up in the northwestern part of the state. "There were four children in the family," he related. "I was the youngest. I went to school in a one-room country schoolhouse. There was music in our home. There were books, although not many children's books. I read what was at hand — Dickens, Thackeray, an encyclopedia. I liked to wander about the farm, which was good-sized, and I got to know every tree and stone in the woods."

Mr. Bulla had no formal training as a writer. "I began very young and proceeded by trial and error. At first I wrote magazine stories, articles, and a novel for adults. I also worked on a hometown newspaper and wrote a weekly column. A friend, who was an elementary teacher and a writer, saw the column and told me the style of it suggested children's stories. So I wrote my first story for children, *The Donkey Cart* (T. Y. Crowell, 1946)." Several of his books have been sparked by his travels. "Until I was grown, I lived in the Middle West. Then I moved to the West, first to Arizona and then to California, where I met Indians for the first time and became interested in them and in their history. One of my most memorable vacations was spent at an isolated trading post on an Indian reservation. I have Indian friends here in Los Angeles," he added.

Mr. Bulla's books reflect his many and varied interests. Several books include songs he has composed: *Riding the Pony Express* (1948) contains four songs, and *Eagle Feather* (1953), a story of present day Navajos, three. He has also written books about opera for older boys and girls.

Regarding his work habits, Mr. Bulla commented, "I like to carry an idea in the back of my mind for awhile, allowing it to develop in its own way and in its own time. One day, when the story seems complete, I begin writing; I write first in longhand, slowly and painfully. The opening paragraph is the hardest; sometimes I write as many as 50 or 60 before turning out one I can use. Every manuscript goes through several complete drafts. Sometimes I try out ideas on children. I hope the boys and girls know from my books that I have sympathy for them and that I remember what it is like to be a child."

SOME OTHER BOOKS BY MR. BULLA (All T. Y. Crowell):

A Tree Is a Plant (1960).
White Bird (1966).
Mika's Apple Tree (1968).

John Ciardi

I MET A MAN!

I met a man who was born in Boston on June 24, 1916. This man grew up in Medford, Massachusetts, and attended public school there. His father, an insurance agent for Metropolitan Life Insurance Company, was killed in an automobile accident in 1919.

I met a man who always wanted to be a poet. He received his B.A. degree from Tufts College and his M.A. degree from the University of Michigan. "I took all sorts of courses in English in college and graduate school," he commented. "John Holmes, a fine poet and my teacher at Tufts, persuaded me to take poetry seriously in my sophomore year. In grad school Professor Roy Cowden gave me great help."

I met a man who has become known as one of America's foremost contemporary poets and who is famous for his translations of Dante. This man used to be an English professor at Kansas City University, Harvard, and Rutgers. After 20 years of teaching he resigned. Since 1955 he has been poetry editor of *Saturday Review,* and is also the director of the Bread Loaf Writers' Conference.

I met a man who decided to write for children because they were around him. "I wrote first for my sister's children, from about 1947–1953, when my wife and I were living with them. Then I wrote for my own children as they came. Now I write for myself. My children (Benn Anthony, 14, John Lyle Pritchett, 15, and Myra, 16) are in a hurry to grow up; I'm not, so I write for my own childhood."

His own favorite book is *I Met a Man* (Houghton, 1961). "It's my favorite because I wrote it on a first-grade vocabulary level when my daughter was in kindergarten. I wanted it to be the first book she read through, and she learned to read from it." This book is a collection of 31 poems. "Almost any child halfway through the first grade should be able to read the first poems. Any bright child toward the end of the first grade should be able to solve the slightly added difficulties of the later poems."

I met a man who has no system of writing. "It's like lazy fishing," he commented. "Drop a line, sit easy. If a fish bites, play it; if not, enjoy the weather!"

Most of his poems for children are funny and make boys and girls laugh. He wrote *The Monster Den* (Lippincott, 1966) about his own children. "It was a way of spoofing them. Kidding, with love and some restraint, can be a happy relationship. We are not a somber family." Many of his books are really spoofs of parent-child relationships. "I often write spoofs. I have written some adult poems *about* children that are not *for* them. The closest I can come to pointing out the difference between poetry for children versus poetry for adults is that most children's poems are *eternal;* adult poems are *mortal.*"

I met a man who, when he isn't at work, plays golf badly but enjoys it! "Because of a bad back I have had to give it up, but I will be operated on and hope I can be back on the course soon. I like playing with my dog, Serendipity ("Dippy"), a great German shepherd. Dippy's favorite game is catching a Frisbee. He is trained to stand in front of me. When I wave the Frisbee behind my back, he scoots around me to get a running start, races up to 50 yards, more in a wind, leaps up, grabs the Frisbee out of the air, and brings it back to me. Aside from being good

35

exercise, it is a beautiful piece of action, and I never tire of watching the speed and grace of his leaps."

Mr. Ciardi (chee *ar* dee) lives in a New Jersey suburban town in a big, old (c. 1890) white house with 14 rooms situated on two and one quarter acres. He collects painting, mostly abstracts, and sculpture "in a necessarily limited way." He is concerned about the times we are living in and thinks seriously about the current turmoil of youth. "Adolescent rebellion is always honorably motivated. The young cannot fail to be right when they identify what they call 'hypocrisy.' We need the violence of their objection. But they are merciless, too, because they lack perspective. In another 20 years or so they will be acting — out of love — in ways their children will scorn as hypocritical, and they, too, may learn to think of mercy as relevant."

I met a man who is truly a poet. "What is poetry? Poetry is where every line comes to rest against a white space."

I met a man.

And through his writing you too can meet John Ciardi.

SOME OTHER BOOKS BY MR. CIARDI (All Lippincott):

The Reason for the Pelican (1959).
The Man Who Sang the Sillies (1961).
You Read to Me, I'll Read to You (1962).
John J. Plenty and Fiddler Dan (1963).
The King Who Saved Himself from Being Saved (1965).

William Cole

WILLIAM COLE WEARS two hats upon his head — he is an author and a famous compiler of poetry books for young children and adults. His anthologies are varied; they include volumes of animal poems, books of funny poems, a collection of poems about children's misbehavior, a book of poems of just eight lines or less, nature poems, and — well, one could go on and on for several pages!

Mr. Cole makes the birth of an anthology sound quite easy. He told me, "Usually I notice a number of interesting poems in my reading — poems that are all of a kind, for example *Eight Lines or Under* (Macmillan, 1967), or on a theme such as animals, *I Went to the Animal Fair* (World, 1958) — and I propose a book to an editor. I recently noticed that there were a lot of good poems about adventurous men — cowboys, fighters, and pirates — so it seemed logical to put them all in one book; I'm working on it now, *Rough Men, Tough Men: Poems of Action and Adventure* (Viking, 1969). I have some 2,000 books of poetry, and I gather a lot of my material from them. The only real problem in doing an anthology is writing the introduction. Writing is terribly hard work for me. My method is to sit down at the typewriter, look at it, stand up, walk around, lie down, have an idea for a sentence, sit at the typewriter, type it, get up, and go through the process again. You must be enthusiastic when you do an anthology; any anthology done without enthusiasm is like a TV dinner — frozen, tasteless, and quickly forgotten."

Mr. Cole's first collection was one for adults, *The Best Cartoons from Punch* (World, 1953). "I was working at Knopf as an editor and had the idea that somebody should do a *Punch* magazine humor collection. After three or four writers refused the assignment, it suddenly struck me that, heck, I could do it. And I did! And then I did another, and another, and another. . . ."

Mr. Cole is in his late forties. He stands 6 feet, 1 inch tall and weighs 190 pounds. "I still have some hair, I'm handsome, though corpulent, right-handed, level-headed, quick-witted, shy with strangers, and forward with friends." He was born in Staten Island, New York, and spent most of his childhood in Port Chester, New York. "I grew up at a time and in a place when there actually was an 'old swimmin' hole' only a short hike distance from home. I was forced through a Catholic elementary school and barely made it through high school, owing to a built-in confusion about anything mathematical, or even arithmetical! I was what was then known as a 'bad boy' and was thrown out of high school twice for disorderly conduct. In other words, school and I were badly mismated."

He never returned to school. He served in the army, worked in the publishing field after his discharge, and then began compiling anthologies. "It's a great pleasure to discover a wonderful poem that has been forgotten and that fits into the theme of a book I'm working on. I enjoy passing on my enthusiasm for poems, cartoons, and songs. It is a great thrill to me to have a child react with excitement to a poem I have discovered and put between the pages of a book. The books I actually write are of two kinds: those that come from inspiration such as *Aunt Bella's Umbrella* (Doubleday, 1969), and those that are simply hard work like *That Pest, Jonathan* (Harper, 1969).

The latter two books are Cole originals; in the past six years he has authored eight books. His favorite of the works he has collected is *Folk Songs of England, Ireland, Scotland, and Wales* (Doubleday, 1951). "This contains a number of beautiful songs that are found nowhere else. It is a very personal selection and contains no song that I do not love. Also, I cannot read one note of music nor play any instrument, and I like the idea of doing a song book under those circumstances."

Mr. Cole is married to Galen Williams. Miss Williams runs the Poetry Center at the Young Men's Hebrew Association in New York City. They have three children, two daughters, 20 and 19, and a son just one year old. The Cole family live in upper Times Square in New York City in two apartments on the same floor. "I fear that my apartment house will soon be torn down, since everything around it is 48 stories high and new, and I'm only six little stories high and old. I like living here — it's noisy, dirty, dangerous, and fascinating."

His spare time activities include "looking at pretty girls, playing tennis, eating, and looking at and conversing with dogs. My work is my hobby and usually my pleasure," he commented. His favorite poets are those who mostly seem underappreciated — Frances Cornford, R. S. Thomas, Andrew Young ("for their clarity and depth") and Wallace Irwin ("he's simply a great unappreciated comic poet"). He believes "The greatest poet of all is Yeats, followed by D. H. Lawrence; these two men give me authentic chills. The great light-verse poet is still W. S. Gilbert."

Mr. Cole has collaborated with Tomi Ungerer on several books. "I give Tomi the manuscript and forget about it. He illustrates it and invariably improves it. He is a thorough professional and doesn't need, or want, me leaning over his shoulder as he works. The only time he needs me is to reinforce a dispute between him and the publisher's art department. He is immensely strong minded, and by golly, when he wants brown on the jacket, he's gonna' get brown or tear the place apart!"

I asked Mr. Cole to define poetry and whether or not he felt there was a difference between poetry for children and poetry for adults. He answered, "Poetry is beautiful shorthand! It doesn't matter who it is written for. I generally use few poems that are written specifically for children. These tend to be too cute, written down to them. What I figure is that if I like a poem and understand it, so will a lot of other people. My motto is 'Scissors and paste and trust your taste.'"

We ended our interview on a note of Cole philosophy: "I have three beliefs: (1) If you have enthusiasm, you can do anything; (2) a well-rounded education is not as important as curiosity; and (3) my advice to the young is to specialize! Know more than anybody else about *one* thing — almost *any* one thing!"

Some Other Books by Mr. Cole:

Frances Face-Maker (World, 1963).
What's Good for a Six-Year-Old? (Holt, 1965).
Uncoupled Couplets: A Game of Rhymes (Taplinger, 1966).
What's Good for a Five-Year-Old? (Holt, 1969).

Anthologies:

The Birds and the Beasts Were There (World, 1963).
Beastly Boys and Ghastly Girls (World, 1964).
Oh, What Nonsense (Viking, 1966).
A Book of Nature Poems (Viking, 1969).

Barbara Cooney

BARBARA COONEY LIVES in an old yellow 16-room New England
house in the center of a small town in Massachusetts. The house
is surrounded by a big green lawn, beautiful shade trees, and
lovely flower, herb, and vegetable gardens. She does a great deal
of gardening and loves flowers, especially fragrant ones. She is
married to Dr. C. Talbot Porter, a general practitioner, and has
four children, Gretel and Barnaby, who are in their early twenties, and Talbot, Jr., and Phoebe, teenagers. "Two of my children are married. Gretel is married to an Indian, and I have a
little Hindu grandchild — a boy named Shetaketu," she said.

Miss Cooney is 5 feet, 2½ inches tall, has blonde hair, and is
a bundle of energy. She has many likes and described them
enthusiastically: "I have only two pieces of furniture that I
cherish — an ancient, worn table and an ancient French dresser,
also worn. And a Polish rug! And I must admit I do like *things,*
elegant, beautiful, interesting things, whether trees or houses
or pebbles or flowers or dishes or jewelry or clothes — the things
must be really delicious. I guess I'm a Sybanite who is also capa-
ble of really roughing it, which I also enjoy. I also like people
and laughing and seeing the world. I love foreign places and
languages and books. I love the country and also cities, but not

suburbia. I love the salt water and lying on my face in the sun, and picnicking, skiing, and fishing. Dogs, too! And walking, mountain climbing, and the great outdoors!"

Her love of travel has taken her to many places. She has been back and forth to France three times as well as to Spain, Switzerland, Ireland, England, St. Lucia, and Haiti. Miss Cooney was born in Brooklyn, New York, and grew up on Long Island and in Maine. Regarding her professional life she declared, "I really don't know why I decided to write and illustrate books. It just happened. I majored in the history of art at Smith College, and I took a course in graphic arts (lithography and etching) at the Art Students League in New York City."

She illustrated her first book in 1940. Eighteen years later Miss Cooney was awarded the Caldecott Medal for *Chanticleer and the Fox* (T. Y. Crowell, 1958), an adaptation of Chaucer's "The Nun's Priest's Tale." In this book she drew many of the herbs and plants from her own garden. Since 1958 she has produced a host of interesting books for children, many resulting from her travels. While in France she gathered the material for illustrations for *Mother Goose in French* (T. Y. Crowell, 1964), which was translated by Hugh Latham. She also did a French version of "Wynken, Blynken, and Nod" entitled *Papillot, Clignot et Dodo* (Ariel, 1954) and *Le Hibou et la Poussiquette* ("The Owl and the Pussycat," Little, Brown, 1961).

"I'm not sure which of my books is my favorite," she remarked. *"Le Hibou et la Poussiquette* was great fun doing; *Papillot, Clignot et Dodo* satisfies my romantic side, *Mother Goose in French* or *Mother Goose in Spanish* (T. Y. Crowell, 1968), gave me the chance to steep myself in two different cultures."

Ideas for her books just happen! "I get interested or fanatic about the woods, or France, or Spain, or medieval life, or mice say, and then the ideas come. Some of my texts take reworking, sometimes much, sometimes little." But she reworks her pictures until they are perfect. To date Miss Cooney has illustrated over

60 books. Her work is a tremendously important part of her life, for it is interrelated with her life. Her books are gay, entertaining, and simple, yet complex. Is it any wonder that children young and old enjoy books by Barbara Cooney?

SOME OTHER BOOKS BY MISS COONEY:

Cock Robin (Scribner, 1965).
A Little Prayer (Hastings, 1965):
A Garland of Games and Other Diversions (Holt, 1969).

From COCK ROBIN by Barbara Cooney, © 1965 by Barbara Cooney. Permission of Charles Scribner's Sons.

James Daugherty

JAMES DAUGHERTY (*daw* er tee) lives in what he describes as a "two-story saltbox that is sort of a house." It is an old pioneer cabin-like house located in Weston, Connecticut. One can still see the adz marks on the hand-hewn beams. "We fixed this place up as far as it would go," he exclaimed, "but that wasn't too far! It does keep out the weather most of the time, and we are used to it now. The community around here is the only thing that sometimes bothers me. It's made up of commuter types — they're all squares!"

Mr. Daugherty was born on June 1, 1889, in Ashville, North Carolina. He remembers growing up on a farm in southern Indiana and in a small town in Ohio. When he was nine years old, his family moved to Washington, D. C., where he attended school. He recalled his grandfather telling him tales of Daniel Boone, "handed down by word of mouth and not from the books," his Virginia-born mother speaking about the Old South, and his father reading aloud from Shakespeare, Poe, and Dickens. "As he read to us, I drew illustrations for the stories," Mr. Daugherty said. "My home, not school, gave me my best education."

After high school Mr. Daugherty attended the Corcoran Art

School in Washington, D. C. Later he studied at the Philadelphia Art Academy in Pennsylvania and then in England. While in London he read the writings of Walt Whitman and became excited over the possibilities of presenting visual images of America. During World War I he worked in shipyards in New England, camouflaging ships for the navy. After the war he painted murals for Loew's movie houses in New York City.

His first book was commissioned by the late May Massee, juvenile editor at Viking; it was to illustrate Stewart Edward White's *Daniel Boone*. His own first book, *Andy and the Lion* (Viking), was created in 1938; it combines fantasy and reality in the tale of a boy who re-creates the adventures of Shaw's *Androcles and the Lion*. Mr. Daugherty told me about the development of this book. "One wintry night, as we sat by the fire with the north wind howling in the treetops, we broke into laughter as we remembered the first New York performance we had seen many years ago of *Androcles*. *Andy and the Lion* leaped into my mind's eye, and I drew the pictures; the words came long after."

I asked Mr. Daugherty how he felt about this book becoming a modern classic. He answered, "If this little fable should continue to give delight to the children of today and tomorrow, I shall humbly thank God that I have not lived and labored in vain. *Andy and the Lion* is my favorite book, although I really enjoyed doing them all, because it was the most fun to do." Following *Andy and the Lion,* he illustrated scores of books and became one of the best known children's illustrators. His biographies for older readers re-create the American scene and include *Abraham Lincoln* (Viking, 1953), *Marcus and Narcissa Whitman: Pioneers of Oregon* (Viking, 1953), and *Daniel Boone* (Viking, 1939), for which he was awarded the 1940 Newbery Medal. His illustrations are powerful, vigorous, and contain a great deal of action and movement.

Regarding his writing, he commented, "Nobody knows where ideas for books come from. I wish a consumers' guide or yellow pages could provide them. I am sure the good ones come from God if you ask Him. He does exist, you know. I don't try out my ideas on anyone. When a book is completed, I *inflict* it on my loving wife, Sonia, who is an author, my best friend, and severest critic."

The Daugherty's have one grown son, Chris. In his spare time Mr. Daugherty enjoys painting abstract pictures. "It is an obsession with me, rather than a hobby," he exclaimed. "I sometimes enjoy reading and even thinking! I am grateful that children have read my books. To give them pleasure is a great privilege." He is adamant about adults imposing tasks on children. "The thousands of fan letters children write to authors are cruelly imposed by their teachers without even the benefit of a self-stamped envelope. Let the authors write, the teachers teach, and the children be their naturally joyous selves." He is also concerned about the lack of peace in today's world. "Ah, Lee," he sighed, "we have had four wars in the last 50 years and have given lip service to Christianity for 2,000 years. This makes me wonder about the children of tomorrow and what they shall inherit."

James Daugherty has lived in America and recorded it for the annals of history. Lynd Ward once remarked that Mr. Daugherty "stands in a kind of symbolic relation to our culture, his talent firmly rooted in American experience, his creative motivation well attuned to the techniques of our age, his voice well able to speak out for the values of democratic life." These words on James Daugherty sum up James Daugherty.

SOME OTHER BOOKS BY MR. DAUGHERTY (All Viking):

Benjamin Elkin, Gillespie and the Guards (1956).
The Picnic (Viking, 1958).

Ingri and Edgar P. d'Aulaire

INGRI MORTENSON WAS BORN in Kongsberg, Norway. "I grew up in a big, happy Norwegian family, the youngest of five. My father was in government service so we moved from one government-owned town house and town to another. We spent every summer at my grandfather's estate in a valley, which you might call the Vermont of Norway. So I consider myself a valley girl. I went through girls' prep school, junior college, and then decided to quit and become an artist."

Edgar Parin d'Aulaire (doh *lair*), her husband, told me, "Some people say I was born in Campoblenio, Switzerland; my Swiss passport says so too! Switzerland was the legal residence of my parents, but actually, I was born in a hospital in Munich, Germany. Both my parents were studying art in Munich. I grew up in almost all of the art centers of Europe — Munich, Paris, Rome, Florence. I spent nine years at the gymnasium, or prep school, in Munich.

"I started to draw and paint at a very early age, and I can't remember ever having had a stronger desire than to be left in peace to draw. My first picture book was made at the age of 11 or 12; it depicted my American grandmother's adventures on the wild prairie being chased by Indians. Later I turned into a serious artist and only worked on illustrations for limited editions and some very sophisticated books."

Mrs. d'Aulaire recalled, "I was spoiled and brought up to know a lot about art and literature. At the age of 15 I revealed to my family that I had shown my paintings to the foremost woman painter in Norway, Harriet Backer; she advised me to start studying in an art school at once. My father, mother, and my uncle, who is a noted philosopher and poet, backed me. I studied in Oslo, Munich, and Paris. Some years later I returned home as Edgar and Ingri Incorporated."

The d'Aulaires met in an art school in Paris and were married in 1925. Four years later they came to New York City. Their first book, *The Magic Rug* (Doubleday, 1931), grew out of an illustrated letter to a little niece in Norway. It was also at this time that they began to do complicated color lithography. They use the old techniques of the artist-lithographer who did all his work by hand instead of using a camera as do most modern lithographers. First, color drawings are sketched on paper in exactly the size needed. Mr. d'Aulaire next draws on a stone with crayon the black parts of the picture. His hand must be absolutely sure of every line, for there is no way to erase or to go over lines once they are drawn on stone or zinc. He then draws the red parts of the picture for a red plate, the blue parts for a blue plate, and the yellow parts for a yellow plate. The four drawings or color separations are combined on the finished stone, and many additional tedious processes are still required to complete a lithograph.

Mrs. d'Aulaire learned the art of lithography from her husband. "You must be a bulldog and stick to it," she said. "Once you have started on a book, finish it. This is where a team of two works so well. When one is down, the other is up. We may rewrite our text ten to twenty times before we are both satisfied, and hundreds of sketches end in the fireplace before the drawings are executed."

Commenting on their life together, she declared, "For 14 married years we, as struggling young artists, could not feed a child and we agreed that we did not want a half-starved, garret-studio baby. Finally we thought we could provide a childhood as happy as our own and Per Ola, our oldest son was born. We were happy in our New York studio, but a child should, if possible, have the pleasure of the country — chickens, pigs, sheep, and unpolluted air — consequently, we bought our Wilton Farm. Nine and one-half years afterwards 'The Lord's little afterthought,' Nils Maarten, came. He was christened at our silver wedding anniversary.

"We were blessed with the three nicest children, Per Ola, Nils Maarten, and Ola's wife Emily, who is the daughter we never had but always hoped for. They all work with us on our books. Taught by his father, Ola has become a good lithographer. All three are very good researchers and co-writers. Like everything we do, our books are a family enterprise."

The d'Aulaires still live on Wilton Farm, an area in Connecticut. They built the house they live in "mostly with our own hands." The walls are covered with paintings, and they have lots of old Norwegian furniture. "As Wilton, where we have lived for 27 years, became a suburb, we started another home in Vermont, a tiny farmhouse with lots of land and a second home for our children. But this time we had grown too old to do it ourselves. We directed! Carpenters got the old decrepit house up again, and it is adorable," she noted proudly.

In 1940 the d'Aulaires won the Caldecott Award for their book *Abraham Lincoln* (Doubleday, 1939). "This book was born out of love," she commented. "We wanted to try to make a wonderful man come alive for children, keeping all of his humility, gawkiness, and greatness. We followed the Lincoln path and pitched our tent wherever he had been staying, to smell the same flowers, be bitten by the same bugs, and have the same thunderstorms burst over our heads. Nearby farmers came out and invited us to come and stay with them if we could not afford to pay for a hotel in the nearest town. And we said, 'Thank you, but we have to know what Abraham Lincoln first smelled and saw when he woke up at dawn.' And maybe that is just what

49

From ABRAHAM LINCOLN by Ingri and Edgar Parin d'Aulaire, copyright 1939 by Doubleday & Co., Inc. Permission of Doubleday & Co., Inc. and C. Combridge Ltd.

makes the book alive to children; you have to see it, smell it, hear it, and really live it before you can tell the story of Lincoln! Children won't take half-measures, and maybe that is why we love our work on children's books."

Regarding collaborating Mrs. d'Aulaire commented, "There are no problems as long as I remember that a plane needs a captain and a navigator. It is clear flying; Edgar is the captain, but it took me quite a few years to become a navigator. Our goals as artists are so different. Our individual paintings so different. But we respect each other *as* painters."

Mr. d'Aulaire replied, "It is always difficult for two completely different artists to work together. We have created a third person, different from each of us, different from my wife's and my own work, yet a combination of us two. This third person has been enriched by our children."

Pleasures in life include painting, farming, remodeling ugly old farmhouses, and commuting between Connecticut and Vermont. "As for me," stated Mrs. d'Aulaire, "I am a wife, mother, cook, doctor, farmer's wife, carpenter, stone mason, and globe-trotter in search of material for our books."

The d'Aulaires lead a close family life and they enjoy it. They have contributed greatly to the field of children's literature by producing excellent biographies of famous people so that young children can know and appreciate their greatness.

SOME OTHER BOOKS BY THE D'AULAIRES (All Doubleday):

George Washington (1936).
Pocahontas (1949).
Benjamin Franklin (1950).
Leif, the Lucky (1951).
Buffalo Bill (1952).
Columbus (1955).

Beatrice Schenk de Regniers

EIGHT THIRTY P.M. in New York City is the time when orchestras begin to tune up and massive curtains rise in darkened theatre houses along Broadway's Great White Way. It was an appropriate hour for me to meet Beatrice Schenk de Regniers (duh *rayn* yay), for she, like the theatre, is a woman of many talents. Her books for children run the gamut from stories about giants to poems about cats. She stated her reason for this diversity in two short sentences: "I don't do books to earn a living. I do the books I have to do, the books that are deep inside me."

Her stage setting is a meadow. "All my books have their own way of working themselves out from me, but most of them begin in a meadow. I take my notebook and my pencil and go away, alone, to a place where I can be physically in touch with nature. I wander through the countryside and work in a kind of meadow trance," she smiled. "Many of my books came out of my visits to the meadow. *The Shadow Book* (Harcourt, 1960; beautifully written and illustrated with photographs by Isabel Gordon) was born in a meadow in Central Park. I had a difficult time getting away when I worked on *Something Special* (Harcourt, 1958; a small volume of ten childlike poems, which is the favorite of her books), so I got up every morning at 5:30 and worked until 7:30 a.m. The dining room table was my meadow for this book. You know how still everything is between five and seven. The house is so quiet."

Her scenery is her apartment furnishings. She and her husband, Francis, live in a stylish New York apartment in the West Fifties. Plants and flowers sprout all over; modern paintings adorn the walls along with works by such well-known illustrators as Irene Haas and Beni Montresor. One has the feeling of visiting a carefully selected museum showing. A large fireplace in the living room adds to the atmosphere of a country place right in the middle of one of New York's busiest areas. "I'm in a little house of my own here," Mrs. de Regniers stated, borrowing the idea from her book *A Little House of Your Own* (Harcourt, 1954), which is her autobiography. "I love it here. We're only a block from Central Park (where she rides her new bicycle), and we're within walking distance of Lincoln Center. Many summer nights we just sit at the Center and watch the choreography of the fountains in front of the Metropolitan Opera House."

She has had a life-long interest in the dance. "I love to dance!" she exclaimed, as her face lighted up as if in a spotlight. "In my reincarnation I'm going to be a choreographer. My writing is a kind of dance. I want all my books to have a pace, a movement, like a ballet. Beni (Montresor) and I are planning an hour-long ballet of *May I Bring a Friend?* (Atheneum, 1964; winner of the 1965 Caldecott Medal). It would be a beautiful ballet, wouldn't it?"

The overture to Mrs. de Regniers' life began in Lafayette, Indiana. At the age of seven, her parents moved to Crawfordsville, Indiana, where she lived "a wonderful kind of free childhood, where I could gather violets, live in a tree, walk in the woods — be!" She attended the University of Chicago and Winnetka Graduate Teachers College. She has traveled extensively both on her own and as a welfare officer with the United Nations Relief and Rehabilitation Administration

53

(UNRRA) during World War II. After the war she served as educational materials director of the American Heart Association. "I got sick of health," she commented, "so I left!"

Her first children's book was *The Giant Story* (Harper, 1953) illustrated by Maurice Sendak. She knows *why* she did each book and how they came from within her.

"I had to write *A Little House of Your Own*. I have a strong sense of privacy. I wanted to give the message to all the children in the United States of America that it is all right to want to be alone someti.nes. I lived the first years of my life under the dining room table. Today it is hard for children. Now we have glass-top tables and no place to hide! If that book didn't get published, I was going to mimeograph it and put it in corn flakes boxes to get it to kids!

"I'm crazy about Lincoln! I would have married him if he had asked me and I'd been alive then. I spent two years researching *The Abraham Lincoln Joke Book* (Random, 1965), going through old newspapers, original memoirs, and the like."

"As gay as *May I Bring a Friend?* is, I wept all the while I was writing it. We had two Siamese-alley cats for 10 and 11 years. One of the cats died of cancer; he died in my arms. A year later the other was dying, and I was so distressed I decided to write to focus on something else. The book was done in an almost mechanized way. I said, 'I'll write and not think of cats. I'll write verse because it demands concentration.' I didn't know what I was going to write about, but when the book was finished, oddly enough it was filled with animals — but no cats. Beni and I worked closely together on the book. We'd call one another and discuss situations on the phone. I wasn't the least bit surprised that it won the Caldecott Award. I expect all the illustrators of my books to win it; they are all great." (And three of them have — Sendak, Montresor, and Hogrogian.)

Currently Mrs. de Regniers is the editor of the Scholastic Book Services' Lucky Book Club. "I work four days a week as an editor, but Mondays are reserved for my own writing. I've trained all my friends *not* to phone me on Mondays."

She likes to ride her bicycle, and she rides it to work each morning, weather permitting. She also reads a great deal. "I'm an avid reader. I can read while walking, while riding up and down in elevators, while brushing my teeth. I haven't yet managed to combine reading and bicycling — although I may bicycle to a secluded rock in Central Park and read when I get there."

She is a petite person who moves with grace, speaks poetically, and dances even when she's sitting still. Before I left her apartment and bade good night, she exclaimed, "I want to make a movie!" And someday she will. And whether it is about children laughing or children hiding or children chasing shadows or children just being children, it will undoubtedly be excellent. Why? Because Beatrice Schenk de Regniers is a child's child.

SOME OTHER BOOKS BY MRS. DE REGNIERS:

Cats cats cats cats cats (Pantheon, 1958).
The Snow Party (Pantheon, 1959).
The Shadow Book (Harcourt, 1960).
Willy O'Dwyer Jumped in the Fire (Atheneum, 1968).

Barbara and Ed Emberley

WHEN ED EMBERLEY won the Caldecott Award in 1968 for *Drummer Hoff* (Prentice-Hall, 1967), many reporters, critics, and biographers referred to him as more than an illustrator; to them he is an *artist* as well. Mr. Emberley has earned this reputation for his mastery in illustrating as well as his ability to put a book together from the initial idea through to the finished product. Jean Reynolds, Mr. Emberley's editor at Prentice-Hall, has written of him as "always aware of the cold practicalities of bookmaking. Having studied printing and production techniques, he applies his knowledge in the development of any new style. . . . When an Emberley dummy is submitted, there is no necessity to compromise the artist's original conception of the book because of technical problems."

Mr. Emberley and his wife, Barbara, have collaborated on a number of books. He said of their work together, "Barbara actively participates in almost all phases of our craft as much as her homemaking duties will permit. For instance, over the past year she has been involved in finding and adapting manuscripts, preparing work sheets for the printer, preparing overlays for my master drawings, gathering material for a book we are doing on clothing, coloring my black line drawings for a series of textbook illustrations, pulling prints from my blocks for two Christmas shows we are preparing, paying the bills, arranging for research trips, and taking most of the photos we use."

Both the Emberleys have art backgrounds. Mr. Emberley holds a bachelor of fine arts degree in painting and illustrating, from the Massachusetts School of Fine Arts in Boston. At the school he met his wife, who was studying fashion design and illustration. After their graduation, they were married. Mr. Emberley then served a two-year stint in the United States Army.

Mrs. Emberley was born December 12, 1932, in Chicago, and grew up in Lexington, Massachusetts. Her husband was born in Malden, Massachusetts, on October 19, 1931. His childhood was spent in nearby Cambridge. He recalls washing dishes at Harvard for one year before entering art school. The couple have two children, Michael, 9, and Rebecca, 11. They live, along with their cats, in Ipswich, Massachusetts, on the rim of the winding Ipswich River. Their home, situated yards back from an unpaved road, is an old red saltbox built in the early part of the 18th century. The living room is large, low, dark, and cool. The dining room, by contrast, is warm and bright. Giant fireplaces big enough to stand in dominate both these rooms; there are five fireplaces in all! Upstairs the rooms are sunny. The children's rooms, like most children's rooms, are cluttered. Adjacent to the house is a barn housing a loom, homemade candles, and homegrown herbs, which Mrs. Emberley lays out to dry. A "bird-in-the-bush" press also stands in the barn; Mr. Emberley told me how it got its name. "Most of us have to spend most of our time working for the bird in the hand. This press will devote its time to working for the bird in the bush!"

Mr. Emberley's first book was *The Wing on a Flea* (Little, Brown, 1961), an imaginative commentary on simple forms such as the triangle of a flea's wing or the beak of a bird. The text had an interesting development. He explained, "I had been waiting five years for a publisher to send me a book to illustrate. I finally decided that the most sensible way to convince an editor that I could indeed illustrate a children's book was to make one up, so I created *The Wing on a Flea,* with text and illustrations, along with a detailed dummy. It was accepted, published, and Barbara and I were off!" Upon publication he bought 30 copies of the book and sent them to all the publishers he could think of with a letter asking them to consider his work for future books. Three publishing houses immediately accepted his offer, and the Emberleys' meteoric career began.

During the summer of 1962, Mr. Emberley began experimenting with woodcuts — one of his favorite media — using ordinary pine planks from a local lumber yard. His work in this media can be seen in *Yankee Doodle* by Dr. Richard Shackburg (Prentice-Hall, 1965), the song that became the clarion call of our forefathers, *One Wide River to Cross* (Prentice-Hall, 1966), a counting book to the tune of an old folk song and sole runner-up for the 1967 Caldecott Award, and *Drummer Hoff. Drummer Hoff* was the fifth book on which the husband-wife team collaborated.

Commenting on work habits, Mr. Emberley stated, "Our work habits are simple. We do not work on Sunday, Thanksgiving, Christmas, or from the time school lets out in the spring till the children go back to school in the fall — all other time is devoted to our work. When doing artwork, we work at adjoining tables; when working on anything to do with writing, we have to be alone — absolutely and positively alone. Since the studio is in our home, our work day tends to be long, from about 8:30 in the morning till about 7:00 in the evening and longer if need be. We decided a long time ago that the reason we got married was to be together, so I have avoided things that would tend to separate us mentally and physically. I can't imagine living any other way."

The family, a warm close one, shares everything. Pleasures include gardening, concentrating on spring bulbs and herbs, traveling and camping in their Volkswagen bus, collecting anything early American, and boating. "We have a canoe, rubber life raft, pram, two small sailboats, and a larger cruising sailboat in which we cruised around Cape Cod and the islands in the summer of '66," he said. The Emberleys enjoy their work: "It is a challenging field. It is a wonderful one to be involved in." And they thoroughly enjoy family life — being together.

One wide river, and that wide river is Jordan,

SOME OTHER BOOKS BY THE EMBERLEYS:

Night's Nice (Doubleday, 1962).
51st Dragon (Prentice-Hall, 1968).
Simon's Song (Prentice-Hall, 1969).

ILLUSTRATED BY MR. EMBERLEY (All T. Y. Crowell):

Franklyn M. Branley. *The Big Dipper* (1962).
———. *Flash, Crash, Rumble, and Roll* (1964).
Judy Hawes. *Ladybug, Ladybug, Fly Away Home* (1967).

WRITTEN AND ILLUSTRATED BY MR. EMBERLEY (All Little, Brown):

The Parade Book (1962).
Punch and Judy (1965).
London Bridge Is Falling Down (1967).

60

Marie Hall Ets

WITH HER SNOW-WHITE HAIR, glasses, and sweater carefully draped over her shoulders, Marie Hall Ets looks as homey as apple pie — like a grandmother from whom you want to hear story after story. Her background explains this warm simplicity. "I was born in a place that is no place at all, North Greenfield, Wisconsin. The name of the place was changed, and it is now a part of Milwaukee — I think!" she explained. "I was the third of six children. My two sisters were older; my three brothers, younger. We moved around Wisconsin a great deal until my father settled down. The happiest memories of my childhood are of summers in the North Woods of Wisconsin. I loved to run off by myself into the woods and watch for the deer with their fawns and for porcupines and badgers and turtles and frogs and hugh pine snakes and sometimes a bear or a copperhead or a skunk. When I was old enough to be trusted alone in a flat-bottomed boat, I used to explore the lake shore or the channels between the lakes."

Many of these childhood memories provided the storylines for several of her books, notably *Mr. Penny* (Viking, 1935), *In the Forest* (Viking, 1944), and *Play with Me* (Viking, 1955). In recent years Mrs. Ets has provided youngsters with such delights as *Gilberto and the Wind* (Viking, 1963), a tender story of one child's adventures with the wind, and *Bad Boy, Good Boy* (T. Y. Crowell, 1967), a stark book about family life among a disadvantaged Mexican family.

"Gilberto is a real child, you know," she told me. "I was vacationing in La Jola, California, and actually looking for a model for a story. Walking down an alley was a young girl with a smaller boy. I knew this was the child I wanted to draw. The children became suspicious of me looking at them and quickly disappeared! A few days later, while I was on the way to the bank, I walked down that same alley again, and I saw the boy! This time he was alone. All I could think of was here I am without my Kodak or drawing materials! Suddenly the child ran across the street and threw his arms around my knees. With my poor Spanish I managed to ask him to take me to his mother. He took my hand and led me to his house. The boy was Gilberto. Actually, Gilberto chose me. His mother let me come to sketch him whenever I wanted to. I really came to know the family quite well."

The same family inspired *Bad Boy, Good Boy,* a true story. Mrs. Ets told me that Gilberto is now about nine years old, speaks English, and goes to a private school. Mrs. Ets sends money to the family to help keep him there.

Her favorite book is *The Story of a Baby* (Viking, 1939), a pioneer text in the field of sex education. "There is no mention of sex in this book," she remarked. "I wanted boys and girls to have definite pictures showing the beauty of life development. I got the idea at the 1933–34 Chicago World's Fair exhibit of human embryos. This book is the most important thing I have ever done."

In 1960 Mrs. Ets won the Caldecott Medal for *Nine Days to Christmas* (Viking, 1959), a book written in collaboration with a close Mexican friend, Aurora Labastida. "Señorita Labastida and I wanted to make a story about a little Mexican girl who lived in the city. Señorita Labastida said that Mexicans resent the fact that all children's books in America about Mexican children make them villagers wearing ponchos and following burros; actually 70 per cent of all Mexicans live in cities. In the book I used actual characters throughout, except for the little girl; the real Ceci was too large and too blonde."

The furnishings in Mrs. Ets' apartment, which is located in New York's Harlem, are an indication of her travels and interest in Mexico. A favorite piece is a wooden chest purchased in a museum there. The chest houses the many books she has written and illustrated.

Mrs. Ets' robust personality fully conceals a chronic illness contacted in Czechoslovakia in the mid-1920's; she was there organizing a permanent children's health program for the Czech government under the auspices of the American Red Cross.

Commenting on her interests, she stated: "I like music — baroque, modern jazz, and folk music, but I *hate* opera. I don't like women who sing in an overstuffed artificial way. I turn down any tickets given to me for the Met."

We lunched together, talked about life, and enjoyed each other's company. I felt richer for having met Marie Hall Ets. She is a warm, outgoing human being who has contributed greatly to the happiness of many children through her beautifully written and illustrated books.

SOME OTHER BOOKS BY MRS. ETS (All Viking):

My Dog Rinty (coauthored with Ellen Tarry; 1946).
Oley: The Sea Monster (1947).
Beasts and Nonsense (1952).
Just Me (1965).
Talking Without Words (1968).

Louise Fatio
Roger Duvoisin

LOTHROP, LEE AND SHEPARD prepared an information sheet about Roger Duvoisin (dyoo vwah *zahn*) for the 1968 Hans Christian Andersen Exhibit. One section lists his awards and honors, which numbers 23 from 1937–1966; another section fills six pages and lists the 122 works he illustrated from 1932–1967; still another section fills four pages and lists work that has been translated and published in countries other than the United States. This seems like a great deal for one man to achieve, but it isn't all — Mr. Duvoisin is married to Louise Fatio, an author who has also been heralded in the field of children's literature.

Mr. Duvoisin commented to me on his diversity. "Ideas for stories come in all sorts of ways: accidentally from an event I hear or read about, something I see, perhaps at home watching children play, or when I reflect about my own childhood. Ideas are also sometimes built around some personal feelings or opinions I would like to express. I note on pieces of paper ideas that occur to me, and I keep them in a folder. I seldom use them, however, for I prefer to work with fresh ideas. Illustrations are always developed from the problems, lessons, or ideas contained in the text I am working from. Nothing comes easily! Although I am known mostly as an illustrator, I enjoy writing as much as drawing. The two are closely related."

Mr. Duvoisin has collaborated with his wife on the popular and delightful "Happy Lion" series, beginning with *The Happy Lion* (McGraw-Hill, 1954). This book was the winner of the first prize for children's books awarded by the West German government; it was published in Germany in 1955. The development of this book was an interesting one. When her two sons were still young, Miss Fatio began to help her husband with his work on children's books, contributing her ideas and assisting him in some aspects of his artwork. She also began formulating ideas for future books, partly from the stories she invented for her own children. While sojourning in France before the war, she first had the idea for *The Happy Lion*. A lion had escaped from a circus in a small French town. The peaceful wanderings of the well-fed lion through the streets of the town contrasted with the excitement he caused and was a natural subject for a book for children. *"The Happy Lion* remains my favorite," she said, "because its hero has become for us almost a real, living pet!"

Regarding their collaborating, Mr. Duvoisin remarked, "There are problems and great pleasures in collaborating. Louise has a sensitive eye. Her criticism is very valuable but sometimes difficult to accept, especially when she tells me that I should do particular illustrations all over again. She is usually right, though!"

Roger Duvoisin was born in Geneva, Switzerland. Throughout his boyhood he drew and painted. He began to study music at the age of seven and later attended the Geneva Conservatory of Music. At the Écoles des Arts Décoratif, he studied mural painting and stage scenery. Upon finishing school, he worked at the Geneva Opera Ateliendes Décors where he designed scenery, painted murals, and did posters and illustrations. His love of working in ceramics led him to managing an old pottery plant that Voltaire had founded in the little town of Ferney-Voltaire and that needed an injection of young blood. He considered settling there, but, the old manager of the pottery plant began to make trouble for him by breaking pottery at night and mixing up orders. The old man even threatened to cut Duvoisin's throat one dark evening. Mr. Duvoisin decided to move to Lyon where he had been offered a position as foreman of a large textile designing studio. In Paris he met the art director and president of one of the largest textile firms in America and was offered a contract to go to New York to design textiles. There he also met Miss Fatio. They were married and sailed to the United States.

His first book, *A Little Boy Was Drawing* (Scribner), was published in 1932. This began a steady stream of books; he had 14 to his credit in the 1930's, including a textbook series that he illustrated.

Miss Fatio was born in Lausanne, Switzerland. She attended the public schools of Geneva, then went to a boarding school in Basel in German Switzerland, where she had some art training and learned to speak German fluently. She finished her education at the College des Jeunes Filles in Geneva.

Today the Duvoisins live in a rural area of New Jersey in a modern house, which they partly designed and built in the 1940's. The house is set on a hillside among woods and orchards. "Last spring we had the unfortunate experience of signing contracts for the enlargement of the house with two contractors who never told us in advance that their undertaking the job would be a spare time project. As a result, we lived all summer in a partly demolished house, under the rains and among building materials of all sorts. Living in the beautiful countryside compensates for these inconveniences, however," Mr. Duvoisin continued. "We have many happy moments here; I can work quietly in my studio, with our woods coming up almost to the windows, except I can't resist going out to join my wife in the endless and pleasant chores that our fruit trees, fowl, pond, house, and garden require! We enjoy the seasons as they come and go. We go to

From PETUNIA by Roger Duvoisin. Permission of Alfred A. Knopf, Inc.

New York when we feel the need of the city, which is very often."

Mr. Duvoisin likes people, travel, reading, music, writing letters, caring for gardens and orchards, work, and seeing intimate friends and his sons, Roger, Jr., a neurologist at the Columbia Medical Center in New York, and Jacques, an architect, and their families. "I also like loafing around our pond and watching the life around it — when book work leaves free time, that is." He dislikes formal clothes, particularly neckties!

Miss Fatio shares many of her husband's likes but added, "I enjoy our books and recordings, paintings, antiques collected during our trips, and our animals — dogs, cats, and fowl." She is also an excellent cook and an accomplished expert in the art of French cooking. (An editor friend told me that she gave her best recipe for Quiche Lorraine to her neighbor and friend, Adrienne Adams.)

In 1948 Mr. Duvoisin was awarded the Caldecott Medal for *White Snow, Bright Snow* (Lothrop, 1947), written by Alvin Tresselt. Commenting on his collaboration with Mr. Tresselt, he stated "An award gives an artist some confidence and a greater sense of responsibility. I have always enjoyed illustrating Alvin's books, because I share his love of nature, a love he expresses with charm and imagination in his poetic texts."

The interview with the Duvoisins ended humorously with some advice Mr. Duvoisin once gave someone requesting biographical information (not me!): "It is too bad that making illustrations requires also telling about yourself. I am sorry that nothing dramatic such as hunting lions in Africa or exploring the North Pole has taken place in my life, but you can make it up if you wish."

Fortunately, I didn't have to!

SOME OTHER BOOKS BY MISS FATIO (All McGraw-Hill):

Red Bantam (1962).
Doll for Marie (1957).

SOME OTHER BOOKS BY MR. DUVOISIN:

Alvin Tresselt. *Hi, Mr. Robin* (Lothrop, 1950).
Petunia (Knopf, 1951).
Alvin Tresselt. *Wake Up, Farm!* (Lothrop, 1955).
Veronica (Knopf, 1961).
Alvin Tresselt. *Hide and Seek Fog* (Lothrop, 1965).
Louise Fatio. *Red Bantam* (McGraw-Hill, 1962).
What Is Right for Tulip . . . (Knopf, 1969).

Tom Feelings

Tom Feelings was born in Brooklyn, New York, grew up in Brooklyn, attended the George Westinghouse Vocational High School in Brooklyn, and now lives with his wife, Muriel, and newborn son on Eastern Parkway in Brooklyn. He is a young, tall, handsome, and well-built man who is on the move and fast becoming one of the top black illustrators in the field of children's literature.

Mr. Feelings told me about his recent experience working and living in West Africa. "I worked in West Africa, in Ghana, for the Ghana Publishing Company. There I illustrated the magazine *African Review* and also worked on syndicated newspapers, booklets, educational materials, and visual materials for both Ghana television and the Ghana Airport. Ghana was my first lesson and experience with 'black power'; my initial impressions were those of pride in seeing every facet of life manned by black people — banks, industries, schools, the mass media including press, radio and television, and commerce. It was an inspiration to work for a black establishment, something I had never before had the opportunity to do. I was not asked 'Why are you drawing black people?' as I was functioning in an all-black country.

"The phrase 'black is beautiful' was unquestionably taken for granted in Ghana as people there had no inferiority complexes about their physical beauty. Their standards were their own. The people proudly wore their national dress with bright colors complementing their black skin. Women wore their hair in a variety of styles — braided, high puffs, in a ball, but most always unstraightened. They walked tall and laughed loudly and freely."

Living in Africa definitely influenced Mr. Feeling's work as an illustrator. "One day when looking through the work I had done in Brooklyn an African artist in Ghana asked me, 'Why are the Afro-American children that you draw looking so sad?' I had never thought of their expressions as sad when I was in the States. I soon saw why they looked so to him. African children are basically happy, stable, and secure children, and this well-being is reflected in their glowing faces. I discovered this as I began to look at and draw them. This was one of the beautiful experiences I gained in Africa. Another thing influencing my work was the colors. I began to depict these colors in scenes showing the dress and outdoor life; something that was absent here."

Before the trip to Africa and after his high school years, he attended the School of Visual Arts; he illustrated a comic strip for the now defunct *New York Age,* entitled 'Tommy Traveler in the World of Negro History.' It depicted episodes in the lives of black heroes and was developed from histories Mr. Feelings had read. He also worked as an illustrator for the graphics division of the air force during his tour of duty in London. After his discharge from the service, he returned to the School of Visual Arts. "By then I had decided that I could best express myself as an illustrator. Illustrating enabled me to depict subjects drawn from life and was a far more diverse and flexible field than cartooning," he declared.

Mr. Feelings decided to illustrate books for young children because he was concerned about the absence of positive imagery among black children, a lack he had felt existed since his own childhood. The first book he illustrated was one dealing with an

African child who wanted to become a master drummer and play for the Oba, "the king." The book, entitled *Bola and the Oba's Drummers* (McGraw-Hill, 1967), was written by Letta Schatz. The author and publisher had seen the work he had done in Africa and felt that his style and African experience would lend itself to the subject.

Mr. Feelings described to me how he works on a book. "After reading through a story, I go back and look at each chapter for an idea that can best capture the essence of that particular part of the story. I write the idea down and develop a list of picture subjects. From this I create the initial layouts and illustrations."

He lives in an apartment in the Crown Heights section of Brooklyn, a residential-commercial area. The possessions he values most are the books he acquires and reads zealously. The subjects usually deal with black people, fiction and nonfiction. He has a guitar he has enjoyed for a number of years. "It's good when I feel like croaking a folk song or such in my leisure hours." He has a record collection that consists of African and Afro-American blues, folk songs, rhythm-and-blues, and ballads. "I enjoy talking with friends, especially people with whom I have some common ground. I like plays and other cultural forms dealing with the black situation primarily. I enjoy jazz and the out-of-doors when time permits," he added.

Of the books he has illustrated, his favorites are *When the Stones Were Soft: East African Folktales,* collected by Eleanor Heady (Funk and Wagnalls, 1968), ("I feel I captured the mood of the tales and the atmosphere of Africa"), and *To Be a Slave,* written by Julius Lester (Dial, 1968), a book by and about slaves and slavery. About the latter Mr. Feelings commented, "The subject matter is one I feel deeply about as an Afro-American and a descendent of African slaves. It was also the first book by an Afro-American I have had the privilege to illustrate. This added to my desire to express the message the author was conveying. I feel the resultant work has strong emotional impact." The book became a runner-up for the 1969 Newbery Medal.

Mr. Feelings is one who is constantly busy, constantly at work. "I basically consider myself and my work inseparable," he commented. "That is, through my work I express my life and environment, the people and the situation — the truth about things as I see it. The African experience did a great deal to reaffirm

From A QUIET PLACE by Rose Blue and Tom Feelings, © 1969 by Rose Bluestone. Permission of Franklin Watts, Inc.

my feeling and belief in the beauty and humanism of black people. My work is one of the greatest satisfactions in my life. My work is my life! I hope that little black children will be uplifted by any positive imagery they discover through the books I have illustrated. I so missed these things as a child and can, therefore, very much understand their need for them. As for adults who likewise have experienced very little that is positive in blackness — for themselves or for their children — I hope my work has begun to fill the vacuum."

Through the efforts of people like Tom Feelings, the vacuum will be filled.

SOME OTHER BOOKS BY MR. FEELINGS:

Osmond Molarsky. *Song of the Empty Bottles* (Walck, 1968).
Robin McKown. *The Congo: River of Mystery* (McGraw-Hill, 1968).
Ruskin Bond. *Panther's Moon* (Random House, 1969).
Rose Blue. *A Quiet Place* (Watts, 1969).
Julius Lester. *Black Folktales* (Richard W. Baron, 1969).

Aileen Fisher

AILEEN FISHER HAS WRITTEN books of poetry, picture books in verse, plays and programs, prose about nature and the American heritage, biographies, Bible themes, and articles for popular magazines and journals. A listing of her prolific writings could easily fill several pages.

She was born and grew up in and around the little town of Iron River, on the Upper Peninsula of Michigan near the Wisconsin border. "I was a lucky child," she remarked. "When I was four years old my father had a serious bout with pneumonia. This made him decide to give up his business in Iron River and more or less retire to the country. He bought 40 acres near Iron River and built the big, square white house where I grew up. We called the place High Banks because it was on a high bank above the river, which was always red with water pumped from the iron mines. Still, the river was good to wade in, swim in, fish in, and skate on in winter. When I was young there was still quite a bit of logging nearby, and my brother and I used to follow the iced logging roads. There was a big landing for the logs on the railroad about a mile from our house. We had all kinds of pets — cows, horses, and chickens. And we had a big garden in summer. I loved it. I have always loved the country."

She began writing while still in college. "I always liked to write verse. My mother had quite a flair for versifying, and I was sort of brought up on it. Mother was an ex-kindergarten teacher, which was fortunate for her offspring. During my last year of college, I wrote quite a bit of children's verse and several puppet plays. My first book was *The Coffee-Pot Face* (McBride Company, 1933), a collection of children's verses, now out of print; about half of the 80 or more verses in it had previously been published in *Child Life*. The book was a Junior Literary Guild selection."

Miss Fisher described her work habits as being quite methodical. "I try to be at my desk four hours a day, from 8 a.m. to noon. Ideas come to me out of experience and from reading and remembering. I usually do a first draft by hand. I can't imagine writing verse on a typewriter, and for years I wrote nothing but verse so I formed the habit of thinking with a pencil or pen in hand. I usually rework my material, sometimes more, sometimes less. I *never* try out my ideas on children, except on the child I used to know — me! Fortunately I remember pretty well what I used to like to read, think about, and do. I find, even today, that if I write something I like, children are pretty apt to like it too. I guess what it amounts to is that I never grew up."

Miss Fisher is tall, solidly built, and "decidedly a country person, addicted to blue jeans and slacks." She lives on a two-hundred-acre ranch about a 20-minute drive from the city of Boulder, Colorado, and two thousand feet higher! With her friend Olive Rabe,* a lawyer-writer, she designed and helped build the cabin that is her home. It has a high beamed ceiling and a big fireplace in the center.

"When we moved to the ranch in 1937, no electricity was available, so we organized our lives very happily without it. And now that we can have it, we don't want it. We have wonderful

---

* NOTE: I recently received a letter from Miss Fisher stating that Mrs. Rabe had died.

views in all directions with no houses in sight. There are a few neighbors here and there, mostly fields, pine-covered hills, dips and swells, and the Arapahoe Peaks and Bald Mountain in the distance, which are always covered with some snow. We don't raise any stock but always rent the pasture for cows in the summer, so we have the pleasure of a ranch without the grief. I'm not a bit gadget-minded. My favorite possessions are books and interesting pieces of Colorado wood from the timberline, which have been enhanced by wood-rasp, chisel, and some sandpaper. Oh, and a 1941 jalopy! My pleasures in life are found through animals (especially dogs), mountain climbing, hiking, working with wood, unorthodox gardening, a few people in small doses, and *reading*. I like centrality in my life and peace and quiet, which means that I avoid commercialized excitement, cities, traffic, polluted air, noise, confusion, travel, crowds, and airports. For me early morning on a mountain trail is the height of bliss."

I asked Miss Fisher if she had a favorite book among those she has written. She replied, "What a terrible question! Which do you like best, peaches or apples? I mean, can one compare verse and biography or natural history? Maybe I can sort it out this way. Of the verse collections I have had published, I like best *Up the Windy Hill* (Abelard, 1953) for it touches more children's interests and is, for me, a sort of record of the things I used to think. Of the nature verse picture books I like *Listen, Rabbit* (T. Y. Crowell, 1964) best. It was one of those books that wrote itself. Of the collections of plays and programs (several coauthored with Olive Rabe) I like best *Holiday Programs for Boys and Girls* (Plays, Inc., 1953). It contains some of my best plays. I rarely write plays anymore. Of the natural history-ecology books, I like best *Valley of the Smallest* (T. Y. Crowell, 1966) because in it I figured out a few things I wanted to know and wanted other people to know. Of the books of fiction and fictionalized biography I guess I'd say *Skip* (Thomas Nelson and Sons, 1958) because it means so much to children and because it meant a great deal to me, too, at the time I wrote it. We had gone through the experience of having a much-loved dog become blind."

In regard to poetry, her first love, Miss Fisher stated "Poetry is a rhythmical piece of writing that leaves the reader feeling that life is a little richer than before, a little more full of wonder, beauty, or just plain delight."

She certainly knows children and children's interests. "Judging from my fan mail, I have found that children want to know the details about everything, especially pets, jalopies, weather, electricity, mountains, and cabins." And children know Aileen Fisher. Whether they are *Going Barefoot* (T. Y. Crowell, 1960), are spending time *In the Woods, In the Meadows, In the Sky* (Scribner, 1955), or taking a *Skip Around the Year* (T. Y. Crowell, 1967), they take to Miss Fisher like a *Cricket in a Thicket* (Scribner, 1963).

SOME OTHER BOOKS BY MISS FISHER:

Runny Days, Sunny Days (Abelard, 1958).
Where Does Everyone Go? (T. Y. Crowell, 1961).
Like Nothing at All (T. Y. Crowell, 1962).
Arbor Day (T. Y. Crowell, 1965).
In the Middle of the Night; illus. by Adrienne Adams (T. Y. Crowell, 1965).
Sing Little Mouse (T. Y. Crowell, 1969).

Don Freeman

Don Freeman was in New York City en route to his home in Santa Barbara, California, when I met him. He had just visited Washington, D. C., where he had completed sketches of The Poor Peoples' March for the *Christian Science Monitor*. New York is not strange territory to Mr. Freeman; he knows it, loves it, and has lived in and for it. Shortly after finishing high school in St. Louis, Missouri, he set off for New York City to study with John Sloan at the Art Students League.

"I played a trumpet in a jazz band," he recalled, "and I came across the country doing one-night stands at dances, banquets, and anywhere else I could find a job. Once I got to New York City, I began drawing life here, everything and anything I saw. Like my father, I loved the theatre. I had little money, so I'd buy standing room to every and any show. I became quite friendly with stage managers and always went backstage. I began drawing intimate glimpses of theatre people and theatre life — my impressions. I submitted several of my drawings to the *New York Times* and the *New York Herald Tribune;* they printed them!"

Mr. Freeman stopped his trumpet playing by accident rather than by choice. "I was riding in the subway, came to my stop, and left without the trumpet case. The door closed, and the train rushed away with my instrument. I never got it back. Somebody's playing it," he remarked with a slight tinge of regret in his voice.

Theatre life continued to be lucrative for Mr. Freeman. He did a series of posters and a series of sketches for the famous American star-studded restaurant, Sardi's. One of his sketches still hangs there. "In New York wonderful things happened to me," he said. "My life was full. My wife and I found life fabulous here."

He recalled one evening, while living on 14th Street in Greenwich Village, when the playwright William Saroyan rang his doorbell. "We went into the night with marvelous talk. Mr. Saroyan looked at my drawings and said, 'I want you to illustrate my new book!' I thought I'd never hear from him again, but I was wrong. I did, and later, I did the illustrations for his *My Name Is Aaron* and *The Human Comedy*." He also did work for the late James Thurber.

Mr. Freeman came into the children's book field via a librarian in California, his friend Marge Raskin. "Marge encouraged me to send in a book I did for my son. 'Send it to a publisher,' she said. It was published, and since then I've been hooked. Illustrating children's books is an expression of the theatre for me. I can create my own theatre in picture books. I love the flow of turning the pages, the suspense of what's next. Ideas just come at me and after me. It's all so natural. I work all the time, long into the night, and it's such a pleasure. I don't know when time ends. I've never been happier in my life!"

A unique Don Freeman habit is that as a book deadline draws near, he checks into a hotel so that he does not become distracted. "I've finished books in hotels in San Francisco, Los Angeles, New York City, and a host of other big cities. *Dandelion* (Viking, 1964), a funny account of a lion who decides to live up to his name, was done in a gloomy hotel room in Washington, D. C."

Mr. Freeman, his wife Lydia Cooley, who is also an author-illustrator of children's books, and their son, Roy, 19, now make their home in Santa Barbara. "If I had a map of the world and someone gave me a thumbtack to place where I would *not* want to live, I'd put it on Santa Barbara. We live in a wooden house, sort of a mountain cabin. When someone asks me about it, I just say, 'It's beautiful — but I don't mind it!' I'm a city guy. I love big cities. I love to be involved with big cities. I only need one bush or one tree — out there I have too many. People keep me going. My hobby is living."

Although people keep him going, his work keeps youngsters going. His books such as *Mop Top* (Viking, 1955) have children rolling with laughter; *Corduroy* (Viking, 1968) relates the universal theme of a young girl's love for a department store doll; *Fly High, Fly Low* (Viking, 1957), a Caldecott runner-up depicts a beautiful tale of two pigeons in one of Mr. Freeman's favorite haunts, San Francisco. Mr. Freeman is big and burly warm and tender, and as friendly as each of his books.

SOME OTHER BOOKS BY MR. FREEMAN (All Viking):

The Night the Lights Went Out (1959).
Cyrano, the Crow (1960).
Turtle and the Dove (1964).
Ruth A. Sonneborn. *Seven in a Bed* (1968).
Tilly Witch (1969).
Robert Burch, Joey's Cat (1969).

81

Lou Ann Gaeddart

IN 1965 DOUBLEDAY published *Noisy Nancy Norris*. The book, written by the quiet, reserved Lou Ann Gaeddart (*ged* ert), caused a great deal of noise in the field of children's literature. The book was Mrs. Gaeddart's first. I became acquainted with it via Bank Street College; its Communications Laboratory Division decided to film the book for one of its "Reading Incentive" series. One of Hollywood's top female stars, Shirley MacLaine, was selected to read the book. Whenever the film is shown to children, to adults, or to mixed groups, howls of laughter erupt throughout the room at Nancy's antics. She bangs on radiators, bounces down the hall, wails like a fire siren, and clumps like an elephant — all to the distress of her apartmenthouse neighbors, especially Mrs. Muffle, the owner of the building who lives in the apartment below the Norris family.

"The book grew out of a common problem that people who live in the city must face," commented Mrs. Gaeddart. "Children can be noisy. My own children, Andrew, 9, and Martha, 6, are noisy! There are very few books that recognize that children *do* live in apartment houses. I think we've got to face the fact that many children are apartment dwellers and that more and more kids will be living in apartments in the future. I am interested in the urban child. Suburban living is a completely different way of life. If there has to be a choice between Daddy and grass, I feel the choice should be Daddy!"

The Gaeddarts live in a cooperative apartment building in Jackson Heights, New York. Mrs. Gaeddart writes between 9 a.m. and 12 noon when Martha is in school. "Soon she will be in school all day, and I can spend more time writing."

Her most recent major project was authoring *The Split-Level Cookbook* (T. Y. Crowell, 1967). "I wanted to write a cookbook that could be used by housewives who had to feed the kids at one time, and fathers at another. The object is to make mothers' lives easier. All the recipes and menus are easy, inexpensive to prepare, and are for those who are far from the gourmet type. I hate to cook! Unfortunately, my poor husband was my guinea pig. He ate a lot of the stuff and only once got up from the table."

The Gaeddarts recently bought a summer home in the Berkshires. "The house was built in 1901, and it's a terrible wreck of a thing. Everything's wrong with it. It costs us every extra penny we have. As a matter of fact," she laughed, "the royalties on *Noisy Nancy Norris* are down the well, and the earnings on the *Cookbook* will be put into a crumbling fireplace and a sagging foundation."

Perhaps the house will be an inspiration for many books to come. Lou Ann Gaeddart is fun, witty, and the humor she created in *Noisy Nancy Norris* will be around to elicit chuckles from children of all ages for years and years to come.

Paul Galdone

THE TOMATOES WERE the largest, reddest, and juiciest I had ever seen. The cucumbers were scrumptious. The breads, cheeses, and meats, all sprinkled with homegrown herbs and spices, resembled a table setting from a great master's still-life painting. "It's all done by us," Paul Galdone said proudly. "We grow all our own vegetables in the garden. There's nothing like the taste of home-grown vegetables. One of the joys of living and working in the country is being able to supply our own food." The "we" include Mr. Galdone's delightful family — his wife Jannelise (Esie), his pixie-like daughter Joanna, 22, and his son Paul Ferencz, 21.

Their sprawling, modern farmhouse is situated on 16 acres in New City, New York. The house was designed by both Mr. and Mrs. Galdone, with the help of her architect brother. "Esie's brother designed it while he was in California," Mr. Galdone noted. "He used descriptions of the land area from our letters; he didn't see the house or the land until ten years after he designed it." We sat around a wooden table in the huge country kitchen, eating and talking. Mrs. Galdone kept tempting me with simple cookery such as corn-on-the-cob, squash, and chunks of salami, all as tasty as the finest gourmet meal.

After our long lunch, Mr. Galdone and I went upstairs to his studio to talk about his life and his work. Paul Galdone was born in Budapest, Hungary. He came to the United States at the age of 14. Not knowing one word of English, he worked at any odd job he could find and studied nights at the Art Students League in New York City with George Grosz, Louis Bouche, and Guy Pene du Bois. For several years he worked in the art department at Doubleday and Company. During World War II he served with the United States Army Engineers. "My father wanted me to come to America to avoid the war," he commented. "So I came here and spent four years in the army!" Upon leaving the service, he designed book jackets for adult and children's books on a free-lance basis and finally had the opportunity to illustrate books of his own.

Mr. Galdone has illustrated scores of books for young children and is one of the country's best-known illustrators. In both 1957 and 1958 he was runner-up for the Caldecott Award for *Anatole* (Whittlesey, 1956) and *Anatole and the Cat* (Whittlesey, 1957), stories about a French cheese-tasting mouse written by Eve Titus. Mr. Galdone characterized his work as being representational and humorous. "Children's books provide me with much freedom of their naturally whimsical nature," he stated. He usually works in pen and ink and wash. He often makes his own color separations with the help of his wife. Many of his picture books are based on well-known poems, ranging from Mother Goose to Edgar Allan Poe and Henry Thoreau.

Mr. Galdone is also a painter and sculptor. His home is filled with canvases of landscapes, still lifes, portraits, and nudes that he has created. The chimney outside his house is adorned with a large, silver grasshopper that has movable legs; the pool-side bathhouse is decorated with an over-sized flying fish. He fashioned these objects from roofing sheet metal. Besides painting and sculpting, he enjoys the outdoors — long hikes, sawing, wood chopping, forestry, and gardening. "One of the most valuable things in life to me is time," he observed. "Time to work, to live, to be out under the sky, and to be with my family."

We rejoined Mrs. Galdone and Joanna for a walk around the grounds. A lively, leaping brook contains a small dammed area that the children used for swimming when they were growing up. The rest of the land is a mass of trees and flowers. A large swimming pool and bathhouse are adjacent to the house. "I love the outdoors," he said. "I love everything about nature. Look at these trees. Trees give you such permanence." He smiled, looking like a young boy getting into mischief for the first time. I could tell he really loved his land, his work, and his family.

From HENNY PENNY by Paul Galdone, © 1968 by Paul Galdone.
Permission of The Seabury Press.

SOME OTHER BOOKS BY MR. GALDONE:

Oliver Wendell Holmes. *The Deacon's Masterpiece or the Wonderful One-Hoss Shay* (McGraw-Hill, 1958; 1965).

Eve Merriam. *A Gaggle of Geese* (Knopf, 1965).

Edgar Allan Poe. *Three Poems of Edgar Allan Poe* (McGraw-Hill, 1966).

The History of Simple Simon (McGraw-Hill, 1966).

Rabelais. *The Wise Fool.* (Pantheon, 1968).

The Horse, the Fox, and the Lion (Seabury, 1968).

Henny Penny (Seabury, 1968).

Pura Belpré. *Oté* (Pantheon, 1969).

The Monkey and the Crocodile: A Jataka Tale from India (Seabury, 1969).

87

May Garelick

MAY GARELICK HAS BEEN in publishing all her working life, holding every job from clerical worker to production manager. For approximately 15 years she was an editor of children's books for the William R. Scott Company.

As we sat in her apartment in New York's Greenwich Village, Miss Garelick commented on her childhood years. "I was born in Vobruisk, a small town in Russia, in a log cabin my father had built with the help of some neighbors. But I don't remember any of this because I was nine months old when my family came to the United States. We lived for several years in Rochester, New York, moved to Newark, New Jersey, and then to New York City, where I have lived ever since. The elementary school I went to was probably the first school built in New York City; it was called Public School #1. This no doubt makes you think that I should be hundreds of years old or at least one hundred! I'm not! And since I am as vain as most women, I won't tell you my age. I won't tell you a wrong age, but I just won't tell.

"When I was about 12 years old, I decided I would read every book in the library. The books were arranged alphabetically by author. I started with the A authors but got restless and began to skip around. By this time the librarian was helping me choose books. I didn't read them all but did read a good many. I went to high school in New York City, continuing on to college for two years. My family couldn't afford to keep me in school, so I quit and went to work, trying to continue my college education at night. It was too hard to work and try to be a good student. I had to work, so I gave up school."

Miss Garelick is a fun person to know. She is animated and speaks quickly and wittily. Throughout her conversation she throws in a sprinkling of Jewish words and phrases; she laughs, jokes, and has a great sense of humor. She likes people, music, theatre, and books. "I'm really interested in everything!" she exclaimed.

Although she has a love for the city, many of her books focus around nature. She commented on one of her popular books, *Where Does the Butterfly Go When it Rains?* (Scott, 1961), which tells where various animals find shelter when the rain falls. "Maybe it's because I was brought up in a city that I became so aware of things in the country. As a child I wondered about a good many things but, I didn't ask questions; therefore, I grew up without knowing many of the answers. But I did develop a sense of observation and found out that you can always look up the answers if you know the question. I wrote this book to encourage children to notice things and ask about them!

"It's funny," she continued, "children don't seem troubled by the question, 'Where does the butterfly go when it rains?' I've had a lot of trouble with grownups though who ask continuously, 'But where DOES the butterfly go? Where? Tell me!' Children have given many answers voluntarily — 'under a leaf,' 'under a rock,' 'in a tree.' One five-year-old remarked to his teacher, 'Mrs. Johnson, I think I know where the butterfly goes when it rains. He climbs way down inside a flower and then the flower closes up and he stays nice and dry until the sun comes out again.' This child knew the important thing — wet wings won't work! Really and truly, does it matter where a butterfly goes when it rains? No! But to think creatively, to make your own discovery, that's pretty important. I like to pose a question in each of my books, to encourage readers to make their own discoveries in nature and in the world around them."

One of Miss Garelick's books, *Look at the Moon* (Scott, 1969), resulted from a question asked by a four-year-old girl on a moonlit night. "We were on the Normandy coast," she recalled. "The moon was full, the night enchanting. We were walking in silence, when Shula asked me, 'Do you have a moon in America?' I assured her we did. 'But is it like our moon — as lovely?' She was startled to find that it was the same moon. After all she had a reason for doubting since we lived in different countries and spoke different languages. I wrote this book, as I wrote my other young nature books, in response to a question. When I write, I always try to keep my audience in mind. I ask myself, what is it that the child wants to know about this? What is the *question*?"

Miss Garelick child-tests her material. She goes into classrooms to read her manuscripts long before they go to the publisher. She accepts children's criticisms and enjoys their comments. Because of her expertise in the publishing world, she has been hired as children's European editor for the E. P. Dutton Company. In her new position Miss Garelick will divide her time between the United States and Europe, seeking out new authors and illustrators and sharing her knowledge of books and book production.

SOME OTHER BOOKS BY MISS GARELICK:

Sounds of a Summer Night (Scott, 1963).
Winter's Birds (Scott, 1965).
Wild Ducks and Daffodils (Scott, 1965).
What Makes a Bird a Bird? (Follet, 1969).

Hardie Gramatky

Bookmobiles serving the Los Angeles area have a name plate that reads *Little Toot*, in honor of the children's classic published in 1939 (Putnam) and still in large demand.

When a recent strike in the tugboat industry was settled, one newspaper reported the settlement under the headline: LITTLE TOOT GETS BACK TO WORK.

For years tugboats in Venice have been called "Little Toot" by most Venetians who, like a generation of Americans, grew up with *Little Toot* among their favorite books.

IF THESE ANECDOTES do not prove that *Little Toot* (Putnam, 1939) is a popular book, consider the following: *Little Toot* was made into a movie by Walt Disney with recordings by Capitol; it is still on many best-books-for-children lists; it is part of the CARE-UNESCO book programs; it has been a float in the Pasadena Tournament of Roses; it has been on television many times; it was made into a filmstrip by Weston Woods Studios; it has been rated by the Library of Congress as one of the all-time greats in children's literature; and it has been translated into

Thai for children of Thailand, and also into Norwegian, Swedish, Finnish, and Danish. In fact, when Hardie Gramatky (gra *mat* kee) was in Viet Nam in 1966 on an assignment for the United States Air Force, he was recognized by a correspondent of *Newsweek,* who filed a report that *Newsweek* published under the heading "Little Toot Goes to Viet Nam."

With all this commotion about one book, I was quite anxious to meet its creator. Mr. Gramatky and his wife, Dorothea, live in Westport, Connecticut. When I arrived at their home, Mr. Gramatky was waiting for me on the front lawn. He is an enormously friendly man, one who enjoys life to the fullest.

He was born in Dallas, Texas. At the age of 9, his family moved to California. He spent his early adult years as a logger, bank teller, and deck hand on a lumber schooner. He began his art career with the late Walt Disney; after six years working as an animator in the Disney studio, he came to New York with his wife to set up his own studio. "We had a studio overlooking the East River," he said. "It was a huge room with three windows and cost only $15 a month! From these windows I would often see the little tugboats going up and down the river. *Little Toot* was conceived from this vantage point."

Mr. Gramatky wrote and illustrated the story but no publisher would accept it. "It was rejected by every major house," he recalled. "One editor told me that it wouldn't be successful 'because children aren't thinking this way this year!' I gave up on Little Toot and shelved it for awhile. Finally Putnam took it; it was their first book published for children. *Little Toot* is one of my favorite books for it is the love story of a personality."

The book was an immediate success; several Hollywood offers came, but Mr. Gramatky finally sold it to his good friend Walt Disney, who featured it in the film *Melody Time*. His next book was *Hercules* (Putnam, 1940), the story of an old-fashioned fire engine, which was conceived after a visit to the Museum of the City of New York. Next came *Loopy* (Putnam, 1941), the disobedient airplane that wanted to fly by itself.

In the mid-1940's the Gramatkys moved to their Westport home, which is situated on two acres of land. He continued writing and illustrating books for children as well as doing work in advertising and for national magazines. The walls of his home are adorned with fine watercolors. Many of his paintings appear in permanent collections throughout the United States. His work has been exhibited in India, Pakistan, and the Philippines, and he has earned over 30 top watercolor awards.

Mr. Gramatky enjoys traveling, the companionship of his wife, and being with his grandchild Andrew Prentice Smith. He is dedicated to children. "I have a great concern for boys and girls. They are the ones who can truly see the world the way it is. If I could reach just a few children through my work to make them greater people, I've done my life's work."

I left Westport feeling happy that I had met Little Toot's creator. In my pocket was an autographed sketch that Mr. Gramatky had drawn for my 12-year-old "adopted" nephew, Philip, who accompanied me on this visit. Although Philip's only love in life is baseball, even he was impressed by the afternoon's visit. "I like Mr. Toot," he commented. "He's cool!"

SOME OTHER BOOKS BY MR. GRAMATKY (All Putnam):

Nikos and the Sea God (1963).
Little Toot on the Thames (1964).
Little Toot on the Grand Canal (1968).

Ann Grifalconi

ANN GRIFALCONI (*grih* fal koh nee) is electric and vibrant —
brimming over with life. She stands tall, her eyes dance and gleam
as she talks, and her brunette hair, streaked with gray, looks as if
she had painted it herself.

Miss Grifalconi was born in New York City and attended
New York City public schools. "I love New York City. New
York's my home. I'm in my own fish bowl here. I can see and I
can breathe — and I even love the air." Recalling her early life
she said, "As a child we lived in Greenwich Village, over an
artist's studio. A sculptor lived there who was working on a
marble bust of Joe Louis, the great prizefighter. My brother
John and I used to see Mr. Louis come and go, day after day.
We watched a huge block of marble take on the resemblance of
the famous champion fighter. Maybe my love for art and for
drawing minority people started there . . . I don't know."

Most of the work Miss Grifalconi has done concerns minority
children, particularly children in the cities. "I find Mexicans,
Indians, and blacks beautiful people with strong features and
very expressive faces. My interest in poor children reflects a great
deal of my own childhood experiences. I was a Depression baby,
and I well remember the Depression days. It seems that we ate

and almost lived on evaporated milk and chopped meat. Mother was a great cook, though, and made wonderful meals from this combination. I never knew what a steak was until I was an adult!" she exclaimed.

Miss Grifalconi worked her way through college doing all kinds of odd jobs. She folded laundry in a laundromat, worked with children in various organizations, and even demonstrated paint-in-the-numbers sets at a five-and-ten-cent store on Times Square.

"I had to leave that job because I really didn't believe in this type of art. I lasted a month, but I had a great time. I even conducted my own art class," she continued. "For students I had a subway motorman — a dear old fellow — an opera buff, and a sculptor who made things from railroad ties. They would come in day after day and we would talk about art — their work and mine!"

After graduating, Miss Grifalconi worked in advertising and display and later was an art teacher for ten years in New York City junior and senior high schools. Her brother John became an architect; her mother, Mary Hays Weik, wrote *The Jazz Man* (Atheneum, 1966), a runner-up for the 1967 Newbery medal. Miss Grifalconi illustrated this poignant story of a young boy and his life in a Harlem tenement house.

"*The Jazz Man* is really the favorite of all the books I've done," remarked Miss Grifalconi. "It was my first attempt at illustrating a children's book in woodcuts. I did the work for this book on old orange crates!"

A second favorite is *The Ballad of the Burglar of Babylon* (Farrar, 1968), an exciting and dramatic poem written by the Pulitzer Prize winner Elizabeth Bishop. This is also illustrated in woodcuts. "*The Ballad* came about because of *The Jazz Man*. I knew I could work in this medium, and I love the poem. I first saw it in an issue of *The New Yorker*. I clipped the poem out and put it on my bulletin board. The adventures of Miçucú, the main character, haunted me, and I knew that I had to depict him in art. I wrote back and forth to Miss Bishop, and two years later I started the book." The book was selected as one of the outstanding books of 1968 by *The New York Times*.

In her Greenwich Village studio apartment, a fourth floor walk-up, Miss Grifalconi and I sat on the floor browsing through her portfolio. She continued to talk and talk and talk — she has so much to give, so much to share. Later in the afternoon I bade good-by. Across the bustling street there were three stores — a laundromat, a spin art center that advertised "spin your own painting," and a music store blaring a jazz beat. I chuckled, took a deep breath of spring air, and continued on my way.

SOME OTHER BOOKS BY MISS GRIFALCONI:

City Rhythms (Bobbs-Merrill, 1965).

Tillie S. Pine and Joseph Levine. *The Africans Knew* (McGraw-Hill, 1967).

———. *The Incas Knew* (McGraw-Hill, 1968).

The Toy Trumpet (Bobbs-Merrill, 1968).

John and Sara Brewton, compilers. *America Forever New* (T. Y. Crowell, 1968).

Lee Bennett Hopkins, ed. *Don't You Turn Back: Poems by Langston Hughes* (Knopf, 1969).

Anne Baldwin. *Sunflowers for Tina* (Four Winds Press, 1970).

From THE JAZZ MAN by Mary Hays Weik, illustrated by Ann Grifalconi, © 1966 by Mary Hays Weik. Permission of Atheneum Publishers.

Berta and Elmer Hader

BERTA AND ELMER HADER live in Nyack, New York, in a house they built from foundation to chimney top; it is situated atop a large, steep hill overlooking the Hudson River and the Tappan Zee Bridge. When I arrived at the house, Elmer Hader was waiting for me. An elderly man with snow-white hair and a moustache, he is vibrantly sharp, witty, and highly animated. After a warm greeting, we entered the charming house. Berta Hader invited me to sit down in front of a crackling, hissing fire in their living room. "It's beautiful isn't it?" she remarked. "Miska Petersham taught us how to make a fire!"

The Haders have interesting backgrounds. Mrs. Hader was born in San Pedro, Mexico; her parents were Americans who were living in Mexico because of her father's business. The family moved to Texas and finally to New York, where she received most of her schooling. Mr. Hader was born in 1889, in Parajo, California. His childhood was spent in San Francisco. He remembers that his high school studies were interrupted by the earthquake and fire of 1906. Before beginning art study at the California School of Design, he served as a silversmith's apprentice, surveyor's assistant, and locomotive fireman. He appeared in vaudeville in Paris prior to serving in the First World War.

The Haders met in San Francisco. "I was living there and met Elmer through a painter friend," Mrs. Hader said. "I had a cottage for $5 a month on Telegraph Hill. Elmer did a painting of Telegraph Hill, which now hangs over the fireplace of Laura Ingalls Wilder's house in Mansfield, Missouri."

The name Laura Ingalls Wilder is a monumental one in children's literature. Mrs. Wilder was the creator of the classic "Little House" books published by Harper; they are stories telling about the growing-up of the Ingalls girls and the Wilder boys. The books were based on the author's own life and that of her husband and portray the hardships, difficulties, and pleasures of pioneer life in the 1870's and 1880's in America. I was curious to know how Mr. Hader's painting ended up in the house of Laura Ingalls Wilder. Mrs. Hader told me. "Rose Wilder Lane, Laura's daughter, and I shared a four-story house in Greenwich Village at one time. I was always friendly with the family. One day, years after Elmer and I had been married, Laura sent me a manuscript to look at, a story called *Little House in the Big Woods*. She used to write accounts for little farm journals, you know. I read it and liked it because of the story's simplicity and homespun quality. I showed it to my agent and to several publishers, but everyone said the same thing — 'No hope in such a story.' One day an editor friend from Alfred A. Knopf visited with me. She told me that the company was looking for some exciting materials about early days in America, written by people who had lived it. I told her I knew of something she might be interested in and gave her Laura's address. They corresponded, but nothing happened.

"Finally Virginia Kirkus, then editor at Harper, took the book. It immediately became a success when it was published in 1932. I really have a sneaky feeling down deep inside me that if it weren't for me the book might not have been. Would you like to see a first edition of it?" she asked. Mrs. Hader went to get the copy. Written an the flyleaf were the words: "In apprecia-

tion of your kindness in introducing my little book to an editor
. . . Yours sincerely, Laura Ingalls Wilder."

The Haders were married in 1919. "We married on a shoe-string," she recalled. "In order to make ends meet, we did illus-trating for national women's magazines and newspapers which at that time had sections devoted to younger children. One of our friends was an editor on one of the magazines and liked an idea we had for a special children's page. This launched us into the field of illustrating for children. During this period we did a series of drawings of Mother Goose rhymes. Our work in this area came to a halt when postal regulations caused the children's feature pages to be eliminated from the magazines.

"This was a time when children's books were just beginning to come alive in the United States. I remember taking our Mother Goose drawings to Louise Seaman at Macmillan with the idea of putting them into a small book. Louise didn't know what to do with them. Harper took it some time later but had to send to Europe to get prices — and some advice. Louise had great foresight, however, and it was she who encouraged and published our first books — a series called 'The Happy Hours.' They were small, inexpensive picture books. We did about seven of them, and they established us in the field."

Following this series, the Haders' work was in great demand. In 1929 they did two books of their own and illustrated five others; in 1930, three of their own and illustrated six others; in 1931, three of their own and illustrated three others. Their pro-ductivity has never slowed down. In 1944 *The Little Stone House* (Macmillan) was published; it describes how they built the house in which they live. "*The Little Stone House* tells the bright side, however," laughed Mrs. Hader. "Although we en-joyed doing most of the labor, there were many backaches."

The house is an extraordinary one. It is situated on an old quarry and is snuggled into a deep hillside. On the roadway leading to the house is a waterfall that leaps and dashes its way down over moss-covered rocks to a pool at the foot of tall willow trees. The floors of the house were made from now-extinct wormed chestnut; the hand-hewn beams add great warmth to this house of wood and stone. The Haders' studio is an astonishing sight. To visit it is like taking a trip through a wonderful old attic. It is cluttered with books, many by friends such as Ruth Sawyer, the Petershams, and Dorothy P. Lathrop; paintings done in the early part of the century by Mr. Hader adorn the walls; materials and supplies needed to produce their own books are everywhere. The studio has a high, 25-foot cathedral ceiling. Long floor-to-ceiling windows let in sunlight and give a view of the animals and wildlife they both so much enjoy. A staircase and balcony lead to their upstairs living quarters. Mr. Hader explained that he had copied the type of studio he had lived in in Paris as a student artist.

In 1949 the Haders won the Caldecott Award for their book *The Big Snow* (Macmillan, 1948), a story of various animals of the woods who prepare for winter and two kindly folk in the country who help them through an unexpected, disastrous snowstorm. "When that big snow came, we could barely see out the studio's windows. Everything was covered!" Mr. Hader said. Mrs. Hader recalled the telephone call that informed them of winning the Caldecott Award. "A member of the Macmillan staff called us to say, 'Berta, I've got the most wonderful news for you.' I replied, 'Oh, I bet you're getting married!' The voice on the other end said, 'No! Something better. You and Elmer won the Caldecott!' "

The question often asked the Haders is, "How do you work together?" In 1937 they created a colorful booklet entitled *Working Together: The Inside Story of the Hader Books*. It was distributed free by Macmillan and is now a collector's item. In it they answer most of the questions one might ask and convey a good deal of information about the behind-the-scenes work in an artist's studio and publishing house. "We both work on the text and the drawing for our books," Mr. Hader commented. "We develop ideas together and criticize each other constantly.

We don't always agree and cling stubbornly to our individual ideas!"

Over fruitcake and sherry we discussed the state of the world. "There's too much revolt today," Mrs. Hader declared. "We're too eager to knock down the establishment. There shouldn't be war. Peace is all-important! With the war, slum conditions, the strikes, and the quick communication of television, children are confused today. Revolution is so terrible, so destructive. We've got to have a plan for peace."

The Haders are a grand couple. Their life has been immersed in publishing books for boys and girls. "We're near 80," said Mr. Hader, "but in the prime of our lives. We have two books in the works now. We want to go on to do just what we've been doing all our lives — writing, drawing, and having a great time in life." And from meeting Berta and Elmer Hader, I believe they will do just that — forever and forever and forever.

SOME OTHER BOOKS BY THE HADERS (All Macmillan):

The Mighty Hunter (1943).
Two Is Company, Three's a Crowd (1965).
Snow in the City (1963).

Nonny Hogrogian

NONNY HOGROGIAN (hoh *groh* gi an) answered the door of her twelfth floor apartment on Manhattan's midtown East Side, smiled, and said, "Oh, come in! I got lost in my work and forgot the time and this place is just a mess!" The first thing one notices about Miss Hogrogian is her smile, for it sums up the delightful personality of this petite bundle of creativity.

In 1967 Thomas Y. Crowell published a tiny volume with a long, long title: *The Renowned History of Little Red Riding Hood*. Miss Hogrogian, who illustrated this volume, explained its development. She and Elizabeth Riley, Crowell's distinguished editor, had visited the Pierpont Morgan Collection in New York City. They came across an edition of *Little Red Riding Hood* that was published in the 1800's; in this rhymed version, the wolf not only devoured grandmamma, but made dessert of Little Red Riding Hood! They adopted the 19th century ending for 20th century children.

After she told me this I exclaimed, "I have a story for you about the book!"

"Really? Tell me!" she enthusiastically answered.

"I was working in Hartford, Connecticut, last summer and introduced your book to teachers. A kindergarten teacher took it and read it to her class. Upon completing the story, a four-year-old looked up from the reading circle and asked with big, bright eyes, Did the wolf really eat up grandmamma?

"The teacher replied Yes, happy that the child comprehended the tale.

" 'And did he *really* eat up Little Red Riding Hood, too?'

" 'Yes, he did!' replied the teacher again.

" 'Why that son of a bitch!' exclaimed the boy."

And Miss Hogrogian howled!

From THE STORY OF PRINCE IVAN, THE FIREBIRD, AND THE GRAY WOLF by Thomas P. Whitney and Nonny Hogrogian. Illustrations ⓒ 1968 by Nonny Hogrogian. Permission of Charles Scribner's Sons.

Miss Hogrogian is a pure-bred New Yorker. She was born in the Bronx, attended public school and high school there, and went to Hunter College in New York City. "I got through school by drawing," she chuckled. "In the geography class, I made maps; in other classes I was appointed to such positions as chairman of the poster committee."

Her family is of Armenian background, and she grew up in a household that emphasized Armenian culture. After graduating from Hunter, she tried her hand at various jobs. "I wanted to go into advertising work," she recalled, "but at that time women were not too welcome. I worked in a resident buyer's house and hated it. Then I took a job with William Morrow Publishers, where I both designed and bought art for book jackets. From there I went to Crowell, where I met Elizabeth Riley. It was she who really gave me a start in illustrating books for children. I worked at Crowell several years, went to Holt, Rinehart and Winston, and then to Charles Scribner's Sons. While at Scribner I illustrated my first picture book, *Always Room for One More* (Holt, 1965), a Scottish folk song written by Sorche Nic Leodhas, which won the Caldecott Award in 1966! Crazy, no? Winning the Caldecott Award changed my life completely. I was able to stop working and devote my full time to illustrating books for children."

Miss Hogrogian is a perfectionist. She works and reworks her material until she is thoroughly satisfied with it. She recently illustrated *Three Sparrows and Other Nursery Rhymes* (Scribner, 1968), with text by the German poet Christian Morgenstern, translated by Max Knight. Upon completing the book she felt "it just wasn't right" and undertook to do the entire book over! "Children's books should be as beautiful as they possibly can be. Kids grow up on picture books, and they should see beauty in them," she commented.

She dislikes deadlines and keeps no schedule for her work. "I can't keep myself to a time schedule. I work and work and work on a book until I can't look at it; then I go back and finish it."

Miss Hogrogian is very close to her family who live in suburban New Jersey. "My dad is a Sunday painter. He has always painted. He did that piece for my apartment," she remarked, pointing to a huge seascape on the living room wall. "My sister Gloria was an interior decorator before she married. She has two children. My niece, 7, and my nephew, 4, are my greatest critics."

She likes many things. "I like all kinds of *good* music, particularly Vivaldi and Bach. I like jazz, too, but I don't know a lot about it. I like to read. I *love* the movies. I could go to movies five times a week, and I love foreign films. I like to cook and sew, but I go through periods when I could live without either. I love New York City — everything about it. It's alive. It's *my* city."

I certainly share this last love with her, and someday soon I am sure we will meet again in the Scribner Book Store on New York's elegant Fifth Avenue where both of us frequently browse.

SOME OTHER BOOKS BY MISS HOGROGIAN:

Henrietta Bancroft. *Down with Leaves* (T. Y. Crowell, 1961).
Sorche Nic Leodhas. *Gaelic Ghosts* (Holt, 1963).
———. *Ghosts Go Hunting* (Holt, 1965).
Beatrice Schenk de Regniers. *The Day Everybody Cried* (Viking, 1967).
Isaac Bahevis Singer. *The Fearsome Inn* (Scribner, 1967).
Thomas P. Whitney, translator. *The Story of Prince Ivan, the Firebird, and the Gray Wolf* (Scribner, 1968).
Theodor Fontane. *Sir Ribbeck of Ribbeck of Havelland* (Macmillan, 1969).

Dahlov Ipcar

"I AM GENERALLY optimistic, cheerful, and patient. I like a lot of solitude but enjoy a few close friends and my family. I love animals, and they have made a great contribution to my life and art. I like to do things the best way possible, even if it's not the easy way. I enjoy my work and don't look for short cuts. The greatest pleasure I know is the thrill of creating a work of art, whether in paint or in writing. I hate repetition. Inevitably certain ideas crop up and repeat themselves, but I always try to find some different viewpoint or some new way of expressing the subject.

"I have very few recreations. I read some and play chess at a club and with my husband, who is pretty good — I am fair. I used to ride horses but haven't now for 15 years. I am too busy to 'play' and most sports bore me unless there is some element of imagination connected with them. I like gardening and farm work, even if it's hard," Dahlov Ipcar (*dah* luff *ip* car) said of herself.

Mrs. Ipcar and her husband, Adolph, have lived year round for the past 32 years on their farm in Robinhood, Maine; for 30 years it was a working farm. "I love country living and visual beauty," she continued. "The country around us is beautiful deep woods, fields, flowers, ocean, and shore. I love animals, as I said before, and have many here on the farm. I don't feel sentimental about animals; I love them simply for their beauty — their diversity of form and movement.

"We are alone on one hundred acres. My parents' house is nearby, but they are no longer living. The village of Robinhood is about a half-mile away. Only three families live there in winter, and we don't see much of them. We are on the water but rarely go boating. I prefer digging in my flower and vegetable gardens. It was very primitive when we first came here and started farming — no electricity and no indoor plumbing."

Mrs. Ipcar was born in Windsor, Vermont, on November 12, 1917, and spent winters in New York City and summers in Maine. "I grew up in a very creative family atmosphere. Both my parents (William and Marguerite Zorach) were artists, yet they never wanted me to go to art school. They felt the academic training they had received had hampered their free development. I learned on my own with their encouragement.

"All my education was in progressive schools. I started at the age of three at City and Country School in New York City, when it was in its early beginnings. I feel strongly that progressive education brings out the best in a creative person. I went on to high school at Walder for one year and to the Lincoln School of Teachers College at Columbia for two. At the age of 16 I spent one year at Oberlin College on a full-tuition scholarship, but it was a disappointment after my more stimulating earlier education. I dropped out and have never regretted it. I feel that a person with creative talent does just as well without a formal education."

After leaving college, Mrs. Ipcar stayed at home and painted. She dabbled in the field of illustrating books for children but soon gave up the whole idea. At 18 she married "a nice, young struggling accountant" and persuaded him to try farm life.

"Many years later, in 1944, I was approached by an ex-teacher of mine, who worked for William R. Scott, to illustrate *The*

Little Fisherman by Margaret Wise Brown (1945). This was my first published book. I illustrated one more for Scott and then wrote one of my own, *Animal Hide and Seek* (1947), which they published. I loved the kind of modern books they were doing and became inspired, I think, by reading samples from them." Since that time Mrs. Ipcar has been producing about two books a year — via the mail.

"Ideas for my books just pop out of nowhere, usually around 4:00 a.m. when I am lying awake trying to get back to sleep. Sometimes I consciously try to tap this underground source. I think of things I would like to do pictures of, and a story idea comes."

Regarding her work habits she told me, "Usually the color dummy goes fast. I slap it out casually, almost unthinkingly. If it's the way it should be, if every line and patch of color seems just right, I try to recapture it in separations. I do all my own color separations. Separations inevitably become tighter and more exact because the outlines must meet exactly or they merely look sloppy instead of free. I make it harder for myself by trying to avoid a complete black outline.

"I don't try out my ideas on children. I depend on vivid memories of what interested me as a child. I like all my own work, although I can see the flaws clearly. My books are a part of me. Like children, you can't decide which is a favorite."

Mrs. Ipcar related the reasons why she likes a number of her works. "I like *One Horse Farm* (Doubleday, 1950) because this was the life we led, *Brown Cow Farm* (Doubleday, 1959) for the idea, *Stripes and Spots* (Doubleday, 1961) because I like jungle animals and jungles, *I Love My Anteater with an A* (Knopf, 1964) because it was fun, and *Calico Jungle* (Knopf, 1965) for the decorative pictures. I also like *General Felice* (McGraw-Hill, 1967) because it is not a picture book and was the most exciting piece of writing I ever did.

Whisperings and Other Things (Knopf, 1967) was my first published poetry. I have written poetry since I was a small child but never tried very hard to get it in print. I write quantities of poetry almost under compulsion. The poems I selected in this collection were the ones I thought children would enjoy. I feel most books of poetry for children fail to touch a child's interests. We are still under the blight of Robert Louis Stevenson whose *Child's Garden of Verses* I hated as a child!

"Alley Cats" (one of the poems in her book) originally included other things such as railroad trains and Hoboken ferries. By a process of metamorphosis, they changed into cats! It was years before I could persuade my publishers to accept the idea of a book of poetry for children. Poetry was *out* for a long time. If I wrote a story in free verse, I had to disguise it as prose. Now, poetry is *in* again."

The Ipcars have two grown sons, Robert William, a free-lance motion picture photographer living in Brooklyn, New York, and Charles, who has just finished three years with the Peace Corps in Ethiopia.

Dahlov Ipcar is a great collector of folk songs. "I have been for years," she stated, "and I know a good many folk singers. Both our boys have picked up this interest and are good banjo players. I have never been able to play anything, in spite of two wasted years of piano lessons at an early age."

Mrs. Ipcar is an accomplished artist ("I consider myself first of all an artist," she said.) and has had exhibitions of her work shown throughout the country. Her oils are in the permanent collection of the Metropolitan Museum of Art and the Whitney Museum in New York City, the Newark Museum in New Jersey, and in Fairleigh Dickinson College and Colby College. Five of her oil paintings are owned by the Laurence Rockefellers, and her work is in many other private collections. She paints and sculpts the things she is most fond of in life — animals. She has created collages entitled "Leopard and Elephant" and "Antelope and Bird," oils of cats, geese, and roosters, and cloth sculptures of weasels, ocelots, snails, and fish.

110

Dahlov Ipcar doesn't come back to New York very often. "The only things I miss in the city are the Bronx Zoo and the American Museum of Natural History!" she added. What else *could* there be for Dahlov Ipcar — a true lover of country living?

SOME OTHER BOOKS BY MRS. IPCAR:

The Wonderful Egg (Doubleday, 1958).
Deep Sea Farm (Knopf, 1961).
The Wild Whirlwind (Knopf, 1968).
The Warlock of Night (Viking, 1969).

Virginia Kahl

I WAS HAPPY TO LEARN that Virginia Kahl's (call) favorite
book is *The Duchess Bakes a Cake* (Scribner, 1955) because it
has always been one of my favorites! She told me about the idea
behind this book. "*The Duchess Bakes a Cake* was based on a
true incident. A friend of mine was baking biscuits and mis-
takenly put in a cup of baking powder instead of flour! Although
she caught it in time, it could have been disastrous. That was the
start of the story; of course the setting, the period, the type of
characters involved, and the plot came after mulling over the
incident. But the story was the easiest of all to do and the one
that seemed to just write itself. It is my favorite of all the books
I have done because it was fun to do. I enjoyed everything about
it — deciding on the characters and medieval setting (her favorite period in history), thinking about the plot, which seemed to
develop logically once the illogical premise was stated, writing
the couplets, and planning the illustrations."

Miss Kahl decided to write for children while working in
Austria as an army librarian after World War II. "I became
aware of picture books on this job," she stated. "When both story
and pictures were original and entertaining, they were a joy to
experience; and I was tempted to try one of my own. Besides,

Austria — colorful, picturesque, and with a fairy-tale quality all its own — could inspire anyone."

Her first book for children was *Away Went Wolfgang* (Scribner, 1954). It was set in Austria, and the main character, a clumsy, not-so-bright dog, was patterned after a real dog who worked in Salzburg and pulled a garbage wagon.

"Certainly one of the most interesting times of my life was spent working for the army," she stated, "helping to set up and run libraries for the military and civilian personnel in Germany and Austria. It was a wonderful opportunity to meet people of other countries and to work with them. My first assignment was Berlin in 1948. Since this was the time of the Berlin blockade, it was an unusual experience. It was fascinating from the moment of my arrival in an airlift plane that was carrying supplies to the city to my departure almost eight months later, just ten days before the blockade ended.

"It was strange to be confined to half a city where there were two governments, two police forces, two kinds of currency, and four occupying powers and where streetcars ran every hour and planes landed every minute. If we attended an opera in the east sector of the city, there was a ride through deserted streets, with mile after mile of rubble from bombed-out buildings, an unheated theatre, and the tense moments during the last act when we wondered if we could catch the last streetcar to the American sector; it left at 11:00 p.m. If we missed it, there would be the unpleasant experiences of wandering through darkened, deserted streets, with only the flashlight we always carried to light the way; and there was the even more unpleasant prospect of being detained overnight or longer.

"There was a real threat of kidnapping hanging over the heads of some of the people who had fled to West Berlin; and when one of the Germans or refugees who worked with us didn't show up some morning, we never knew if he were ill and it was a temporary absence, or if he had disappeared permanently. I grew to admire the Berliners, who lived on an island in East Germany;

when an election was held during this tense time, they voted overwhelmingly for a non-Communist mayor. Although it was an experience I was glad to have had, I was ready to be transferred to Austria, with its cheerfulness, its relatively undamaged towns, its relaxed atmosphere, and the chance to travel about more freely."

Miss Kahl was born in Milwaukee, Wisconsin, and attended school there, graduating from Milwaukee-Downer College. Later she received a master's degree in library science from the University of Wisconsin. Although her immediate family was small, there were innumerable aunts, uncles, cousins, and friends for companionship. While growing up during the Depression years activities were of the simple inexpensive kind — "excursions to nearby lakes, vacations at camp or farms of relatives, and always, regular trips to the well-stocked public libraries."

Miss Kahl has lived most of her life in the Midwest. Recently she bought a house in Virginia near Mount Vernon. "After living in cities all my life and in an apartment for a number of years, I must adjust to life in another part of the country, to living in the suburbs, to owning a house, and to many more responsibilities than I've ever had. I have no possessions that are special favorites, except for a few lithographs by Kathe Kollwitz; and I have a sentimental attachment to a set of poetry books that once belonged to the tragic Crown Prince Rudolf of Austria. His name is inscribed on the flyleaf of each of the four volumes. When there is an opportunity, I enjoy travel in Europe, visiting the medieval towns, castles, cathedrals, and all the art museums. Although France, Italy, and Greece are runners-up, my favorite country will always be Austria.

"I enjoy meeting new people but prefer one or two at a time rather than large groups. And I like all animals and would love to have, as Noah had, two of every kind living with me. Just now, though, I'm limited to six cats who traveled with me from Wisconsin to Virginia. And, of course, being a librarian I can't imagine a life without books on any subject — art history, mysteries, cookbooks, or anything else that happens to interest me at the moment."

Regarding work habits she said, "My work habits are not very commendable because I work neither regularly nor steadily at writing. However, almost everything I've done has followed a pattern. Usually I visualize the main characters; they never have a great deal of native intelligence, but all have, I hope, good hearts. Before I think of the story, I have a pretty good idea of how they look and might act; it is the characters who bring about the story. Before I put it down on paper, I have the story nearly worked out, so that when the story *is* written, a minimum of re-working is needed. And I know that if it isn't written quickly and completed within two or three weeks, it isn't going to be right. So, although it may take quite awhile to think about the plot and to work it out mentally, the writing goes quickly.

"Very often some small thing will serve as a jumping off place for a book. It may be an anecdote, a picture, an incident, or a remark that will set off my imagination. I suppose anyone who writes stories goes through the same process. With such a beginning, one asks himself, 'What would happen if . . . ?' and he's off."

SOME OTHER BOOKS BY MISS KAHL (All Scribner):

Maxie (1956).
Plum Pudding for Breakfast (1956).
The Perfect Pancake (1960).

Ezra Jack Keats

To go from a Brooklyn, New York, tenement house to the Shah's palace in Iran is a giant step for any man to take. Ezra Jack Keats took it! Mr. Keats was the youngest of three children and grew up in Brooklyn during the Depression years. He has been drawing since he was four years old. "I trained myself by experimenting," he said. "I first realized that my drawings meant something when one day I covered our enamel-topped kitchen table with a host of sketches. My mother came in, and I expected her to say, 'What have you been doing?' or 'Get the sponge and wash off that table!' Instead she said, 'Did you do that? Isn't it wonderful!' Rather than washing it off, she covered it with a tablecloth and showed it off periodically to the neighbors and friends who visited her."

Mr. Keats' father did not give him the same open encouragement. Working as a waiter at a beanery in Greenwich Village, he was painfully aware of how difficult the life of an artist could be. "Occasionally he would bring home some materials — a tube of oil paint or a set of brushes for watercolors — but they all came with a lecture about starving artists. Years later after I had grown up, my father suffered a fatal heart attack away from home, and I went to identify him. As part of the procedure, the

116

police asked me to look through his wallet, and I found myself staring deep into his secret feelings. There in his wallet were worn and tattered newspaper clippings about the awards I had won. My silent admirer and supplier had been torn between dread of my leading a life of hardship and real pride in my work."

Mr. Keats went into a closet in his studio and pulled out an oil painting he had done at the age of 17. On the canvas stood his parents. His father was dressed in a T-shirt, with his pants held up by suspenders; his mother stood gray-haired, wearing glasses, with a look on her face carved by the hardships of Depression years. Mr. Keats vividly recalls the days when he gave one of his paintings to a dentist in exchange for his mother's false teeth and another to a doctor to have his own nose repaired after a neighborhood street brawl.

Before Mr. Keats became a top illustrator of children's books, he was a muralist and designer of book jackets. He illustrated his first book, *Jubilant for Sure* by E. H. Lansing (T. Y. Crowell), a story for older readers, in 1954. Since that time he has steadily illustrated books, always searching, experimenting, and trying to find a style of his own. The technique of using collage came to him in 1962 when Peter, a young black boy, was born in the now-modern classic, *The Snowy Day* (Viking, 1962).

"With *The Snowy Day* I started all over again. My use of collage developed naturally. I used a bit of paper here and there and immediately saw new colors, patterns, and relationships forming. When I finished the book, I myself was startled!"

And so was the world! *The Snowy Day* won the 1963 Caldecott Medal and has since been a phenomenon in the field of children's literature, it has led the way in portraying black children in natural settings, and it began what is referred to as the "casual approach" to Negro life in books for children.

One morning in 1967 Mr. Keats received a telephone call from his friend Morton Schindel, producer of the Weston Woods

117

audio-visual materials in Weston, Connecticut. "Are you sitting down?" asked Mr. Schindel.

"I'm lying down," answered Mr. Keats. "Why?"

"I just received a cable from the Empress of Iran. The Shah and Empress Farah have invited you for a two-week stay as their guests!" The Empress had seen the film version of *The Snowy Day*, which won the Venice Film Festival Award for children's film shorts. Several weeks later Mr. Keats was attending palace parties and meeting important dignitaries from the world over. In discussing this work, Mr. Keats remarked, "I decided to make young Peter a Negro child. I had been illustrating books by other people showing the goodness of white children, and in my own book I wanted to show and share the beauty and goodness of the black child. I wanted the world to know that all children experience wonderful things in life. I wanted to convey the joy of being a little boy alive on a certain kind of day — of *being* for that moment. The air is cold, you touch the snow, aware of the things to which all children are so open." *The Snowy Day's* success gave impetus to his later work. He created additional books about Peter — *Whistle for Willie* (Viking, 1964), *Peter's Chair* (Harper, 1967), *A Letter to Amy* (Harper, 1968), and *Goggles* (Macmillan, 1969), a 1970 Caldecott Honor Book.

Now an established writer as well as an illustrator, Mr. Keats remarked to me, "Writing is not too difficult for me. I read into a tape recorder, constantly dropping a word here and there from my manuscript until I get a minimum amount of words to say exactly what I want to say. Each time I drop a word or two, it becomes a sense of victory to me!"

Mr. Keats receives letters by the score from children and adults about his books. "I save every letter and every picture that a child draws," he stated. "I bundle them together, mark the year on the package, and put it into my closet. I have some prize letters from the late Langston Hughes, Harry Golden, and the widow of James Weldon Johnson about my various books — and, of course, many wonderful comments from young readers.

Many boys and girls have sent me scraps of interesting paper, which I use in my collages. I find other papers in trash cans, fruit stores, anywhere and everywhere!" Mr. Keats' books have been translated into other languages, and he now receives mail from children in many parts of the world.

From JOHN HENRY by Ezra Jack Keats. Permission of Pantheon Books.

Mr. Keats lives high on a twenty-second floor in New York's East 80's. His apartment is large, light, spacious, and tastefully decorated with modern furniture. He has walls of artwork, and plants are carefully placed among old relics and sculptures he has collected over the years. His studio contains many books; on its walls, when I visited, hung the original illustrations for the book he was working on, *The Little Drummer Boy* (Macmillan, 1968), a beautiful, tender Christmas song about a boy too poor to bring a gift "fit to give a king."

The work of Ezra Jack Keats has given a new look to children's books. He gave us Peter, he made collage a household word, and he has given of himself his sensitive and poignant feelings for all the world to share.

SOME OTHER BOOKS BY MR. KEATS:

Richard Lewis, editor. *In a Spring Garden* (Dial, 1965).
John Henry (Pantheon, 1965).
Jennie's Hat (Harper, 1966).

Ruth Krauss
Crockett Johnson

I SPENT A HILARIOUS summer afternoon with Ruth Krauss and her husband, Crockett Johnson. Their home is situated in a small Connecticut town on the north edge of Long Island Sound. As I approached the house, Mr. Johnson was standing outside, apparently waiting for me. He is a big man — tall, husky, and completely bald, just like the famous character Barnaby whom he created. Looking at me and chuckling Mr. Johnson exclaimed, "I draw people without hair, because it's so much *easier*! Besides, to me, people *with* hair look funny." Discussing New York he said, "I'm probably the only person you've ever met who was born on East 58th Street in New York City." On living in Connecticut he remarked, "It was a nice neighborhood here until the young fogies moved in and spoiled it. The lake is so crowded now that there isn't even enough room to go sailing." He continually interrupted his conversation with guffaws of laughter.

Soon Ruth Krauss joined us on the sun porch. At the precise moment she entered, a clap of thunder exploded, lightning flashed, clouds darkened the sky, and rain began to pour from the heavens. As we were all being nicely drenched, Miss Krauss looked at me and said in a most relaxed manner, "Oh, hell-o. Do you think we should move inside?"

Miss Krauss is as funny and as clever as her many books. She was born in Baltimore, Maryland, studied art and music at Peabody Conservatory, and graduated from the Parsons School of Fine and Applied Art in New York City. She also studied anthropology at Columbia University. Her books are milestones in the field of children's literature. Children simply adore them. One of the reasons for this, perhaps, is that Miss Krauss studies boys and girls.

When preparing *A Hole Is to Dig: A First Book of First Definitions* (Harper, 1952), she carefully observed children around the community. "I went to the beach every day and would ask five- and six-year-olds the question, 'What is this for?' or 'What is that for?' — questions about things that children held personally dear to them. Actually I got the idea from child psychologists who write that five-year-olds are pragmatists. I wanted to see if they were right! The kids thought I was crazy," she laughed. "I asked one boy what a hole is for, and he looked at me like I was nuts, frowned, and walked away from me. Another child, however, said 'A hole? A hole is to dig?' And that's how the title was born."

The first children's book Mr. Johnson illustrated was his wife's *The Carrot Seed* (Harper, 1945), which is typical of her work in that it contains very few words. "I wrote it in 45 minutes" she commented. It tells a simple tale of a boy who planted a carrot seed. His mother, father, and big brother all tell him it won't come up. The child, however, ignores the negative advice, gives it great care, "And one day a carrot came up just as the little boy had known it would." When *The Carrot Seed* was published, a copy was sent to San Francisco where the United Nations was being organized. "I guess the message came through. Look what it did for the U.N.!" she laughed.

Mr. Johnson has since collaborated with his wife on several other books including the comic *How to Make an Earthquake*

(Harper, 1954). "Do you know what the librarians did with *How to Make an Earthquake*?" he asked. "They catalogued it with other how-to books such as how to collect stamps and how to sew a seam," he roared.

Mr. Johnson has also written and illustrated the famous "Harold" series, beginning with *Harold and the Purple Crayon* (Harper, 1958), amusing tales that relate the adventures of a small boy who "draws" himself in and out of curious situations. Also to his credit are *Ellen's Lion* (Harper, 1959), and *The Lion's Own Story* (Harper, 1963), his personal favorites.

The work habits of this husband-wife team vary. Miss Krauss stated, "I'm haphazard, flighty, and eccentric. I'm fresher in the morning and like to work on the kitchen table." Mr. Johnson declared, "And I can work any hour of the day. I'm a steady worker."

From BARNABY, copyright 1943 by Crockett Johnson. Permission of Crockett Johnson.

The Johnsons do have a serious side to them. Mr. Johnson is avidly interested in executing geometric paintings — paintings that require the mathematical computations of a computer. His large canvasses, covered with dramatic color, have been exhibited in a New York gallery.

Miss Krauss is a serious student of poetry and has been devoting much of her time to writing poem-plays. Several seasons ago she had "A Beautiful Day," 17 poem-plays strung together, produced off-Broadway and directed by Remy Charlip. Mr. Johnson described the reception the play received. "I caught the second night's performance. At the end of the play the audience cried out 'Bravo! Bravo!' and wild applause rang from the theatre's rafters. I have never heard such response. 'Isn't this wonderful?' I asked Ruth. She merely looked at me disappointedly and remarked, 'I'm crushed! This audience is not as enthusiastic as the one we had last night!' "

Miss Krauss also teaches poetry at a local art center and is doing poetry workshops at Daytop Village, an institution for the self-rehabilitation of narcotic addicts.

My day in Connecticut turned out to be filled with fun, good humor, and interesting anecdotes. I even learned that Crockett Johnson is not really Crockett Johnson! "Crockett is my childhood nickname. My real name is David Johnson Leisk. Leisk was too hard to pronounce — so — I am now Crockett Johnson!" he exclaimed.

Before I left the sun came out. Even today I can hear the strains of Ruth Krauss's "hee, hee, hees" and Crockett Johnson's "ho, ho, hos" whenever I pick up *A Hole Is to Dig* or *Barnaby*!

SOME OTHER BOOKS BY MISS KRAUSS:

The Happy Day (Harper, 1949).
The Backward Day (Harper, 1950).
What a Fine Day For . . . (Parents, 1967).

SOME OTHER BOOKS BY MR. JOHNSON:

Emperor's Gifts (Holt, 1965).
Upside Down (Whitman, 1969).
A collection of the best of the Barnaby cartoons is available in a paperbound edition, *Barnaby* (1967) from Dover Publications, Inc., 180 Varick Street, New York, New York 10014.

Dorothy Lathrop

DOROTHY LATHROP HAS the distinction of being the first woman to receive the Caldecott Award: it was given to her in 1938 for her illustrations of *Animals of the Bible: A Picture Book* (Lippincott, 1937). The text was selected by Helen Dean Fisher from the King James version of the Bible. Miss Lathrop declared, "I still get letters from children about the book; however, most of them are at the well-meant instigation of teachers. Adults write too. The book is still selling well, and I think — and hope — that new plates are about to be made to replace badly worn ones. *Animals of the Bible* is, perhaps, my favorite book because of the diversity of illustrations in it."

Of her own books, she likes best *Hide and Go Seek* (Macmillan, 1938). "Why? Because I knew the little squirrels whom I wrote about — knew each one so well."

The author-illustrator was born on April 16, 1891, in Albany, New York. She grew up in an active and creative household. "My mother, I. Pulis Lathrop, an exhibiting painter, undoubtedly influenced both my work and that of my sister Gertrude, who is a sculptor."

Miss Lathrop became interested in books through her paternal grandfather who owned a book store in Bridgeport, Connecticut.

After high school she attended Teachers College, Columbia University, where she studied art under Arthur Wesley Dow and writing under several Barnard professors. Later she attended the Pennsylvania Academy of Fine Arts. "I decided to illustrate books for young children because I like children's books," she commented. "I began to illustrate in 1918, while I was teaching art in the Albany High School." One day at lunch she and a fellow teacher were looking at an illustrated book. "I wish I could draw like that," she remarked. "I may not be a Howard Pyle but I *want* to illustrate."

Her first attempt was for a book called *Japanese Prints* by John Gould Fletcher (Four Seasons, 1919). The company went bankrupt before it could pay her for the drawings. She obtained other work, however, and illustrated several books in the 1920's for Alfred A. Knopf, Inc. In 1931 Macmillan published *The Fairy Circus,* a book she both wrote and illustrated. Since that time she has illustrated over a score of picture books, most of them about the animals that she lived with and loved.

"I don't know where my ideas come from," she said. "Open your mind and they come! They develop as I work. Do I rework material? Of course! Do I try out my ideas on children? Never!"

Miss Lathrop and her sister lived for many years in Albany. Their two-room studio was set back amongst apple trees, and they had all the animal models that they needed to sketch and study. Miss Lathrop now lives in a small town in Connecticut. She has a house with a big studio on nine and one-half acres at the foot of a mountain. Among her favorite possessions are her dogs, some of them show dogs and champions. Her pets are actively engaged in dog snows, one of her favorite pastimes.

I asked Miss Lathrop what she thought of children's books today as compared to those of the 1940's and 1950's *"Don't ask me!"* she exclaimed. "Most of them are dreadful, tossed off by persons too lazy to draw! They are under the mistaken impression that children can understand and enjoy such pictures as they themselves can draw. Most of today's books, I feel, are also badly tainted by present-day trends in art."

Dorothy Lathrop has been devoted to creating books for children. She concluded our interview by giving some sagacious advice to adults on how to encourage children to read. "Let them browse," she declared. "Let them browse in libraries. Don't force books on them." Today children are surrounded by volumes of good literature — books they certainly will be tempted to open if adults follow Miss Lathrop's advice.

SOME OTHER BOOKS BY MISS LATHROP (All Macmillan):

An Angel in the Woods (1947).
The Littlest Mouse (1955).
Follow the Brook (1960).
The Dog in the Tapestry Garden (1962).

Munro Leaf

1934 WAS A GOOD YEAR for children's literature — it marked the date of Munro Leaf's first book, *Grammar Can Be Fun* (Lippincott), the first in the series of his ten "Can Be Fun" books. The book came about as a result of a distraught mother who was trying to break her five-year-old's habit of saying "ain't." Mr. Leaf put the book together along with some stick-figure suggestions for illustrations. When the editors looked at the manuscript with the curious drawings, they laughed and kept them in the original form, establishing Mr. Leaf not only as a writer but as an illustrator as well.

Mr. Leaf is a dynamic man. He is short, thin, humorous, and highly intellectual. He speaks quickly, his facial expressions change from second to second to match his words, and he talks with pride and love about his life and his work. I first met him for a brief second in my office. As usual, he was in a hurry. "I've got a cab waiting downstairs to whisk me off to the airport. Boston-bound," he commented. "I'll see you next week, Wednesday. Let's make it Wednesday." And he dashed out of sight like Santa Claus leaving a rooftop.

Next Wednesday came — and went. He didn't show up. A week later, however, I strolled into the office. It was Yom Kippur, a quiet day in New York, and fewer people than usual were at work. While turning into a corridor, a voice said, "There you are! We must talk before I whisk off to Boston!" It was Munro Leaf again. While we talked, Mr. Leaf sipped black coffee and smoked tiny cigars one after the other. He explained that Boston, New York, and Washington, D. C., are his three home bases. Comically he remarked, "My next book should be *A Tale of Three Cities*. I'll be 63 years old this year, and I've lived about 20 years apiece in these cities."

He was born in a little town called Hamilton, now a part of Baltimore, Maryland. His childhood was spent in Washington, D. C. He attended public schools there, graduated from the University of Maryland in 1927, and then went on to Harvard University, where he received a master of arts degree in English literature. The next period of his life was spent in New York City where he began a career in publishing. Currently he is living in Washington with his wife Margaret, commuting constantly between the three cities to do his work.

Mr. Leaf and I discussed his books at length. Each has a fantastic story behind it, each unbelievable in its own way. "I wrote *The Story of Ferdinand* (Viking, 1936) in 25 minutes on a rainy Sunday afternoon. I wrote it for Rob (Robert Lawson, the late author-illustrator). I had known Rob for about two years. He was doing illustrations for children's books but was unhappy having to conform to publishers' ideas. I gave him *Ferdinand* and told him, 'Rob, cut loose and have fun with this in your own way.' I picked the story of a bull 'cause dogs, cats, rabbits, and mice had been done thousands of times. I thought out the plot — bull, Spain, bullfight, no fight. The bee became a mechanical device for the book to have a plot. The bull needed a name, of course a Spanish name, so, I took it right out of a fourth-grade textbook. Ferdinand was the name of the husband of Isabella, the queen who financed Chris Columbus's expedition in 1492. You can't get a more Spanish name than that!"

Mr. Lawson was delighted with the manuscript. He took the book and completed the illustrations in two months time. Mr. Leaf then brought it to May Massee, editor at Viking Press.

"She read it and told me to get out! She said, 'I'm locking this up in the safe!'" The book was published in September 1936 and immediately received a great deal of free publicity because the Spanish Civil War had started in June of that year. Because of *Ferdinand,* Mr. Leaf was accused of being a left-winger, although neither the author or the illustrator had ever set foot in Spain, taken sides in the war, or even viewed a bullfight! *Ferdinand* has continued to be a children's classic. The character has been the basis of films, recordings, parade floats, and television discussions. In 1966 *Ferdinand* celebrated its thirtieth birthday, and since published it has been translated into 60 languages.

In 1936 *Manners Can Be Fun* (Lippincott) was also released; more copies have been sold of it than even *Ferdinand!* "It's my best eating book," the author exclaimed. "We have many a good meal from that one!" *Wee Gillis* (Viking, 1938), the story of a Scottish lad, was another product of the Leaf-Lawson team.

Mr. Leaf also collaborated with the well-loved Ludwig Bemelmans. He told me how he met Mr. Bemelmans. "My wife, Margaret, ran the children's section in Brentano's book store in New York City. There was a young girl there who was employed to paint murals. Margaret thought she was quite good. 'Write a story for her to illustrate,' Margaret told me. I wrote about my neighbor's 11-year-old dachshund. [He was the basis of the story *Noodle* (Lippincott, 1937.) (His neighbor was Hendrik Van Loon, author of *The Story of Mankind* (Boni and Liveright, 1921); Mr. Van Loon was the first author to win the John Newbery Medal.] I gave the story to this young girl to illustrate, but I did not like what she did with it. I threw the whole thing up on the shelf. One day Ludwig came into Brentano's to see how his book *Hansi* (Viking, 1934) was selling. My wife chatted with him. One night he and his wife, Madeline, came to dinner. I told him, 'Ludwig, I've got a story for you.' I gave him *Noodle,* and we were a team!"

In addition to children's books, Mr. Leaf has collaborated with Dr. Seuss on an army field manual on malaria, which was published in 1934 by the War Department. It was entitled *This Is Ann* — "Her full name is Anopheles Mosquito!" He has also written with Dr. William C. Menninger, the noted psychiatrist. Recently he has written and illustrated a booklet entitled *I Hate You! I Hate You!* (Sterling Institute Press, 1968), a rather disturbing look at the times in which we are living. "It took me 62 years to think this up," he said, "and it is my most satisfying work." The book is a result of his world travels for the U. S. State Department. In 1961 he covered the Middle East, in 1962 Western Europe and Scandinavia, and in 1964 the eastern countries, doing chalk talks for children and speaking to educators, publishers, and librarians in 26 countries.

Mr. Leaf loves his work. "Kids have been my patrons," he said. "I've had all the luxuries that a writer in the 18th century received if he had a patron. I love kids. They've made my life worth living. If I weren't me, I'd envy me!" His life is something to envy. He has made a tremendous impression on millions of people — young and old — throughout the entire world.

The last lines in *The Story of Ferdinand* read:

> And for all I know he is sitting there still, under his favorite cork tree, smelling the flowers just quietly. He is very happy.

Like Ferdinand, Mr. Leaf is happy, but unlike the famed bull, Mr. Leaf is *not* sitting still, and I doubt if he ever will!

SOME OTHER BOOKS BY MR. LEAF (All Lippincott):

Robert Francis Weatherbee (1935).
Gordon, the Goat (1944).

Lois Lenski

I WAS PLEASED to receive a photograph of Lois Lenski doing what she enjoys most — gardening. Of course, when she isn't potting, pruning, fertilizing, seeding, weeding, watering, and transplanting, she is busy writing books for America's boys and girls. Miss Lenski has written for every age level. Her books for younger readers include the humorous and gay *Cowboy Small* (Walck, 1949) and the many other Mr. Small books that followed. Her important and exciting regional books are written for older readers. Among the regional books, *Strawberry Girl* (Lippincott, 1945) won the 1946 Newbery Award.

Miss Lenski was born in Springfield, Ohio, on October 14, 1893. She was the fourth of five children. Her childhood and early youth were spent in Anna, Ohio, a small farming town of about two hundred people, where her father was a Lutheran minister. In 1915 Miss Lenski received her bachelor of science degree in education from Ohio State University. Although she prepared for a teaching career, her interest in art persuaded her to train further in drawing and painting. One of her teachers at Ohio State encouraged her to go to New York City to study at the Art Students League. She took the advice, went to New York, and studied there for four years, working part-time at odd jobs to meet her expenses. In 1920 she went to London to study at the Westminster School of Art.

Miss Lenski commented, "It was while studying in London that I did my first illustrations for children's books. I illustrated one by Kenneth Graham and one by Vera Birch." Upon returning to the United States, she found that children's book publishing was beginning to develop at a rapid pace. In 1927 Frederick A. Stokes published her *Skipping Village* and in 1928 *A Little Girl of 1900,* stories drawn directly from her own childhood experienecs.

Miss Lenski married Arthur Covey, the famous mural painter, and moved to Connecticut. The place aroused her interest in the history of Connecticut and New England; and her historical books resulted. In 1941, because of poor health, the Coveys began going south for the winter with their son Stephen. Miss Lenski's sensitivity to life and its surroundings produced a series of highly acclaimed stories about American life, her regional books. These stories became so popular that she was "forced" by her fans to write books with the same focus for younger boys and girls. This resulted in the "Roundabout America" books published by Lippincott.

Miss Lenski's artwork is characterized by its simplicity. She uses ink drawings for most of her books because she feels they mean more to a child than a confusion of color; for the regional books she draws in pencil. Besides writing and illustrating stories, she has composed countless numbers of poems, which she gathered together in *The Life I Live: Collected Poems* in 1965 (Walck). Of all her work, this is her favorite. She remarked, "These poems are the culmination of my life's work and represent my entire philosophy of writing for children."

Regarding her work habits, she declared, "My travels have taken me to all parts of the country — the mountains of North Carolina, the oil fields of Oklahoma, and the corn fields of Iowa. I have tried to describe how people live in these different places. Actual people, seen and known in different regions, become my main characters. Each time I draw a character, I hold in my memory the image of the real person I saw who inspired it." She does not like to write a story if she cannot visualize both the characters and the setting. Her pre-school picture "Davy" books (Walck) were all inspired by a four-year-old during the course of a summer. "Writing and drawing each take a turn; each reinforces the other. My stories are tried out on children of the age the book is intended for. If a drawing is not clear or a word is unfamiliar, the child will let you know. I respect a child's thinking and direct appraisal — his spontaneous reaction to a story or pictures — far more highly than my own adult notions."

Miss Lenski has two hobbies: working with children in creative painting and gardening. She recently moved from Connecticut to Florida. "In Florida I can enjoy year-round gardening," she stated.

The love of Lois Lenski's work is evidenced in many ways: her books have appeared in languages spoken from Britain to Burma; her work is utilized in schools across the nation and is translated into creative dramatics and art expression; and her books cause children, teachers, librarians, and parents to sit down and write her an annual avalanche of letters. She receives hundreds of letters during each school year, and she answers each one in longhand.

Some Other Books by Miss Lenski (All Walck):

I Like Winter (1950).
Papa Small (1951).
Policeman Small (1962).

Blair Lent

BLAIR LENT'S WORDS ARE POETIC; they are put together like his beautiful illustrations for picture books. He told me about his childhood. "I was an only child living in a world peopled by imaginary friends. The friends were often first encountered in story books my father brought to me from secondhand-book stores. It was during the Depression years, and my family could not afford new books. I was born in Boston, but I grew up in a small town where I was rarely happy. Books and some wonderful summers spent away from the oppressive suburban atmosphere brought me what pleasures I had as a child. My mother, father, and I used to stay in a cottage on a New Hampshire lake. There was no electricity and no plumbing in the cottage; we rowed to a village on the other side of the lake for provisions. There was a general store there — I can still smell the spices and the coffee.

"My parents encouraged my early efforts at writing and illustrating stories, and my grandmother told me many of her own stories. She and I often collaborated on wild tales, and I knew then, as a small boy, that what I hoped to do with my life was to travel around the world and write about and draw pictures of my many adventures."

His childhood dreams came true at the age of 23. In 1953 he graduated from the Boston Museum School and was awarded the Cummings Memorial Traveling Scholarship by the Museum of Fine Arts. "I spent one year (1953–1954) studying in Switzerland and Italy. I spent some time in a Zurich printing plant where they often used lithograph stones in their presses. They were huge blocks the size of posters, which were then drawn upon inside the plant by the artists and their apprentices."

In 1968 Mr. Lent received a second traveling scholarship from the Musuem, one that took him to the Soviet Union. "I sketched old but rapidly modernizing villages in the far north, in the vicinity of Leningrad and Moscow, and in the south in Georgia and Armenia. I traveled over the Steppes, down the Don, through birch forests, and into Volga villages. I studied the fantastic wooden architecture of Kizhi and the kremlins of Novgorod, Zagorsk, Suzdal, Rostov, and Moscow. I talked with the art director of a children's book publishing house in Moscow and visited painters, printmakers, and illustrators in many Soviet cities. On my way back, I revisited the plant in Zurich and found that the place had been completely mechanized. The manager proudly showed me all the new automatic equipment, and I was glad I had seen the place at the time when printing was an art rather than just a business."

Mr. Lent's first book was *Pistachio* (Little, Brown, 1964), a story inspired by a roadside circus performance he watched one evening in Paris on the banks of the Seine. His working habits are inconsistent. "Every book presents a different problem in finding and developing story and pictures. Every child's opinion differs from every other's, so I rely on the child within myself, remembering what interested me as a child," he said. He feels that his most successful book in terms of creating a mood is *John Tabor's Ride* (Little, Brown, 1966). "I like the way the words and pictures move together. I used a colorful, nautical vocabulary, with phrases like 'Past fishbones and scrimshaw they climbed, past rusted cringles, mildewed mizzens, and a figurehead of Minnie Small from Gloucester'" words that children enjoy hearing and saying over and over again. The pictures are detailed. A child can keep going back to the book and finding new things to enjoy as well as rediscovering what he had noticed before."

Another of his popular books is *From King Boggen's Hall to Nothing-At-All* (Little, Brown, 1967). "I decided to do a book about nursery rhymes because I am a frustrated architect. The strange houses found in the rhymes presented an opportunity for me to express some of my architectural fantasies. Illustrations that show houses under trees, rooms under the ground, and the like have always fascinated me, and I thought it would be enjoyable, both for myself and for children, to create a book full of just such places."

The original art for the book was printed from cardboard cuts, a technique he uses in most of his work. "It is an excellent medium for illustration because the results resemble a woodcut, but the surface of the cardboard is much easier to cut into, so my ideas are realized sooner," he explained. "I can vary the texture by cutting into the cardboard to different depths. I can also use different methods of cutting, like pricking the surface of the cardboard with a pin or drawing with the edge of a razor blade. I make many prints of each illustration and then study the different prints and scissor the most interesting parts from each. For example, I can combine a blotty print with a dry print. The collage made from the different prints is sent to the printer, who in turn reproduces the artwork on another printing surface from which the book itself is printed. I work with color overlays, so that I can have more control over the final result; I never see a finished illustration until after the book has been on the press." This same technique was used in *The Wave*, written by Margaret Hodges (Houghton, 1964), which was selected as a 1965 runner-up for the Caldecott Award.

In 1969 another of his books, *Why the Sun and the Moon Live in the Sky* (Houghton, 1968), an African folktale adapted from

From WHY THE SUN AND THE MOON LIVE IN THE SKY by Elphinstone Dayrell and Blair Lent. Permission of Houghton Mifflin Co.

Elphinstone Dayrell's *Folk Stories from Southern Nigeria* (Longmans, Green, London), was sole runner-up for the Caldecott Award. This tale expresses a primitive society's concern with the natural elements — the sun and the water. The tale is simply told; the illustrations are brilliant and exciting to look at.

Mr. Lent's studio has always been the most important part of his home setting, and his favorite ones have been on Beacon Hill in Boston and in Gloucester, Massachusetts. "They were in old buildings, with easy access to the outside. On Beacon Hill, French doors led from my studio on the top floor of a carriage house to a tiny roof garden; in Gloucester I was able to work

138

outside my studio, which was located in a ship repair yard. There was enough space so that I could always have an easel set up with a painting in progress. Most artists prefer north light, but I prefer to work in a studio full of sunshine," he commented.

He now lives in Cambridge, Massachusetts, in an apartment filled with books, plants, his own paintings, and paintings and sculptures by friends. "I have never, and never will, live anywhere where there isn't a working fireplace," he declared. "I am always building shelves! I can *always* find some reason for needing more shelves. When I reach an impasse in my work or in my life, building shelves is one of the most therapeutic things I can do." And in his studio every bit of wall space that does not have shelves is covered with tackboard on which he pins a constantly changing array of photos, postcards, children's drawings, unanswered letters, scattered memos, and illustrations that he is currently working on. There are also several strings of clothesline stretched from one side of the room to the other, for drying the prints he makes for much of his work.

"What do I enjoy most in life? Being in love, and good wine, and hiking, picnicking, or doing almost anything outside in the country or by the sea. I don't really know how to describe myself, except that I swim a mile every day at the neighborhood indoor pool, but here is what a friend says about me: 'Blair is thoughtful, often brooding, strongly affected by moods. He tends to disappear in a crowd, but among close friends he has plenty to say. He has his own unique way of looking at the world and is able to make his viewpoint clear in conversation that is always original, often controversial.' "

Unique is a word that well describes Blair Lent. His books are unique, his artwork is unique, and he is a unique type of person who has been duly heralded for his work.

SOME OTHER BOOKS ILLUSTRATED BY MR. LENT:

Hans Christian Andersen. *The Little Match Girl* (Houghton, 1968).
Arlene Mosel. *Tikki Tikki Tembo* (Holt, 1968).
Jan Wahl. *May Horses* (Seymour-Lawrence-Delacorte, 1969).

Richard Lewis

IN LATE JUNE 1967, I hurried through the huge Lincoln Center complex in New York City to Hechscher Oval, the small, intimate children's theatre located on the second floor of the Library of Performing Arts. Adults and children were awaiting to see a performance of The Touchstone Players' production of *I Sing to Myself*. There were three people in the cast — a boy and a girl in their early twenties, who danced and mimed, and Richard Lewis, who narrated poetry against a background of tape-recorded musical effects.

The audience sat spellbound by the performance. Poem after poem flowed into one another, all carefully selected, well-balanced, and imaginatively produced. After the performance, I spoke to Mr. Lewis and received an invitation to visit him to talk further about his work, an invitation I gratefully accepted.

Perhaps the most significant event in Mr. Lewis's life was the collection and publication of *Miracles* (Simon and Schuster, 1966), an anthology of nearly two hundred poems by children of the English-speaking world. This collection took Mr. Lewis to countries throughout the world. New Zealand was one country he particularly loved, probably because here he met and married his wife, Nancy, and became close friends with Sylvia

Ashton-Warner, the famous teacher and author who later became the godmother to his young daughter, Mandy. The Lewis' have one other child, a son, Sascha.

"I was speaking to a training college for teachers there; Nancy was sitting in the audience. Afterwards we talked and talked late into the evening. The following morning I left for Sydney, Australia. Nancy and I wrote to one another for nearly a year. Then, one day, I received an offer from the New Zealand government to tour the island for ten months, lecturing and teaching creative writing. I was intrigued with the idea and, naturally, looked forward to meeting Nancy once again. We were married during that period I spent in New Zealand. Our honeymoon took us on nearly the same route I had traveled while collecting material for *Miracles*."

The Lewises now live on New York's East Side in a huge apartment filled with art and sculpture from the world over. "I was born and bred in New York City," commented Mr. Lewis. "I have spent my whole life here. As a child, summertime provided the only opportunity to leave the city's concrete walls — to get into and in reach of nature. Some of my most moving and profound moments in childhood were spent in the summers in Maine. I felt more at home in the seclusion of the wood than I did in the city."

Many of Mr. Lewis's anthologies reflect the poetic spirit of nature. *The Moment of Wonder* (Dial, 1964) is a collection of Chinese and Japanese poetry showing "the smallest magical details of nature and of living"; *In a Spring Garden* (Dial, 1965), a wedding gift to his wife, is an anthology of haiku selected for children, with exquisite mood drawings by his friend Ezra Jack Keats; *Out of the Earth I Sing* (Norton, 1968) is a handsome volume of poetry and songs of primitive peoples of the world.

Mr. Lewis leads an active life. Besides spending many hours researching for his anthologies, he is on the teaching staff of the Manhattan Country School and the New School for Social Research. He also moderates "Directions in Children's Literature," a radio program on WRVR that features interviews with top personalities in the field of books for children, continues his work with The Touchstone Players, and edits *The Touchstone Magazine,* a periodical reflecting children's work of high quality.

More traveling is planned for the future. "Both Nancy and I have a strong wanderlust," he remarked. Readers enjoy his travels, too, for during them he looks, he sees, he finds, and he shares the many miracles of childhood and youth that might otherwise be forever lost.

OTHER COLLECTIONS BY MR. LEWIS:

In Praise of Music (Orion Press, 1963).
Moon, For What Do You Wait? (Atheneum, 1967).
The Wind and the Rain (Simon and Schuster, 1968).
Of this World (Dial, 1968).
Still Waters of the Air: Poems by Three Modern Spanish Poets (Dial, 1969).

Joan M. Lexau

YOU WALK UP ONE FLIGHT, then another, and another, and you finally reach Joan M. Lexau's (*lex* ou, as in "loud") third floor walk-up apartment located near New York's Lower East Side. Miss Lexau is single, young, round, and jovial, with a delightful sense of humor.

"I was born in St. Paul, Minnesota, spent my first five years in Washington, D. C., and then returned to St. Paul," she remarked. "My father came over from Norway at the age of 17; he was a bridge engineer and a bookworm. He had hoped that some day he would become an author. Mother was born in St. Paul of Czech parents. She taught me, by example, that if something needs doing, you don't waste energy wondering if you can do it but just forge ahead. My brother, Henry, a magazine editor and writer, is a year older than I. He used to make up fantastic mystery stories for me and the other kids in our building; we acted them out as he invented them.

"I grew up from poverty, a broken home, and all that bit. When a small child, I went to the little store for bread one day and heard the store manager telling a customer about a courageous woman who lived nearby and was bringing up two kids on very little money. I went home and told my mother about this marvelous creature and then wondered why she didn't have anything to say about it. It wasn't until years later that I recalled the scene and realized that she was the woman. Ours was a home in which there was a great love and respect for the printed word. Before I could read, my mother read *Alice in Wonderland* to my brother and me because we had seen a copy of the first edition on display at the Library of Congress. One year, I remember, she read to us every night from one of those story-for-every-day-of-the-year books. She didn't know what the best books were, and it didn't matter because she put joy and excitement into every page she read. As I grew older, sometimes my father sent me books for gifts — Grimm, Andersen, Dickens, Rawlings, and so on."

Her brother, Henry, "was a brain," but Miss Lexau disliked her school years. "The regimentation and routine were intolerable, and it went on forever. The subject matter had no meaning to me. When the teacher said to trace a map, I traced it, but I had no idea why I should learn the shape of another country. The teacher said when you multiply fractions, you are actually dividing and when you wanted to divide fractions, you had to turn one of them upside down and multiply them. It didn't make any more or less sense than anything else. I received decent marks since I did what I was told and didn't ask questions because I didn't expect the answers would be any improvement."

She graduated from Central High in St. Paul. "No one told me it was possible to drop out, so I finished high school. I was supposed to receive a college scholarship, but there was a mix-up, which I didn't learn about until I went to register, and by that time it was too late to do anything about it. Later I took some philosophy courses in night school at the College of St. Thomas where I worked. Other jobs included selling underwear, filling permanent wave kits, typing letters to delinquent debtors, waitress, library clerk, bookkeeper, secretary, advertising production manager, and reporter."

145

Then for four years she worked in the children's book department at Harper and Row, where she fell in love with children's books. She decided that working on them, perhaps someday editing them, would be her life's work. "One day as I was feeling envious of the authors, it occurred to me that since before I could remember, I had intended to be a writer, and I asked myself what I was waiting for. That weekend I began writing children's books. It is the work I most enjoy, and it has also meant an escape from the 9 to 5 daily grind, which always made me feel like a machine. I still have nightmares about trying to get to work at 9:00 a.m., something I rarely achieved. I've had little sense of time since I was 13 and read in a book on Einstein's relativity that time was just a yardstick, and a yardstick to me was just a hunk of wood!"

Olaf Reads (Dial, 1961) was her first published book. It was inspired by a news item about a beginning reader who pulled a fire alarm because he could read the word "pull"; her second book, *Cathy Is Company* (Dial, 1961), was written before *Olaf Reads* and was based on the fun she had "visiting cousins and Uncle Frank and Aunt Ethel as a child."

Miss Lexau's books are quite varied. She has written books from pre-school to adult levels. She commented on this diversity: "Writing for different ages is not a problem if you can become not only the age of your characters but the characters themselves, including minor ones, while working on the story. It's something like being an actor and taking all the parts. You need a good memory of your childhood to begin with, not only some of the things that happened but how you felt about them. And you have to cut down on rationalizing as much as possible so you can understand yourself — so you can use this knowledge to understand others and their motives.

"When I wrote about Archimedes (*Archimedes Takes a Bath,* T. Y. Crowell, 1969), I was Archimedes, based on the research I did on him and his times and what I know of human nature. My Archimedes, of course, may or may not be close to the original. When I wrote about Olaf, I was Olaf, not just any six-year-old boy but that particular bumbling, naive, and well-meaning child. I was also his mother and teacher. That way it's easy to show characterization and motivations and have realistic conversation. Besides, I don't know any other way to do it. It's a bit more difficult to become a rhinocerous or a cat or a crocodile, but I do my best. When writing stories about animals, I usually do some research about that kind of animal. I like talking hens to be otherwise henlike. The main problem for me in writing for older children is the length of the books, and, therefore, the time they take. Lately, my books have been somewhat longer intentionally, and I have several long books planned for the day I am able to get at them."

Several of Miss Lexau's books portray children of minority backgrounds. Two such titles are *Benjie* (Dial, 1964) and *Maria* (Dial, 1964). While working on the first draft of *Maria,* Miss Lexau developed a craving for barbecued chicken. "Two or three times I went to buy some, but each time they had just run out. That's why there is so much about chicken in the book!" she exclaimed.

Miss Lexau is a busy person — one who is constantly thinking about her next work and always working diligently at her current task. "For some years I haven't even had any time for hobbies and such, but I'm beginning to have a little spare time now. I enjoy taking photographs, particularly of kids and animals; swimming (Minnesota is the "Land of 10,000 Lakes"), listening to talk shows and country music on the radio, watching baseball and football on TV, talking to most people, and, of course, reading — mysteries and nonfiction. I like to grow things and would love to have a garden some day. I'm crazy about bicycling and have a bike in Minnesota, where I visit every year at state fair time. In Minnesota I have three nieces, three nephews, two young first cousins, nine young second cousins, and neighbors of my nieces and nephews who also call me Aunt Joan" — and she is in love with all of them! She is also fond of an old battered rolltop desk, "which will probably not withstand one more moving since moving men will never follow instructions on how to take it apart."

In less than ten years Miss Lexau has produced approximately 30 books for young readers, which is a remarkable feat for any author. "Books made so much difference to my childhood," she commented, "that I hope in some way to help other children discover what reading can mean. Many of my books have a big-city background because I live in a big city, and more books with that background are needed. But I hope in the future to be able to live in, and write about, various backgrounds — a big city other than New York, a small Southern town, the Appalachians, or Puerto Rico."

SOME OTHER BOOKS BY MISS LEXAU:

That's Good, That's Bad (Dial, 1963).
I Should Have Stayed in Bed (Harper, 1965).
The Rooftop Mystery (Harper, 1968).
Striped Ice Cream (Lippincott, 1968).
Crocodile and Hen (Harper, 1969).

Leo Lionni

THERE IS A MAN who creates large imaginative picture books for young children. He and his wife, Nora, live in a large house in an olive grove overlooking the Gulf of Genoa in the Italian city of Lavagna. This man's name, of course, is Leo Lionni (lee *oh* nee).

His house is filled with works of art and folk objects. His collection includes works by such friends as Ben Shahn, Alexander Calder, and Giorgio Morandi and by people who have been important to him as a painter and designer, such as Hans Arp, Paul Klee, and Alberto Giacometti. Dr. Lionni has traveled a great deal, and many of his folk objects were acquired during his travels. He was born in 1910, in Amsterdam where he lived the first 12 years of his life. "I lived within two blocks of two of the best museums in Europe," he stated. "I spent most of my time there and quite naturally assumed that one day I would become an artist. In grade school nature studies were very important to me. I remember how we collected plants and kept all sorts of animals; we drew leaves and animals. I relive these early experiences over and over again. I haven't changed very much." The rest of his childhood was spent in Holland and Belgium.

In 1939 Dr. Lionni came to the United States and for several years was art director of N. W. Ayer and Son, a large advertising agency in Philadelphia, Pennsylvania. In 1950 he became art director of *Fortune* magazine and also served as a design director for the Olivetti Corporation of America. He has continued to do work for large corporations and publishing firms.

Dr. Lionni's first book was the charming tale of two torn circles, *Little Blue and Little Yellow* (Obolensky, 1959). "This first book just happened," he commented. "I told a story to my grandchildren, made it into a dummy, and showed it to an editor friend. The book was successful. I was asked to do more and little by little discovered the joys of this profession, which was totally new to me."

The following year, the author-illustrator wrote and drew the pictures for *Inch by Inch* (Obolensky), a story of an inch-worm who saves himself from death by proving that he can be useful. The text was widely acclaimed in the field of children's literature. In 1961 it was a Caldecott Award runner-up; in 1962 it was awarded the Lewis Carroll Shelf Award, which is given to books worthy enough to sit on the shelf with *Alice in Wonderland*; in 1963 he won the Children's Book Prize in Germany. Following *Inch by Inch* Dr. Lionni produced other award winners such as *Swimmy* (Pantheon, 1963; Caldecott runner-up in 1964), *Frederick* (Pantheon, 1967; Caldecott runner-up in 1968), and *Alexander and the Wind-Up Mouse* (Pantheon, 1969; a 1970 Caldecott Honor Book).

His books combine a diversity of technique. "I like inventing a technique for each story," he declared. "I've used drawings, crayon, collage, and gouache painting in various books. Since technique and style are related, my style varies from book to book." Regarding writing and illustrating his work, he told me, "The important thing is the story. I eliminate many stories before I am convinced that I have the right one. Once the idea is clear, illustrating it is rather easy — the difficulties are always there, of course, but solving them is exciting. I am not greatly concerned about children. I deal with large themes; my books are fables and parables. They express something I think and feel. The fact that the form is suited for children is a happy coincidence. And perhaps it disciplines my work to invent forms, both literary and visual, that are so simple as to be acceptable to children." All of his books have been translated into foreign languages. His favorites are *Swimmy* and *Frederick,* "Perhaps because they are more autobiographical than others."

He makes no distinction between work and leisure. He is a designer and painter and occasionally gives lectures. Although self-taught as an artist-writer, Dr. Lionni's formal education brought him a Ph.D. in economics from the University of Genoa, Italy. His other interests include playing the flamenco guitar, his two sons — one an architect, the other a painter and a poet — and his two grandchildren.

Some Other Books by Dr. Lionni (All Pantheon):

Tico and the Golden Wings (1964).
The Biggest House in the World (1968).
The Alphabet Tree (1968).

From THE BIGGEST HOUSE IN THE WORLD by Leo Lionni.
Permission of Pantheon Books.

Myra Cohn Livingston

MANY ADULTS LEARN about childhood by reading books on child development, by listening to lectures, and/or by carefully observing children in various situations and settings. But there is another way to learn about childhood. One can go to the local library or bookstore and get a stack of books containing the poetry of Myra Cohn Livingston. Sit down and read poems like "Bump on My Knee," "Wide Awake," or "The Night" to learn how children feel and think, or look at "For a Bird," a mere eight-line verse that sums up the feeling of sadness, loss, and death.

I have not only read the poetry of Mrs. Livingston but had the privilege of hearing her read poetry aloud on several occasions. When she speaks, she has something important to say. Her poetry and thoughts about poetry are refreshing and contemporary. For her poetry is a total experience that is often destroyed when it is stripped apart and classified into little compartments such as ideas, parts of speech, metaphors, or similes. "Too often the form is put ahead of the force," she declared.

She warmly welcomes the new poetry of today's youth. "I feel that it is time we pay attention to the young people who listen, really listen, to pop music. They are not asked here to define meanings, discuss each symbol, or comment on the meter or rhythm; they are only asked to enjoy and take what they will, feel what they will. I believe we have forgotten that poetry is to *enjoy*. And I fear that in sharing poetry, too many adults do not recognize that they offer, through their choice of poetry, a world the child does not know, a tune he has no desire to hear, emotions that are not a part of childhood, a metaphorical guise that also has no meaning for him.

"It seems to me that in the popular music of today, especially when done by the Beatles, Simon and Garfunkel and a few others, the essential core of what good poetry does is met by letting the force of what is being said create the form — and not the other way around. The rhythms are the rhythms of what is being felt and said; the musical inventions support this force. And the young people are listening, imaginatively involved in the symbolism that is much the same symbolism that man has always used, the rain, wind, sun and fantasy-escape symbolism — yellow submarines, tangerine trees, marshmallow skies. They are responding to the *total involvement*, which is at the basis of poetry, with the head, mind, heart, and body. 'No meaning, just feel!' said a young man about this music. 'You can read into it anything you want or nothing at all.' This is what I believe of poetry too — to be able to choose, to respond without imposed standards. It is time that we take the clue from our young people. These songs fulfill their need to find an outlet for senses, sensitivities, and emotions."

Mrs. Livingston began writing poetry while a freshman at Sarah Lawrence College. "I turned in some poems ("Whispers" and "Sliding" among them) that my professor felt were for children. She urged me to submit them to *Story Parade* magazine; some were accepted. In 1946 "Whispers" became my first published poem. I submitted a complete manuscript, *Whispers and Other Poems*, to several publishing houses; it was rejected. Margaret McElderry of Harcourt urged me, however, to con-

153

tinue writing. Twelve years later I sent the manuscript back to her at Harcourt; it was accepted and published in 1958.

Commenting on her work habits, Mrs. Livingston said, "My work habits are erratic. Poetry comes in strange ways and never at the moment when one might think it should come. There are poems I have tried to write for 20 years that have never come out right. Others seem to come in a flash. Searching for the right form to express certain ideas takes time. I try to put poems away, once written, and take them out much later. Many are discarded."

Besides being a poet, Mrs. Livingston is a wife and mother of three children. Josh, 14, is interested in math and space, plays the piano, and loves classical music; Jonas, 11, works on antique and classic cars and plays the French horn (Mrs. Livingston herself had played the French horn and was a professional musician in earlier years); Jennie, 7, is keenly interested in art, writes her own stories, and likes to sew and read. Mrs. Livingston's husband, Richard, is a C.P.A. In 1968 he had his first book for children published, *The Hunkendunkens* (Harcourt), a series of stories he had told his children over the years.

"Music is an important part of our life," stated Mrs. Livingston. "One of our closest friends is Jascha Heifetz, and this enables us to hear chamber music in the home as it should be heard and to be with many fine, outstanding musicians. As a family we enjoy visiting the zoo and museums, whale-spotting when the gray whales are migrating and going to the beach. We enjoy nature and walking, our friends, and attending car concours (my father is a collector of antique and classic cars); we play bridge for relaxation, and we read together almost every evening we are home. We enjoy home life — swimming, playing ping-pong, being together."

The Livingstons live in an Italian villa built on three levels in the Santa Monica Mountains in California. They have a garden of over 80 camellia bushes and assorted flowers; in the summer they grow tomatoes. Their view looks out across Beverly

Hills down to the Pacific Ocean, "And on a clear day we can see Catalina!" Mrs. Livingston exclaimed. Her favorite possessions are her books. "I collect Joyce, Yeats, and Caldecott children's books as well as pictures, stories, and items that my children have done for me over the years. I also prize the pictures and prints illustrator friends have given me."

Mrs. Livingston was born on August 17, 1926, in Omaha, Nebraska. "I had an ideal, happy childhood. I had wise and wonderful parents who taught me that a busy creative life brings much happiness. Today, I am a woman with a very full life. I have family, friends, a home I enjoy, a career that enables me to stay home most of the time, the opportunity to live in an exciting community, teach writing, share poetry with children, share my ideas with teachers and librarians, collect books, do bookbinding, and grow and pick flowers — and to keep the joys ahead of the troubles!"

My interview with Myra Cohn Livingston ended with a discussion of today's times. She commented, "To quote Bob Dylan, 'the times, they are a changin'.' I believe that one of the most difficult things for all human beings is to keep up with changes in a meaningful way; not change for change's sake, but to retain from the past what is important and yet bend a little to new tunes, new rhythms, new ideas. In my anthology *A Tune Beyond Us* (Harcourt, 1968), I used Wallace Stevens' phrase 'a tune beyond us, yet ourselves.' I think all men need the tune beyond, something they apprehend if not comprehend, yet it must be something that relates to 'ourselves.'"

SOME OTHER BOOKS BY MRS. LIVINGSTON (All Harcourt):

Wide Awake and Other Poems (1959).
I'm Hiding (1961).
I'm Not Me (1963).
The Moon and a Star and Other Poems (1965).
I'm Waiting (1966).
A Crazy Flight and Other Poems (1969).

Anita and Arnold Lobel

ANITA AND ARNOLD LOBEL live in a duplex apartment in the pleasant Victorian section of Park Slope in Brooklyn, New York, with their two children, a boy, 10, and a girl, 13. Both Mr. and Mrs. Lobel are artists and writers, yet they have never collaborated.

Mrs. Lobel was born in Poland on June 2, 1934. "I was born into a relatively comfortable merchant family," she commented. "Hitler put a stop to those comforts. My parents separated for practical reasons, believing we would all have better chances for survival, which proved to be true. My brother and I were left in the care of a Polish woman with whom we stayed and drifted around Poland for the next four and one half years. Toward the end of the war, my brother and I were captured and sent to a concentration camp in Germany, from which we were rescued in 1945. We were eventually reunited with our parents in Stockholm. I did not go to school until I was 13, but was taught how to read and write. I came from Sweden to New York against my will because my parents wanted to reclaim some long, lost relatives they had in this country."

Mr. Lobel was born on May 22, 1933, in Los Angeles, California. "My parents had gone from Schenectady, New York, to

Los Angeles to find their fortunes," he told me. "Of course there were not fortunes to be found in 1933, so they returned to Schenectady and to eventual divorce. There I continued to live through a rather unhappy and neurotic childhood until I finally escaped to college in my late teens."

The Lobels met while attending Pratt Institute in Brooklyn. Mr. Lobel was directing a school play in which Mrs. Lobel had the lead part. "I wanted to be in the theatre at one time. When I am illustrating a manuscript, I do it as if it might be a staged play," Mrs. Lobel remarked.

Their work and work habits are highly individualistic. Mr. Lobel explained, "I decided to do books for children because I found it was the one thing I could do well. My first book was *A Zoo for Mister Muster* (Harper, 1962), which I suppose developed out of stories that I made up for my own kids when they were quite small. I'm not sure; it was a long time ago." His second book, *A Holiday for Mister Muster* (Harper, 1963), was selected by the *New York Times* as one of the ten best illustrated books of that year.

"My stories usually emerge out of a visual idea, a situation, or a sequence of situations that I think would be fun to draw. Sometimes the story pops into place in just the right way, but more often than not it is a struggle for me. I never try my ideas out on children — they should see the finished performance, not the rehearsal. My favorite book is always the next one, the one I haven't done yet. Once a book comes out, it is just an anticlimax, a sort of haunting object."

Mrs. Lobel's first book, *Sven's Bridge* (Harper, 1965), developed from a pictorial idea and a character sketch of a kindly man. The format and design of this book dictated the contents of the story. "At first I thought only of illustrating stories by other authors but found, with a little effort, I, too, could supply a story to go with the pictures. When I begin a book, I have a specific style in mind, for instance, a historical period. *The Troll Music* (Harper, 1966) was mainly inspired by the

From THE WISEST MAN IN THE WORLD by Benjamin Elkin and Anita Lobel. Permission of Parents' Magazine Press.

bottom parts of medieval tapestries with all the vegetation and little animals running around. I got the idea for *Potatoes, Potatoes* (Harper, 1967) partly from childhood memories of Poland."

Potatoes, Potatoes is an exciting volume that tells a powerful story of two brothers who become enemies in war and of their wise mother who will not give them or their starving comrades so much as one potato peel until all of them promise to lay down their swords and their guns. "I like *Potatoes, Potatoes,*" she said, "because of its theme. But I do not take it as seriously as some of the reviewers have."

The Lobels both work at home. She declared, "I like working at home. Our children seldom feel alienated from us. We are always there when they come home from school. The idea of work and home and living doesn't seem so fragmented to any of us. Although Arnold and I have never collaborated on anything, we do act as each other's critics."

As for pleasures in life, Mr. Lobel likes "eating, sex, and sleep — probably in that order." Traveling frightens him; he enjoys puttering around at home. The theatre irritates him, but he loves going to the movies. "I also get much comfort from the companionship of my wife and a few close friends."

Mrs. Lobel loves traveling and lots of new clothes. "I love to work! Leisure of the idealized American sort bores me. I like foreign languages, and sometimes I like to cook. I play the piano and guitar, not especially well. Political activities and causes are embarrassing, and I do not like to align myself with groups of any kind."

Books by the Lobels are artistically designed and exciting to read. One wonders what kind of a book might result if they pooled their many talents and worked together on a volume. Perhaps one day they will.

OTHER BOOKS BY MRS. LOBEL:

F. N. Monjo. *Indian Summer* (Harper, 1968).
Benjamin Elkin. *The Wisest Man in the World* (Parents, 1968).
Barbara Borack. *Someone Small* (Harper, 1969).

SOME OTHER BOOKS BY MR. LOBEL (All Harper):

Millicent Selsam. *Greg's Microscope* (1963).
The Great Blueness and Other Predicaments (1968).
Judith Viorst. *I'll Fix Anthony* (1969).

From THE STAR CHIEF by Andrea DiNoto and Arthur Lobel. Illustrations © 1967 by Arthur Lobel. Permission of The Macmillan Co.

Winifred and Cecil Lubell

IF YOU LOOK ON PAGES 2 and 58 of Winifred and Cecil Lubell's book *In a Running Brook* (Rand-McNally, 1968), you will see them at work with Andy, their French poodle. Working in a running brook, a flowering garden, or tree inhabited by caterpillars is not unusual for this writing team.

Mr. Lubell was born in Leeds, England, and came to the United States when he was about 12 years old. He attended the Boston Latin School and went on to Harvard University, where he received both his bachelor of arts and master degrees in English. He is currently the editor of *American Fabrics Magazine,* an important and lavishly designed trade journal.

Mrs. Lubell is a native of New York City and studied at the Ethical Culture School, the Art Students League, and the Duncan Phillips Museum School in Washington, D. C.

The Lubells met in New York, married, and moved to Croton-on-Hudson, New York, where they have lived since the 1940's. Their home, situated on a well-tailored acre and a half, is filled with artwork — tapestries from Egypt, paintings from Mexico, wood sculpture, and art pieces galore. The house and its surrounding countryside act as a laboratory for the team. Many of their books stem from the lush, natural resources that envelop them.

160

Although Mrs. Lubell has been writing and illustrating books for children for the past 15 years, her husband joined the juvenile production scene only recently. In 1960 he wrote the text for *The Tall Grass Zoo* (Rand-McNally). "We had a house for the summer on Martha's Vineyard," recalled Mr. Lubell. "Since I had little to do but vacation, I thought I'd try to help Winnie with her newest project. I always looked down my nose at children's books, thinking they were quite easy to put together. I learned quickly that I was wrong! Working as a team was a satisfying experience not only because I took pleasure in the writing but also because Winnie and I found that a new way of life opened up to us."

Mrs. Lubell has collaborated with authors other than her husband. She coauthored *The Stitchery Book: Embroidery for Beginners* with I. P. Miller (Doubleday, 1965). "I had always been interested in stitchery. Mrs. Miller and I got together and went to a publishing house with a basket of stitchery we made, discussed the book, and received the go-ahead to do it. We persuaded our husbands to work on it too; Cecil edited the text, and Michael, a free-lance photographer, took pictures of our winter's long labor of love!" Naturally animals and insects in stitchery are described in one section of the volume.

Mrs. Lubell has also collaborated with science writer Millicent Selsam on a series of books and on another series with Dorothy Sterling. "When Dorothy and I worked on *Creatures of the Night* (Doubleday, 1960), her son, Pete, was working at a Carvel stand. It was a wonderful place to collect bugs, but Pete preferred that 'us two dames didn't come around while he was working.' My son, David, was working at a Volkswagen agency and was terrified that we'd show up there, so we hit the golf course. The people there were ready to call the police, for they thought we were bats! I love to work with another person — it inspires me and it's so much fun."

The Lubells enjoy working together. "We take a magazine approach," stated Mr. Lubell. "I do the writing, Winnie does the pictures, and we constantly react to each other's work."

161

They are both constant learners. "Cecil couldn't tell, and didn't know, a dandelion from a tulip until I got him interested in nature," she laughed.

"I wasn't that bad," he answered, "but it is true that I have to really dig for information before I begin to write. Winnie is an eternal student. She's always learning. If she isn't doing stitchery, she's studying Greek; if she isn't collecting caterpillars, she's sketching primitive art forms."

It is easy to see how the Lubells' children found their places in life. David, 26, is an archaeologist; Steven, 23, is an art student in London, England. Mrs. Lubell considers herself "one of those

From IN A RUNNING BROOK by Winifred and Cecil Lubell, © 1968 by Winifred and Cecil Lubell. Permission of Rand McNally & Co.

incredibly lucky people. I have done what I like to do in life. And my work has naturally sprouted out of things I like doing — raising children, living in the country, and drawing. And what's even more idyllic, I have a husband who aids and abets me in all this, and children, too, who have helped."

Perhaps the greatest praise an author of children's books can receive is from a child. I had the opportunity to use the Lubells' *In a Running Brook* in a Harlem classroom — far from any running brook. One child became so completely fascinated with the text that he exclaimed, "There isn't a brook around here, but there's one in Central Park. I'm gonna' take this book with me all summer and I'll bet I'll learn a lot of things that I never knew about before."

Countless children look forward to Winifred and Cecil Lubell's work, and they look at it as they would a road map, as a guide through the world of nature.

SOME OTHER BOOKS BY MRS. LUBELL:

Millicent Selsam. *The Birth of an Island* (Harper, 1959).
Dorothy Sterling. *Caterpillars* (Doubleday, 1961).
———. *Spring Is Here.* (Doubleday, 1964).
Jean Craighead George. *Moon of the Mountain Lions* (Crowell, 1968).

IN COLLABORATION WITH MR. LUBELL (All Rand-McNally):

Up a Tree (1961).
Rosalie, the Bird Market Turtle (1962).
Green Is for Growing (1964).
William Wise. *Nanette, The Hungry Pelican.* (Rand-McNally, 1969).

163

Robert McCloskey

WHAT COULD BE MORE EXCITING than to answer the telephone in one's office on a cool autumn morning and have the voice at the other end say, "Mr. Hopkins? This is Bob McCloskey. I'll only be in New York for the next few hours. I've got to catch a plane back to Maine. Can we get together?"

Within one-half hour, Mr. McCloskey arrived at my office at Scholastic Magazines, Inc. He is tall and heavy set, has a graying crew cut, and wears large, round dark-rimmed glasses that dominate his face. He speaks quietly and is rather shy and quite self-conscious about being himself.

Mr. McCloskey has been greatly heralded in the field of children's literature — and justifiably so. From 1940–1963 he wrote and illustrated six picture books for children, two of which were awarded the Caldecott Medal, making him the first man ever to win the award twice, and two others were Caldecott runner-ups! Other works by the author-illustrator include the ever-popular *Homer Price* (1943) and *Centerburg Tales* (1951), both published by Viking Press.

Robert McCloskey was born in Hamilton, Ohio, on September 15, 1914. He spent his entire childhood in Hamilton, leaving there in 1932 to accept a scholarship to the Vesper George School in Boston. He received the scholarship through Scholastic Magazines Annual Art Awards. (After his visit, I looked in Scholastic's library and found the issue of *Scholastic* announcing his first prize, in Prints; it was dated April 30, 1932. The work he had entered was a dramatic and bold woodcut engraving.) Two years later he received his first important commission, executing the bas-reliefs for Hamilton's municipal building. The following fall he moved to New York City and studied at the National Academy of Design. Here he received the President's Award and began exhibiting his artwork at the Academy as well as at the Tiffany Foundation and the Society of Independent Artists in Boston. During the summers he painted and studied on Cape Cod.

While in New York, he went to call upon May Massee, the late editor of junior books at Viking Press, with his portfolio under his arm. "She looked at the drawings," recalled Mr. McCloskey, "was rather polite, and we spent the time talking about *Ohio*!" Before returning to Ohio, he began to draw everyday life as he saw it. Shortly afterwards he returned to New York and worked in the field of commercial art. He called on Miss Massee once again, this time with his "new styled drawings" and a story about a boy and his harmonica. Miss Massee took the book, as she took all his subsequent books, and *Lentil* was born in 1940.

Lentil is autobiographical in part and reflects the author's own childhood. In one of his illustrations, Lentil is sitting in the bathtub playing his harmonica. "The bathroom, with its old washbasin, is the one upstairs in the house where I grew up," he said.

On the strength of his new paintings, he acquired a job in Cambridge, Massachusetts, assisting Francis Scott Bradford in making huge murals of famous socialites from Beacon Hill for the Lever Brothers' Building. It was on this job that he noticed the ducks who were part of the Boston Public Gardens' scenery. It was here also that the idea of *Make Way for Ducklings* (1941) evolved. The book didn't develop until nearly four years later when he returned to Boston. He had noticed the traffic problem of the ducks and had heard several stories about them. Then the book began to take shape. Mr. McCloskey researched and studied the habits and the anatomy of mallard ducklings in every conceivable way. He sketched them in the Boston Public Gardens, observed stuffed specimens in the American Museum of Natural History in New York City, and even sought the aid of an ornithologist at Cornell University. When he felt he needed "live" models, he went to the old Washington Market in New York City and bought four squawking mallards; two of them turned out to be fakes! Mr. McCloskey was then sharing an apartment in an old house in Greenwich Village with the illustrator Marc Simont. The ducklings were kept in the apartment until there were too many complaints about their noise. Finally, in 1941, the book was published; the following year it won the Caldecott Award.

In 1943 *Homer Price* appeared, a collection of six stories about Homer's adventures. *Homer Price,* like *Lentil,* reflects Mr. McCloskey's humor and affection for life in midwest America. The book is filled with preposterous tales and with zany inventions such as the famous doughnut machine created by Uncle Ulysses and the fabulous musical mousetrap belonging to Mike Murphy. *Centerburg Tales,* a sequel to *Homer Price,* carries Homer through further absurd experiences, causing millions of young Americans to chuckle every time it is read.

The McCloskey's first child was Sally (Sal). His wife, Margaret (Peggy) Durand, is the daughter of the world famous storyteller and writer, Ruth Sawyer. Three years later, their second daughter, Jane, arrived. "Sal (now 22) was married this past year," remarked Mr. McCloskey. "She and her husband are living in Maryland. Sal is teaching there while working for her master's degree in linguistics. Jane is 19 and a junior at Mount Holyoke College. The old house is kind of quiet now. But we have two dogs, and by mistake, we're going to have some puppies come November."

Several years ago the McCloskey family bought an island in Penobscot Bay, Maine, near Deer Isle, and there they spend long May-through-October summers. His later work, *Blueberries for Sal* (1948), *One Morning in Maine* (1952), and *Time of Wonder* (1958), developed from their life on the island. Sal, in *Blueberries for Sal,* is Mr. McCloskey's daughter, and the mother is his wife. The kitchen on the endpapers is their kitchen, except for the old stove, which he borrowed from his mother-in-law's house in Hancock, Maine. In *One Morning in Maine,* Jane is introduced, and their English setter, Penny, and black cat, Mozzarella, appear also. *Time of Wonder,* also awarded the Caldecott Medal, took the author-illustrator three years to create and was his first full-color picture book. *Burt Dow: Deep Water Man* appeared in 1963.

Mr. McCloskey hasn't worked on a book of his own since *Burt Dow.* "I'm chasing a new way of life," he told me. "I have been quite involved for the past three years in constructing puppets — a new type of puppet. My studio now looks like a machine shop. I had to learn a great many new techniques such as operating a lathe and cutting into rubber. I suppose I got interested in movement and in animation from watching Morton Schindel put several of my books on film and seeing the development of *The Lively Art of Picture Books,* a film produced by Weston Wood Studios, Weston, Connecticut, in 1964. I want to do something new with puppets. I think it is too bad that they are usually confined to a television box. I'd like to find a way to eliminate that. Puppets suffer from claustrophobia!"

I asked Mr. McCloskey about the letters he receives from children. "The mail falls into several categories," he laughed. "One category is pictures of ducks sent to me from the world over — from California to Scandinavia, from Holland to Turkey. The same situation exists everywhere, I guess — ducks and duck traffic!

"Then," he continued, "hardly a mail goes by without my getting a question about *Homer Price.* In the first story I referred to four robbers and I drew five. The book was in production, and I was being inducted into the army. I hadn't reread the story after the publisher asked me to do another drawing. I drew it, and drew five! That book came out in 1943, and I still get kids writing to me telling of their 'discovery.' When the book was translated into Japanese, they took the fifth man right out of the bed!

"Another kind of letters I receive are pictures kids have drawn of either ducks or doughnuts, and still another are from students in colleges asking me for the story of my life. They sometimes say, 'Add some new details and please return it to me in three days!' "

His favorite book? "Perhaps it is *Homer Price,* yet I don't think I have a favorite. I cannot bear to read or even listen to anyone reading my books. They are so much a part of me and part of my past."

Mr. McCloskey was in New York City working on a May Massee memorial collection. "I am going to give some of my original sketches to the collection," he commented. "Yet it is so difficult to even sort out my old drawings. I have them all in a big box; it contains my whole life. I can't bear it!"

We ended our talk on a lighter note — one of Mr. McCloskey's many experiences that have evolved from *Make Way for Ducklings.* One day a mallard duck flew into the penthouse garden of the secretary of a big life insurance company in Boston. The duck laid eggs, and the man didn't know what to do. Promptly he contacted Mr. McCloskey to ask, "How the hell do I get them all back to the park?" Obviously, the world considers Mr. McCloskey a duck expert!

SOME OTHER BOOKS BY MR. MCCLOSKEY (All Viking):

Ruth Sawyer. *Journey Cake, Ho!* (1953); (Caldecott runner-up).
Keith Robertson. *Henry Reed, Inc.* (1963).
———. *Henry Reed's Journey* (1963).
———. *Henry Reed's Baby-Sitting Service* (1966).

David McCord

IT IS ALWAYS A TREAT to hear a poet speak about poetry! David McCord did so for me. "Poetry is so many things besides the shiver down the spine. It is a new day lying on an unknown doorstep. It is *Peer Gynt* and *Moby Dick* in a single line. It is the best translation of words that do not exist. It is hot coffee dripping from an icicle. It is the accident involving sudden life. It is the calculus of the imagination. It is the finishing touch to what one could not finish. It is a hundred things as unexplainable as all our foolish explanations."

Mr. McCord writes poetry for both children and adults. Of this duality he said, "Poetry for children is simpler than poetry for adults. The overtones are fewer, but it should have overtones. Basically, of course, it isn't different. Children's verse sometimes turns out, or is turned out, to be not much more than doggerel: lame lines, limp rhymes, and poor ideas. By and large, verse written for children is rhymed; it is nearly always brief, though an occasional poem in the hands of a skilled performer like Ogden Nash may tell a story. But poetry, like rain, should fall with elemental music, and poetry for children should catch the eye as well as the ear and the mind. It should delight; it really *has* to delight. Furthermore, poetry for children should keep reminding them, without any feeling on their part that they are being reminded, that the English language is a most marvelous and availing instrument."

Mr. McCord was born on November 15, 1897, near New York's Greenwich Village. He grew up on Long Island, in Princeton, New Jersey, and in Oregon; he was an only child. "Long Island was all fields and woods when I was a boy. We lived next door to a poultry farm and not far from the ocean. My love of nature began there. When I was 12 I went with my father and mother to live on a ranch in the south of Oregon on the wild Rogue River. This was frontier country then: no electric lights, oil, or coal heat. We pumped all our water out of a deep well and pumped it by hand. I didn't go to school for three years, but I learned the life of the wilderness, something about birds, animals, and wild flowers, trees and geology, and self-reliance. I learned to weather seasons of drought and weeks of steady rain. I sometimes panned gold for pocket money — a very pleasing and exciting art once you can control it! I learned to recognize a few of the constellations and to reverence the night sky — Orion is still my favorite skymark! I saw and experienced the terror of a forest fire. I can honestly say that I was a pretty good shot with a rifle, but I have never aimed at a living thing since I was 15. My love of all life is far too deep for that." His love of nature can be seen in many of his poems.

As a child, Mr. McCord was stricken with malaria. Recurring bouts of fever kept him out of school a great deal. This, however, did not stop him from graduating with high honors from Lincoln High School in Portland, Oregon, and from Harvard College in 1921. Harvard thereafter became an integral part of his life. Prior to his retirement in 1963, Mr. McCord spent well over 40 years at the university, serving in many capacities, but principally as alumni editor and fund raiser. In 1956 Harvard conferred on him the first honorary degree of Doctor of Humane Letters it ever granted. President Kennedy received his LL.D. at that same commencement.

Mr. McCord told me how he came into the field of children's poetry. "Two years after I finished my master's degree in English at Harvard — I had previously studied to become a physicist — I wrote a number of poems for children. One was published in the then *Saturday Review of Literature* and got into some anthologies." He published his first volume of serious poems in 1927. His first book for children was *Far and Few* (Little, Brown, 1952). "I have a weakness for *Far and Few*. It is dedicated to my twice-pioneering mother, a lady of great imagination and courage, who died in 1956 at the age of 93."

As to his writing for children, he continued, "I seemed to know instinctively that to write for the young I had to write for myself. I write out of myself, about things I did as a boy, about things that are fairly timeless as subjects. I do not believe that one can teach the art of writing. You are born with the urge for it or you are not. Only the hardest self-discipline and considerable mastery of self-criticism will get you anywhere.

"Children still love words, rhythm, rhyme, music, games. They climb trees, skate, swim, swing, fish, explore, act, ride, run, and love snow and getting wet all over; they make things and are curious about science. They love humor and nonsense and imaginary conversation with imaginary things. I pray that I never am guilty of talking down to boys and girls. I try to remember that they are closer to the sixth sense than we who are older.

"Sometimes poems come to me full-blown — nonsense verses in particular. More often I work at them, rewriting for choice of words and for sound and smoothness. I never use an unusual word unless I can place it as a key word so that it will make the reader look it up. Poems should open new horizons. They are vistas — familiar as well as strange."

Besides being an accomplished poet whose work is included in 200 anthologies, Mr. McCord has written and edited 32 books. *Time* magazine has called *What Cheer: An Anthology of American and British Humorous Verse* (Random House, 1955) "the classic in its field." He paints watercolor landscapes and has had several one-man shows. He was once an avid amateur wireless operator and holds a 1915 first-grade amateur wireless operator's license. Mr. McCord remembers when he heard on a pocket set he had made "one of the original experiments in what we call radio broadcasting — a man playing the banjo!" He belongs to several clubs, is a trustee of two colleges, a hospital, and a library, and is an overseer of the Perkins Institute for the Blind. He loves people, the theatre, and for five of his young years was a music and drama critic on the old Boston *Transcript*. He likes foreign movies, most good comedians, and travel. He is fond of all animals, except cats, and loves all birds. He has a collection of 60 owls made of ivory, glass, pottery, metal, wood, stone, amber, and porcelain. He also collects watercolors, etchings, wood engravings, prints, aquatints, and drawings, and books — 5,000 of them. He declared, "I have been a fly fisherman since I was 13 — trout, first; salmon, second. I am fond of professional baseball; I'm a Red Sox fan!

"One of my best high school teachers once told us, 'Never let a day go by without looking on three beautiful things.' I have tried to live up to that and have found it isn't difficult. The sky in all weathers is, for me, the first of these three things."

Today I took David McCord's advice. I looked at three beautiful things — his books of verse for boys and girls (all Little, Brown) — *Far and Few* (1952), *Take Sky* (1962), and *Every Time I Climb a Tree* (1967). It wasn't difficult to live up to — not at all!

ANOTHER BOOK BY MR. McCORD:

All Day Long (Little, Brown, 1966).

Phyllis McGinley

"I WAS A LONELY CHILD who grew up on a prairie ranch in Colorado. My family had a couple of sections of land east of Denver. The nearest town was about six miles away. It looked like a scene from a television western with its muddy main street, hitching posts, and false-fronted stores. My brother and I rode horseback to school, which was about three miles from home, *when* there was a teacher," recalled Phyllis McGinley.

At the age of 12, her father died, and her mother took the family to Ogden, Utah. Miss McGinley attended school in Ogden and continued her education at the University of Utah and the University of Southern California. She had always wanted to become a poet and was rhyming words at the age of six. While in college she began selling poetry to various national magazines. Encouraged by her success, she came to New York in 1928 and taught high school English in New Rochelle for four and a half years. Then she moved to New York City to take a job with an advertising agency. She finally gave up this position to become the poetry editor of *Town and Country* magazine.

In 1937 she married Charles (Bill) Hayden. The Haydens now live in the pleasant surburb of Larchmont, New York, in a 165-year-old house hidden behind tall hedges. The house has a secret room that was used before the Civil War as part of the Underground Railroad; the house also contains her favorite possessions — English antiques that she has spent over 40 years acquiring.

In addition to her writing career, Miss McGinley enjoys "people, my grandchildren, rose gardening, and reading detective stories. Besides being a writer, I am a mother, wife, and grandmother." She did not wish to discuss her children. "My children's lives are their own and belong to them, not me."

She said of her work, "I never had any training in writing. I am a writer for grownups. But about once every year or so, I write a book for children in which I expand every bit of art knowledge and technique I have acquired in my lifetime." Her first book for children was *The Horse Who Lived Upstairs* (Lippincott, 1944). "I decided to write for children because Helen Stone, an artist friend, had done a portfolio of horse drawings and wanted a text. She thought they might inspire a poem or two. I put the drawings aside on a table in the living room, and they sat there for two years! Finally, I was shamed into doing something about them." The book tells a delightful tale of Joey, a city horse stabled in a second-story Greenwich Village barn, who longs for the country. To do the book, Mrs. McGinley studied the field of children's literature and then began studying horses. "I went down to Greenwich Village and watched how horses in the city live. It was quite a revelation. I discovered one stable that cried out for storytelling. The horses were all kept on the upper floors of the building, and they surveyed the world from their second-story windows as calmly as though they were standing in country pastures. When I noticed that their watering trough was an old cast-off bathtub, I knew I had a book."

Of the books she has created for children, her favorite is *The Year Without a Santa Claus* (Lippincott, 1957), a rollicking Christmas poem. This book started out to be a play for a very private audience. "It was written to be dramatized by both our family and our friends, Jean and Walter Kerr's children, for a common celebration."

In 1961 Miss McGinley was awarded the coveted Pulitzer Prize for Poetry for her book *Times Three: Selected Poems from Three Decades* (Viking), a book of gay, deft verse. I asked the famous poet if she felt there was a noticeable difference between writing for adults and writing for children. She answered, "No, there is no difference. One does the best one can for both."

Some Other Books by Miss McGinley:

All Around the Town (Lippincott, 1948).
The B Book (Crowell-Collier, 1962, 1968).

Ann McGovern

Attractive young woman + Interest in betterment
of world problems = Ann McGovern.

THIS EQUATION REPRESENTS a person who is concerned about
children growing up in today's confused world and one who sets
out to do something about it whenever she takes her pen in
hand. If one takes a selection of her many texts and reads them
at one sitting, her words seem like a social treatise delivered by
a reknowned historian.

Miss McGovern and I discussed several of her books. "*Little
Wolf* (Abelard-Schuman, 1965; illustrated by Nola Langner, a
close friend of the author's) is my anti-war book," stated Miss
McGovern. It is the story of a young Indian boy who, instead
of hunting, brings home animals who cannot run, cares for them,
and makes them well again. He is a disgrace to his father and
to his tribe:

> "How can I be a hunter if I have to kill you?" he asks the
> deer.
>
> "Never, never will I hunt if I have to kill . . ."

In 1965 she also wrote *Runaway Slave: The Story of Harriet
Tubman* (Four Winds Press). "Harriet Tubman was an ad-

venturous woman. I thought I would try to do a book for young people about a heroine that girls could identify with. And I wanted my heroine to be meaningful to white children as well as black." The book is a dramatic biography of Harriet Tubman, the Negro woman who led hundreds of slaves to freedom during the Civil War era via the Underground Railroad. The dedication reads:

Remembering —

Cynthia Wesley
Denise McNair
Carol Robertson
Addie Mae Collins

These four girls were the ones who were killed in a racist bombing of the Sixteenth Street Baptist Church in Birmingham, Alabama, on September 15, 1963. "You might want to see the poignant letters I received from the girls' parents and friends," remarked Miss McGovern.

I shall never forget the day the brown envelope reached my desk. My first reading of the letters brought tears to my eyes and sent chills down my spine. One of the mothers wrote:

We are sincerely hopeful that through writings and actions that injustice to mankind will be eliminated, both in the courts as well as in the hearts of man;

Another said:

I shall read (the book) to all the children that I can and teach them the importance of having courage and patience in this struggle for freedom.

After the assassination of Dr. Martin Luther King, Jr., Miss McGovern attended a rally held in New York City's Central Park's Sheep Meadow. "Black is beautiful, baby. Black is beautiful. Know it!" echoed throughout the crowds. Returning home, she sat at her typewriter and began writing *Black Is Beautiful* (Four Winds Press, 1969):

At the top of the stairs in a secret place
Black lace
And a black face.
Black is beautiful.

Sunlight and shade — look back;
The color of everyone's shadow is black.

The work of Ann McGovern sums up Ann McGovern. She was born and raised in New York City, attended New York public schools, and went to the University of New Mexico "because it was far away. I was a poor student, got an A in horseback riding, married the English professor, and left after my first year!"

She has traveled extensively and has 101 anecdotes about her journeys. "I was stoned, literally, in a small town near Guatemala for wearing a white sweater, white skirt, and white sandals. The natives probably thought I was a missionary. In Mexico I killed a scorpion, dated a bullfighter, and danced with the Royal Presidente. In Duvalier's Haiti, I was followed. They thought I was a spy!" she exclaimed.

Stateside Miss McGovern leads just as exciting a life. She lives in New York's Greenwich Village with her dog, Frisky, in a house that has two distinct features: it was once the home of the poet Edna St. Vincent Millay, and it is the narrowest house in New York — only 9½ feet wide. The house is like a Hollywood movie set; it has four floors, five fireplaces (only one works), and is filled with original paintings, sculpture, and artifacts that Miss McGovern has collected over the years. The top floor is her studio, the place where she writes, relaxes, and listens to the music of Bach, Vivaldi, and Jacques Brel.

When not writing, she is doing things such as editing the bulletin for the Council on Interracial Books for Children. She was also the original editor of the See Saw Book Club of Scholastic Book Services, a book club for children in kindergarten and first grade.

For relaxation and when there's time, she likes flower growing, bird watching, swimming, theatre, ballet, and doing something about the world. She also enjoys spending time with her teenage son, Peter. She loves clothes and wears them beautifully, and she loves her writing work. She has also played a feature role in a film short and has published adult fiction.

At the age of 19 Edna St. Vincent Millay created a poem of more than two hundred lines entitled "Renascence." Four lines from the poem read:

> All I could see from where I stood
> Was three long mountains and a wood;
> I turned and looked another way,
> And saw three islands in a bay.

Miss McGovern "turns and looks" also. With her keen perception and feeling for life, she writes books for children, she tells them something, and she opens new worlds for them. Lucky are the children who know her!

SOME OTHER BOOKS BY MISS McGOVERN:

If You Lived in Colonial Times (Scholastic Book Services, 1964).
Zoo, Where Are You? (Harper, 1964).
If You Grew Up with Abraham Lincoln (Scholastic Book Services, 1966).
Too Much Noise (Houghton, 1967).
Robin Hood of Sherwood Forest (T. Y. Crowell, 1968).

Eve Merriam

EVE MERRIAM, THE AUTHOR-POET, and I had a difficult time getting together in the spring of 1968. Our first appointment had to be canceled because of the tragic assassination of Dr. Martin Luther King, Jr.; the second, because of an unexpected trip she had to make to New Hampshire where she was participating in the McCarthy campaign; the third, because of the Columbia University student uprising. But we finally made it and spent a lovely afternoon together.

Miss Merriam is a petite woman filled with vim and vigor. She was born in an industrial section of Philadelphia, Pennsylvania, and while still a young girl, her family moved to the suburbs of Philadelphia. "I remember growing up surrounded by beautiful birch trees, dogwood trees, and rock gardens. I enjoyed watching birds and just walking through the woods. My mother always had a great feeling for nature and gardening. I probably inherited it from her," she commented.

Miss Merriam came to New York City in 1939 to do graduate work at Columbia University. "I was a born poet," she said. "While in school I had my poetry published in various school publications. I wanted to get away from home; I wanted to meet other poets and to be in New York, the literary mecca. I began studying for my master's degree, but one day while taking a walk across the George Washington Bridge, I decided *not* to walk back to Columbia. I quit my studies and decided to find a job. It seemed like a good idea — but what could a poet do? I remembered reading somewhere that Carl Sandburg once worked in advertising, so I would, too. I got a job as an advertising copywriter on Madison Avenue and progressed to become a fashion editor for glamor magazines."

While working full-time she continued to write poetry. "When my first poem was published in a poetry magazine, I could have been run over!" she exclaimed. "It was in a little magazine printed on butcher paper, but it was gold to me!"

Her first book of poetry, *Family Circle,* was written for adults, won the Yale Younger Poets Prize, and was published by Yale University Press in 1946. Several other volumes of poetry for adults followed, along with articles, essays, and several biographies revolving around her major interests — social and political satire and the status of women in modern society. Miss Merriam's first children's book, *The Real Book About Franklin Delano Roosevelt* (Watts), appeared in 1952. Her children's books naturally reflect her adult interests. Regarding her work habits she told me, "Being a wife, mother, and writer is difficult work. I try to write in the mornings, but it doesn't always work out. You have to see my workroom! I have the smallest room in the world! That's the reason I write short lines of poetry!" she laughed.

Miss Merriam, her husband-writer Leonard C. Lewin, her two teenage sons, Guy and Dee, and the family cat, Towel, all live on Riverside Drive in New York City. She loves travel. "I particularly love Scandinavia. It is so beautiful physically. It has a little bit of San Francisco, water, and hills; it has the advantages of American technology without the drawbacks of slums and white racism." As for other likes she added, "I'm a great walker! I love the city; I love secondhand book stores and cheese stores. I love lilacs, lily of the valley, evergreens, mountain air, walking on beaches, collecting stones, the Far West, the state of Washington, and parlor games."

Miss Merriam's trilogy of poetry (all published by Atheneum), *Catch a Little Rhyme* (1966), *It Doesn't Always Have to Rhyme* (1964), and *There Is No Rhyme for Silver* (1962), has been widely acclaimed in the field of children's literature. To increase enjoyment of the books, she has prepared a brochure for each. "I want children to love poetry," she stated, "not memorize it! The brochures are explanations *for* children and for those who work *with* children. Since I can't package myself up inside the books and go around to all the kids personally, I said what I wanted to say in these short pieces." A careful look at these brochures will reveal this poet's philosophy about her work. For example, praising poetry in the brochure entitled *What Is a Rhyme?,* she explained:

> A rhyme is a chime
> that rings in time.
>
> > *Ding, dong,*
> > *Come along.*

In *Inside a Poem* she stated, "When something is too beautiful or too terrible or even too funny for words: then it is time for poetry. And in *What Can a Poem Do?* she answered:

> A poem . . . is very much like you, and that is quite natural, since there is a rhythm in your own body: in your pulse, in your heart beat, in the way you breathe, laugh, or cry; in the very way you speak . . . What can a poem do? Just about everything — even though there is no rhyme for silver.
>
> > (Or orange.
> > Any others?).

Eve Merriam is poetry! Catch a little Merriam. Your life will be richer for it!

SOME OTHER BOOKS BY MISS MERRIAM:

A Gaggle of Geese (Knopf, 1960).
Miss Tibbett's Typewriter (Knopf, 1966).
Epaminondas (Follett, 1968).
Independent Voices (Atheneum, 1968).

Katherine Milhous

IF YOU VISIT PHILADELPHIA, Pennsylvania, you will want to see the Philadelphia City Institute Library located on historic Rittenhouse Square. On a wall of the library hangs a modern adaptation of a rooster blowing his horn; the original rooster appeared on an old Pennsylvania Dutch fractur painting. This same rooster also appeared on the jacket of *The Egg Tree* (Scribner, 1950), winner of the Caldecott Award in 1951 and selected by the Institute of Graphic Arts as one of the best designed books of the last five years. The book was both written and illustrated by Katherine Milhous (*mil* house).

Philadelphia is the natural place for the rooster to appear, for it is the city Miss Milhous has lived in, worked in, and loved her entire life. Miss Milhous is of Irish-Quaker ancestry. She became interested in Pennsylvania Dutch design when she worked as a supervisor on the Federal Art Projects of Pennsylvania with Frances Lichten, who was the state supervisor and a woman who became a life-long friend.

Miss Milhous received her art training at the School of Industrial Arts and the Academy of Fine Arts in Philadelphia. During the Depression she designed a series of Pennsylvania Dutch posters, which were exhibited at a publishers' convention in Philadelphia in 1938. Alice Dalgliesh (*dal* gleesh), an editor at Scribner at that time, saw her work and wrote asking her to do a book. At a recent celebration dedicated to Miss Milhous, Miss Dalgliesh remarked, "And so Katherine came up to New York to meet her editor-to-be, and we went on from there. She was diffident. She hadn't an idea for a book and didn't know if she could write one. After some thought, we put together a book of old folk tales, which the color and design of the posters seemed to suggest. The book was *Once on a Time* (1938), and it was followed by *Happily Ever After* (1939)."

One of Miss Milhous's most popular books for children, *The Egg Tree,* came about because of her interest in Pennsylvania Dutch designs. "One day, in a scholarly volume, I came upon a picture of an egg tree. I had hoped to find an account of a charming Pennsylvania Dutch custom," she said. "My enthusiasm was soon deflated, for the scholar pointed out that the egg tree was a symbol of fertility and was hung in the yards of isolated farmhouses where the woman was childless!"

Miss Milhous put the idea aside for several years. "The urge to do another Pennsylvania Dutch book kept nagging at me, however, and I began to think of a book of eggs — the decorated eggs with traditional Pennsylvania Dutch designs." The book had many more ups and downs before it finally developed into the simple story of a grandmother who made an egg tree for the children. The acknowledgments in the book will give an idea of the time, research, and work went into its preparation.

Miss Milhous has written nearly two dozen books during the past 30 years. In 1964 *Through These Arches: The Story of Independence Hall* (Lippincott) was published. "This is my most important book," she declared, "for my love for Philadelphia and its history is depicted in it." The book, written for adults, shows the author's interest in the city where she is active in organizations such as the Society of Architectural Historians, Independence Hall Organization, and the Historical Society of Pennsylvania.

Miss Milhous lives in a house next to a printing shop. "The sound of a printing press has been following me all my life," she remarked. "My first studio was in my father's printing shop. I would sit dangerously near the presses and draw on scrap paper." On her studio wall hangs a rug she carried from Bolivia to Venezuela to Philadelphia; it is a heavy Indian rug she bought from natives in the Bolivian mountains. This treasure later became the jacket of a book written by Alice Dalgliesh entitled *Wings Around South America* (1941), which she illustrated.

Perhaps the work of Miss Milhous can best be summed up in a citation written by the author Marguerite de Angeli. It

From THE EGG TREE by Katherine Milhous, copyright 1943 by Katherine Milhous. Permission of Charles Scribner's Sons.

185

was presented at the Drexel Institute of Technology, Graduate School of Library Science, on April 8, 1967 and reads:

KATHERINE MILHOUS

For her distinguished and lasting
contribution to children's books
For her dedication to our national shrines
For her fidelity to truth
and
For her faithful portrayal of Pennsylvania's
Amish and Mennonite ways
which have endeared her to us all
and to millions of children throughout
the whole world

OTHER BOOKS BY MISS MILHOUS (All Scribner):

Lovinia (1940).
Herodia, The Lovely Puppet (1942).
Appolonia's Valentine (1954).
With Bells On (1955).

Else Holmelund Minarik

"MR. HOPKINS?" the voice on the phone asked.

"Yes!" I replied.

"This is Else! Else Minarik (*min* ah rik)."

"Oh, are you in New York City?" I asked.

"No, no. I'm at home. In New Hampshire. But I'm coming to New York to help my sister move. Perhaps we can get together when I'm in the city. I'll be in early next week, and I'll stop by your office. . . ."

Next week came and went, as did the following week. But one October morning Mrs. Minarik called again, and within an hour she appeared in my office. It was strange meeting her. I had imagined from her hearty voice that she would be tall and stocky. The opposite was true, for she is petite. All I could see was a tiny face peeping out from under a floppy fur hat that completely enclosed her head.

Mrs. Minarik is very shy and retiring. Her private life is extremely guarded; she isn't interested in publicity of any kind. In fact, I received the impression that she wasn't even interested in becoming part of this book. I asked, "Why *did* you come to meet me?" She answered, "Only because you're a friend of Maury's (Maurice Sendak), and I didn't want to hurt him!"

After several struggling moments, Else Minarik warmed up to me. She saw that I was "on the level" and told me to "go ahead and probe." Respecting her feelings I shall sum up our interview briefly. She was born in Denmark and was brought to the United States at the age of four. She attended school in New York City. After completing courses at Queens College, she worked as a reporter for the *Rome Daily Centennial,* a local newspaper. She married and later had a daughter, Brooke.

During World War II when there was a teacher shortage, she began teaching in a rural school in Commack, Long Island. As a result of this experience, she became interested in writing for young children. "I never felt I had enough books to give my first-graders — at least those that they could *read, really* read for themselves. I looked for such books and couldn't find them, so I wrote one. Actually, all I did was respond to the need of my little first-graders."

Her first book, published by Harper in 1957, was "An I Can Read Book" simply titled *Little Bear.* It contains four stories about the charming character Little Bear; the text was carefully selected and written so that upper first-graders and beginning second-grade readers could handle it on their own. "I used bears as a vehicle for the simple reason that I could draw them on the chalkboard for the children," she stated. "Bears have always haunted me throughout my whole life. As a child a dream that kept recurring was one in which I was being pursued by a big bear. I would run and run but always awoke up before the bear caught up with me. One night I got tired of running. I stopped. The bear stopped. And we began talking with each other. Ever since we've been good friends," she laughed.

The same year *Little Bear* was published, Random House began issuing a similar type of series, "Beginner Books." Its first title was *The Cat in the Hat* by Dr. Seuss. "We both had the idea at the same time," Mrs. Minarik remarked. "It wasn't easy selling the idea at first, but look at how many there are now!"

Harper and Row selected Maurice Sendak to illustrate her books. "He made the books come alive so beautifully," she said. "I love the Victorian era. I live in an old Victorian farmhouse, and Maury just seemed to capture the Victorian way of life. He made Mother Bear Victorian with her costumes, her furnishings, and her whole manner. The illustrations couldn't be greater."

Mrs. Minarik continued to create Little Bear books: *Father Bear Comes Home* (1959), *Little Bear's Friend* (1960), *Little Bear's Visit* (1961; a Caldecott runner-up), and *A Kiss for Little Bear* (1968; selected as one of the ten best illustrated books of 1968); Maurice Sendak continued to illustrate them. The author has also written other books in the "An I Can Read Books" series. One title, *No Fighting, No Biting* (1958; also illustrated by Mr. Sendak), was inspired by a Walt Disney television show that depicted baby alligators hatching from their eggs.

Mrs. Minarik enjoys her life in New Hampshire — the climate, the pace, and the serenity of country life. Later in the day, over manhattans and Italian antipasto, she talked about things that were foreign to me, a city-dweller. She gave me tips on working in apple orchards with old varieties of trees, especially the grimes golden apple tree, quails' eggs ("Hurrah for quails' eggs! I'll send you some boiled; that keeps them from breaking in transit!"), and terms such as "pied" and "rose-moles all in stipple."

After lunch I walked Mrs. Minarik up 43rd Street to Fifth Avenue where she was going to do some shopping. We shook hands and parted. We had come a long way in a few hours; we had become friends of a sort. Several weeks later, on a cold, wet November day, I received a note from Else Holmelund Minarik. It read:

> One of these days I shall send you some New Hampshire
> maple products, syrup, etc., in the hope that you can make

pancakes. If the city gets too smoggy — you are welcome to visit us in New Hampshire. I don't think I told you enough for your book, so if you give up on me, I'll understand.

Come to New Hampshire someday. We set our clock by the seasons. I wish I could hibernate all winter.

> Alt godt,
> Mother Bear

SOME OTHER BOOKS BY MRS. MINARIK (All Harper):

Cat and Dog (1960).
The Little Giant Girl and the Elf Boy (1963).
The Winds That Come from Far Away and Other Poems (1964).

Beni Montresor

IF BENI MONTRESOR'S (*bay* nee *mohn* tre sor) career had taken him onto the stage rather than behind it, he might very well have become the matinee idol of millions of female theatre-goers. He is dark and handsome, and his features look as though Michelangelo had fashioned them. He is pure Italian and was born in Bussolengo, near Verona, on March 21, 1926, to Angelo Silvino and Maria Fantin Montresor. "I think I was born with a pencil in my hand," he declared. "I vividly recall my grandfather going to Verona each Friday and returning home with toys and cakes for me. I remember one day, when I was about two or three years old, saying to my grandfather, 'Next time you go to Verona, bring me some colored pencils instead of cakes so I can draw a picture!'"

Verona became both a source of pleasure and a nightmare to Mr. Montresor in following years. He went there to buy art materials of all kinds, visited the ancient Roman arena with the biggest stage in the world where such operas as *Aïda* and *Carmen* were performed under the stars, and attended the High School of Arts, leaving his country home every morning while it was still dark.

"While attending high school, the war broke out. The bus stopped running so I went to school by bicycle. One morning I looked out the school window and saw airplanes flying over Verona. Seconds later bombs fell on the city. I was 14 years old at the time. I remember corpses lined up along the sidewalks covered with dirt and rubble and tiny pieces of flesh strewn in the streets. Verona is restored now. It is impossible for me to explain to my nephew, Luca, how terrible were the things that happened to this city."

In 1952 Mr. Montresor put his artistic talents to work designing sets and costumes for films and the theatre in Rome, Paris, Madrid, and Morocco. In 1960 he came to the United States for the first time. "I came here, to New York City, on a Christmas vacation," he stated. "I saw the city, and it was love at first sight! New York City is the moon; it is almost unreal. Sometimes I think it will just all disappear at any moment. Don't you get me wrong, though," he told me, "I love Rome, too. But in Rome you see the same stores, the same vendors, even after ten years. This is not so in New York — it is always changing!"

It was in New York that someone suggested that he illustrate a children's book. "I wasn't too sure about this," he remarked. "I didn't have books as a child. American children have so many books. They are more sophisticated than Italian children. I didn't know what to do, but I did it!"

Constantly traveling between the United States and Europe, he has illustrated such books as *House of Flowers, House of Stars* (Knopf, 1962), *The Witches of Venice* (Knopf, 1963), and two books by Beatrice Schenk de Regniers, *May I Bring a Friend?* (Atheneum, 1964), which won the 1965 Caldecott Award, and *Willy O'Dwyer Jumped in the Fire: Variations on a Folk Rhyme* (Atheneum, 1968), which was selected by the *New York Times* as an outstanding book of the year. Mr. Montresor has also designed sets and costumes for productions at the New York's City Center and Metropolitan Opera House,

From WILLY O'DWYER JUMPED IN THE FIRE by Beatrice Schenk de Regniers and Beni Montresor. Pictures © 1968 by Beni Montresor. Permission of Atheneum Publishers and Wm. Collins Sons & Co., Ltd.

Milan's La Scala, London's Covent Garden, and Venice's La Fenice — sets that have been hailed by every major critic in the music world.

Mr. Montresor is a man with a great deal to say about his work, his friends, his life, and the world scene. "I illustrated *I Saw a Ship A-Sailing* (Knopf, 1967; a fascinating picture book of Mother Goose rhymes) because Mother Goose had never been done properly. No one took care of the craziness in Mother Goose, the color, the magic of the poems or of their music." This book was selected by the American Society of Illustrators as the best illustrated book of 1967. He continued, "I like the theatre but *not* theatrical people! I love working with my good friend Federico Fellini. (He dedicated *I Saw a Ship A-Sailing* to Mr. Fellini "who, too, was born from a flower plant.") Children are ruined by teachers and parents; adults want to change you to be like them. *Education* they call it! Then, you have to spend much of your life undoing what they've done — finding yourself! Youth today are freer, and it is a great result. You see *faces* today! When I first came here, you did not see faces; everyone was the same."

Mr. Montresor works intensively on his projects. "I only think of what I like, and I do only what I like! I love what I do, and I need what I do!" His apartment in New York is located in Greenwich Village. It is light, airy, and filled with fascinating mementos of his theatrical productions. Before leaving the apartment, Mr. Montresor remarked, "I have a lot of things to say, and I hope to go much further." On the elevator going down, I couldn't help think what a richer, brighter, and gayer world it is because of Beni Montresor's diverse contributions to it — contributions that touch us from early childhood through to our adult years.

Viva la teatro!
Viva ragazzi libri!
Viva Beni Montresor!

SOME OTHER BOOKS BY MR. MONTRESOR:

Margaret Wise Brown. *On Christmas Eve* (Scott, 1961).
Mary Stolz. *Belling, the Tiger* (Harper, 1961).
———. *The Great Rebellion* (Harper, 1961).
Stephen Spender, adapter. *The Magic Flute* (Putnam, 1966).
A for Angel (Knopf, 1969).

Lilian Moore

THE FINGERLIKE SKYSCRAPERS of New York's Wall Street rise almost in greeting to the teeming Brooklyn waterfront they face. Above this waterfront lies Brooklyn Heights, one of the few neighborhoods in New York City that retain some of the look of the community they once were. One can easily imagine being in 19th century New York as he picks his way through the crisscrossed blocks of brownstones and carriage houses, buildings that were here when Abraham Lincoln came to speak at the Plymouth Church where Henry Ward Beecher was pastor and when Walt Whitman was editor of the *Brooklyn Eagle*.

Lilian Moore and her teenage son, Jonathan, live in such a brownstone in the heart of Brooklyn Heights. When one enters Mrs. Moore's home, one has the feeling of taking a step back in time. "The idea is," she said, "to get out of the subway, walk home, and close the door." In the high-ceilinged living room, plants climb luxuriously up a great leaded-glass window, and original paintings adorn the walls, many by artists she knows and admires. "They are varied, aren't they? What these drawings have in common is someone's honest, personal, and intense reaction to life." Commenting on her love for real flowers, Mrs. Moore declared, "Maybe this *is* the age of the plastic philodendron, but I must confess to a feeling of outrage in the presence

195

of artificial flowers." Mrs. Moore is an avid gardener; behind the brownstone where she lives is her secret garden. "It is a city garden, and a city garden constantly struggles for survival against that layer of soot we laughingly call soil. The garden is at its most triumphant in the spring. Then, for a few glorious weeks, the garden glows with an abundance of tulips, hyacinths, and daffodils. And one waits for the first forsythia as if *this* spring the world would really change. Did you know, by the way, that forsythia is Brooklyn's flower? Ever hopeful Brooklyn!" In her recent book *I Thought I Heard the City* (Atheneum, 1969), a delightful collection of poems, Mrs. Moore writes about "the sudden light of forsythia," which "one morning without warning explodes into yellow and startles the street into spring."

Mrs. Moore, who needs to grow flowers and whose city poems are about the smell of fresh-cut grass and foghorns and the changing sky, is a dyed-in-the-wool New Yorker. She was born in New York, grew up there, attended the public schools, went to Hunter College, and did graduate work at Columbia University. "I studied Elizabethan literature," she stated. "I wanted to teach Christopher Marlowe to college freshmen!" She began teaching in New York City and because of her skill in working with children who could not read, became a staff member of the Bureau of Educational Research. Here she worked in reading clinics, wrote professional materials, trained teachers, and did research into the reading problems of elementary school children.

"When did I become a writer? Why, I can't remember when I didn't in some way think of myself as one. One of my earliest memories is of sitting on a big metal box outside a hardware store on the street where I lived. There was a group of kids around me — the friends with whom I went roller skating and sledding — and there I was telling them a series of yarns. I can still remember saying 'to be continued tomorrow!' I wrote the plays I put on in the summers I worked as a camp counselor, and of course, I guess like everyone else, I had half a novel in my drawer that it took me years to bring myself to throw out!"

196

It was while working with youngsters who needed special help in reading that Mrs. Moore began to write for children. "I've been identified for a long time now with what's called easy-to-read material. It's true that I learned from the children the basic difference between dense and open material, but I never understood why people thought that easy-to-read material for children had to be clunky and dull. As an editor, I found out later that what I had sensed was true; writers often use too many words! On their way to independence in reading, young children often need easy material, sometimes for only a very short time.

Mrs. Moore admits that what she enjoys writing most are poems for children. "I think I wrote most of the poems in *I Feel the Same Way* (Atheneum, 1968), on my way to work. I think of them as my subway songs. Often when I seemed to be staring vacantly at subway ads, I was working intensely on a new idea. And sometimes when it didn't come off, I put it to bed at night, with a profound faith in my unconscious where the special truth I'm seeking usually begins."

In 1957 she became the editor of Scholastic's Arrow Book Club. "This was one of the most satisfying things I ever did, helping to launch the first quality paperback book program for elementary school children. It was a job that brought together my experience as a teacher, my interest in children's books, my work as a writer, and my downright pleasure in the endearing middle-grader. Imagine making it possible for these youngsters to choose and buy good books for the price of comics! It was years before I could even simmer down. Talking to me about Arrow is like taking a cork out of a bottle. Even now I remember the endless wonderful letters from children and teachers. They made it clear we were irrigating a drought area and raising a whole new crop of readers. Whatever I may have contributed to this program was due in part to my almost total recall of the children I had known and taught. They seemed to haunt me and were specters at my side, vigorously approving or disapproving books we chose for them."

Besides the work she has done at Scholastic, Mrs. Moore had edited a series of easy readers for Wonder Books, a series of hero tales for Thomas Y. Crowell, and has been reading specialist and contributor to *Humpty Dumpty's Magazine* since its inception. Currently Mrs. Moore is directing another kind of program for Scholastic. "We are creating a series of history and biography books for middle-graders, which will portray the experience of black Americans and other ethnic groups in our country's history. The children who are going to have to cope with the problems of our future need to be clear-eyed about their own history." As a founding member of the Council on Interracial Books for Children, this program is close to her heart.

For relaxation, Lilian Moore turns to Mozart "and almost any good chamber music." She likes to bike, ice skate, garden, and, "at the drop of a reservation," will travel. "The truth is, though," she says thoughtfully, "relaxation isn't such a problem when you love the work you do."

SOME OTHER BOOKS BY MRS. MOORE:

The Terrible Mr. Twitmeyer (Random House, 1952).
Everything Happens to Stuey (Random House, 1960).
Little Raccoon and the Thing in the Pool (McGraw-Hill, 1963).
Just Right (Parents, 1968).

Lillian Morrison

MID-JULY HEAT in New York City can be almost unbearable,
so I was very happy to be on my way to the air-conditioned
Donnell Library on West 53rd Street, just off Fifth Avenue.
Lillian Morrison, the Coordinator of Young Adult Services,
met me there in her second floor office. Within minutes, this slim,
well-tailored woman shattered the stereotype of what people
think a librarian is like. Her world is not confined to the acres of
books that are in her keeping. Although modest, she talked about
herself with a twinkle in her eye, telling me how thrilled she is
with her life and her work as an anthologist, poet, and library
worker.

Miss Morrison was born and raised in Jersey City, New
Jersey. She attended Douglass College, Rutgers, the State University, where she majored in mathematics. She came into library
work by accident. "I met a friend of mine coming out of the
New York Public Library on 42nd Street" she recalled, "who
told me that there was a job opening. I went in, applied, and got
a job as a filer. I loved it. It was quite a relief from my work in
the statistical department at Bamberger's, a large department
store in Newark, New Jersey. I was surrounded by books. The
whole world opened up to me. I knew I was in heaven!"

Miss Morrison received her graduate degree from the School of Library Service at Columbia University and has worked in public libraries throughout the city. "I worked in the Aguilar Branch Library on East 110th Street. Children would bring me their autograph albums to sign. I used to love to write in their books and became curious as to what others had written. I began to collect the comments for fun — I'm a collector from way back! — realizing that the simple messages and the funny verses were actually a form of folklore that could be traced back to the Elizabethan era. I had thousands of these sayings, each written on a 3x5 inch card and stored in shoeboxes. Finally I approached several publishing houses with the idea of doing a compilation of the verses. When I came to Elizabeth Riley, editor at Thomas Y. Crowell, *Yours Till Niagara Falls* (1950) was born." Crowell has continued to publish all her books.

Following this volume came other compilations such as *Black Within and Red Without: A Book of Riddles* (1953), in which each item was selected because it has "some feeling of myth or mystery or some catchy quality of rhyme or rhythm;" *A Dillar, A Dollar: Rhymes and Songs for the Ten O'Clock Scholar* (1955), a collection of folk sayings about school arranged by school subjects; and *Touch Blue* (1958), a collection of wishes and prophecies, spells, and folklore all based on superstitions and all in rhyme.

In 1965 she finished compiling a different type of anthology, *Sprints and Distances: Sports in Poetry and Poetry in Sport,* a volume that took nearly ten years of research and collecting. Almost every sport is represented; the verses range from ancient writers such as Virgil up to the modern poets such as Ogden Nash and David McCord. "This book grew out of my own love of sports. As a kid I was great on the street. I played everything. As a child I lived for two years in an apartment house where there was a boxing ring in the basement and watched the fights that took place there. Being with my brother a great deal helped me to become acquainted with sports. I still love tennis and golf."

Besides sports, Miss Morrison is interested in jazz — "the vitality of jazz! I remember catching Billie Holiday's first morning show at the Apollo Theatre in Harlem before going to work. In those days you could see Holiday, Ellington, and Armstrong all on one bill. I grew up on jazz and was high on it."

In 1967 Miss Morrison published an original collection of poems for adults titled *Ghosts of Jersey City* and in 1968 a volume of original poems for teenage girls, *Miranda's Music,* coauthored with Jean Boudin.

She lives in New York's Washington Heights in an apartment house rising above the Hudson River. She detests shopping, cooking, cleaning, ironing — any type of housework — but loves traveling and her own work. Compiler, poet, lecturer, librarian, and now general editor of the "Crowell Poets" series, Miss Morrison is a bundle of creative energy. The next time you start to think of a librarian being shy and withdrawn, think sports and jazz, vim and vigor, mathematics and poetry — and Lillian Morrison.

Evaline Ness

WHEN EVALINE NESS'S *Sam, Bangs, and Moonshine* (Holt, 1966) was published, *The New York Times'* review of the book commented, "Another old pro . . . continues to demand from herself an uncompromising level of quality in book design." The "old pro" is tall, thin, blond, and attractive and has been creating books for less than a decade. She was born on April 24, 1911, in Union City, Ohio, and grew up in Pontiac, Michigan. "After one year of college (Muncie State Teachers College, Muncie, Indiana), I decided that I wanted to be an artist more than anything else, so I went to the Chicago Art Institute for two years and had a break! I did a whole page of fashion drawings for the large department store, Carson Pirie Scott, in the *Chicago Tribune* and decided that I would take this little triumph to New York, where I had always wanted to live anyway. And so I did."

In 1946 she came to New York and began illustrating for the magazine *Seventeen*; this led to fashion drawing for Saks Fifth Avenue store. "I traveled a good deal, plus I made a lot of money, which was nice," she stated. In 1957 she illustrated *The Bridge,* written by Charlton Ogburn (Houghton). Six years later, after illustrating many book jackets and books, she wrote and illustrated her own, *Josefina February* (Scribner), the tale of a Haitian girl. "*Josefina* developed at the suggestion of Nancy Quint, who was children's book editor at Scribner," she recalled. "She saw some large woodcuts I had made after a year's stay in Haiti and simply said, 'Why don't you write a story?' After a lot of simpering and protestations that I wasn't a writer, I wrote the story around the pictures; this is something I haven't done since. The only thing that came close to this was that Sam, in *Sam, Bangs, and Moonshine,* was a drawing *fait accompli;* one of the many I keep in a portfolio of drawings I am always making for myself."

In 1967 *Sam* won the Caldecott Award. The book was again a result of prodding by an editor, Ann Durrell of Holt, Rinehart and Winston. "Ann and I talked through lunch one day, and all afternoon at my apartment, about things we could remember as children. I always lean toward the child with faults — is there any other kind except in people's imaginations? I decided Sam would be a liar, the same kind I was when I was a child, except that I made up new lies for her to tell." To illustrate the book, Miss Ness used a line and wash technique.

Miss Ness recently moved from New York City to Nassau in the Bahamas. "I love to be near, but not particularly in, water — large, turbulent bodies of water, like seas," she declared. She is a designer and executor of wall hangings in her spare time. "I call my wall hangings tapestries, although they are not woven on a loom. I sew them by hand in colored yarns. Wherever I happen to be usually suggests the subject matter. I started them when I lived in Rome, Italy, for two years; consequently, there are quite a few Italian ones. I did the nine muses and have been inspired to do themes from the Virgin Islands, Spain, and Portugal. Undoubtedly there will now be Bahamian ones. They seem to sell very fast. Out of about 35, I have only six left. Right now I am doing them in mixed media, sometimes sewing, sometimes gluing things to the canvas, and if need be, I paint. I love to work more than anything else." She also saws and hammers, building bookcases and anything else that may be needed to make order in her house or studio. She loves Siamese cats, riding her bicycle, and sometimes wearing gold earrings five inches long. And she is an "old pro" at whatever she does — but a youthful one!

SOME OTHER BOOKS BY MISS NESS:

A Gift for Sula Sula (Scribner, 1963).
Exactly Alike (Scribner, 1964).
Pavo and the Princess (Scribner, 1965).
A Double Discovery (Scribner, 1966).
Tom Tit Tot (Scribner, 1966).
Sorche Nic Leodhas. *Kellyburn Braes* (Holt, 1968).

From TOM TIT TOT by Evaline Ness, © 1965 by Evaline Ness. Permission of Charles Scribner's Sons.

Nicolas (Mordvinoff)

NICOLAS IS A BIG and burly man. The day I met him in New York City, he was handsomely dressed and impressive looking with peppered gray hair and a sculptured mustache. He immediately presented me with the accompanying photo, explaining that he had shaved off his beard. "It was too hard and too expensive to keep up. Besides, today everyone has one, and I wanted to be different!" He somewhat resembles the late Ernest Hemingway, and he has been stopped many times by people who thought he was.

Nicolas has a fascinating background, and he tells about it cheerfully and warmly, even though it was not all pleasant. He was born on September 27, 1911, prior to the Russian Revolution, in St. Petersburg, Russia, which later became Petrograd and then Leningrad. He remembers his family's escape by way of Finland to Paris, where he grew up. "I was barely seven years old, but I remember traveling in a horse-drawn sleigh."

He attended schools in Paris, and studied at both the Lycée Jeanson de Sailly and the École des Roches before going to the University of Paris, where he received a degree in Latin, philosophy, and languages. At the age of 18, while still in school, he sold cartoons and illustrations to leading French newspapers and magazines.

"From the time I was three I always wanted to draw and paint," he recalled, "and I always drew horses. I love horses."

Paris of the 30's was gay, vibrant, and experiencing a cultural explosion. Nicolas felt the need to escape the pace and find himself. He had read of the romantic islands of the South Pacific, and in 1934 he decided to go there. For the next 13 years he lived in the South Pacific, traveling from island to island and painting and developing a style of his own.

Nicolas told me of an incident on Mango River, an island about 900 miles east of Tahiti. "While I was in Tahiti, World War II broke out. I wanted desperately to fight in the war, but I couldn't get into the army. The French wouldn't take me, the Russians wouldn't take me, and neither would the United States. I decided to make my way as close to the fighting as possible, but I never managed to! I got to Mango River, and I stayed there for two years, painting and living among the natives. I was the only white man living on the island. There was a schooner that came twice a year. If you wanted to leave, you had to do it when it came or wait another six months.

"The natives bought my work. They called them photographs. They paid me in pearls. One day the chief of the island, a descendant of South Pacific kings, came to me and asked if I would make a photograph of his wife. I told him I would and asked if I could meet her. 'She's dead,' he replied. However, he did have a poor photograph that had been taken of her by a visitor.

"I did a portrait painting from the photograph and, when it was ready, the chief came to my studio. I put it on the easel. The chief sat down, looked at it, walked up to it, touched it, and said, 'She's alive again!' He pulled out a huge, beautifully colored pearl to pay me for the portrait. It was the biggest pearl I had ever seen."

Returning to Tahiti, Nicolas met William S. Stone, the author, who was finishing a book manuscript. Mr. Stone persuaded him to do the illustrations, and his first book, *Thunder Island* (Knopf, 1942), was born. He collaborated on two more books with Mr. Stone, and their success induced him to come to the United States.

In 1946 he came to New York. "This was a terrible experience," he remarked. "I couldn't find a job, and I had no money. For one year I starved." A kindly editor sent him a box of chocolates. "Better she should have sent a ham or a cheese," he laughed. "But chocolates! To this day I have hated the candy!"

He rented an apartment on St. Mark's Place in Greenwich Village East, a Bowery area. "I became very ill. One day while I was in bed, I remembered a man I had met in Tahiti who told me to look him up if I ever came to New York. I did. The man invited me to his cottage in Massachusetts. I missed three trains because I was too weak to pack my few things."

Upon his arrival in Massachusetts, Nicolas was taken to a private island; the friend turned out to be Crane, the plumbing tycoon. He spent two years painting on the island before returning to New York City. He returned to St. Mark's Place and held a one-man show of his paintings in a 57th Street gallery. "I sold two paintings; one was returned!" he exclaimed. During this period he met Maria Cimino of the New York Public Library. Miss Cimino is the wife of Will Lipkind, the author.

"Will is an anthropologist by profession and a poet by inclination," Nicolas remarked. "We talked of doing a book together over a glass of sherry. I saw a red cat on the windowsill and said, 'Let's do a book about that.' Will told me we needed more for a story. Returning from shopping that same night, I saw a boy with red hair. So *The Two Reds* (Harcourt, 1950), the cat and the boy, became the book."

The Two Reds was one of the earliest books to depict life in a slum situation. The story is set in New York City; both reds become involved in trouble — the cat steals a fish from the fish market, and the boy spies on the Seventh Street Signal Senders. The two reds end up seeking refuge and friendship in each other.

"Upon publication of the book a nice young man at F. A. O. Schwarz (the toy store on New York's Fifth Avenue) did a whole window on the book. (The "nice young man" was Maurice Sendak.) The book was immediately banned in Boston. People claimed it was subversive — especially when the two people who created it had names like Lipkind and Mordvinoff." (The team used the pseudonyms Will and Nicolas; however, their full names appear on the copyright page.)

Despite the controversy, the book was runner-up for the 1951 Caldecott Medal. Will and Nicolas collaborated on a second book, *Finders Keepers* (Harcourt, 1951), the story of two dogs who quarrel over a bone, which won the Caldecott Award in 1952. "Winning the Caldecott Medal? It was everything. It changed my whole life," Nicolas remarked. "Instead of going around hungry with my samples under my arms, I had to fight editors off on the telephone!" The team went on to do another dozen books together, the last of which was *The Boy and the Forest* (Harcourt, 1964).

"I have stopped doing children's books," he told me. "It was an interlude in my life. I do not want to get stuck doing one thing until the day I die." He has again returned to painting. He does enormous boldly designed canvasses that depict our turbulent times.

He lives in Hampton, New Jersey, in an old farmhouse with his wife and three children, Michael, 12, Alexandra, 9, and Peter, 7. "The children are not too impressed with me," he laughed. "But I'll tell you a story about an incident that happened the other day. I received a letter from Lynda Bird Johnson on White House stationery. She is very interested in children's books. I showed the letter to Michael. 'Is this real?' he asked. 'Are you serious?' I explained to him that his father was a famous illustrator. 'Yeah, but that famous?' he puzzled."

Nicolas is an extraordinary man who has led an adventurous life. From Russia to Paris, from Tahiti to the United States, these are long distances for any man to travel! He has graced our shores with enormous talents and has left a lasting impression on the field of children's literature. It is a shame he has stopped illustrating books for boys and girls. Perhaps one day he will change his mind. He has been the finder and the keeper, but all of us, young and old, are the losers and the weepers if we will have no more books illustrated by Nicolas.

OTHER BOOKS BY NICOLAS:

Will. *Chaga* (Harcourt, 1955).
———. *The Magic Feather Duster* (Houghton, 1958).
———. *Russett and the Two Reds* (Houghton, 1962).

Maud and Miska* Petersham

MAUD PETERSHAM WAS BORN in Kingston, New York. Her father, a Baptist minister, longed to have a son to follow in his footsteps; instead, he had four daughters. Commenting on her childhood years, Mrs. Petersham declared, "A parsonage with four lively girls was certainly not a dull place. One of the many clergymen who visited our home once said that the only way to sleep in our house was to put a pillow over one's head as well as under! Leaving Kingston we went to live in Sioux Falls, South Dakota, then on to Newburg, New York, and finally to Scranton, Pennsylvania. My sisters and I fidgeted about through long church services and daily morning prayers, but the stories told by visiting missionaries at our table were as exciting as fairy tales to me. We were busy with school and play in winter and

---

* Miska Petersham died on May 15, 1960. He was born in Törökszent-miklos, a small village on the Hungarian plains. From the age of seven, he had always wanted to become an artist. He attended art school in Budapest, struggling to meet expenses. In 1911 he went to England and one year later arrived in the United States. He quickly became known as a fine young commercial artist. After marrying Maud Fuller, the Petershams became a team and began to write and illustrate books for young children. The contributions they made to children's literature will long be appreciated by young and old.

spent beautiful summer months with our Quaker grandfather. We were a bit in awe of Grandfather who believed that children should be seen, not heard, and should share in household duties."

I asked Mrs. Petersham how she came to do books for children. "I loved picture books as a child and was always happy with pencil and paper in my hands. After graduating from Vassar, I studied for one easy-going year at the New York School of Fine and Applied Art, living at the Three Arts Club. My first job was in the art department at the International Art Service, an advertising firm. Here I met Miska. After our marriage we started working on our own, free-lancing. May Massee, who was then with Doubleday, gave us our first chance to illustrate a book for children, *The Poppy Seed Cakes,* (1929) written by Mary E. Clark and Margery Quigley. My real art training came from working with Miska. He had graduated from the Budapest Art Academy and received several years of intensive training in different forms of art.

"At first we illustrated books written by others, but often we found no place in the text that lent itself to illustration, so we decided to plan a book of our own with both pictures and text. Again encouraged by May Massee, we laid out a dummy for *Miki* (Cadmus, 1946), working out the pictures first and then a text, which we thought would have to be rewritten by an author of children's books. We sent the dummy to May, and her answer was, to our surprise, 'We want the book just as it is!'

"Miska and I worked long hours in the studio with everything else neglected or forgotten. Ideas for books were not found by searching for them. They came out of the blue and were connected with life around us, with places we had visited, or what was foremost in our thoughts at the moment. The ideas took shape on scratch paper that was cut and folded to form a small book. Playing with roughs of pictures and text — it seemed easier to think with pictures than with words — the ideas grew to a dummy of the size and format of the book as we wanted it. If we were lucky and the dummy was accepted, the serious work

211

of making finished drawings began. This meant hours of research as we were careful of fine details of costumes and local color where we felt this was important. Also, to cut the printing cost of full-color illustrations, we ourselves made the color separations on glass or acetate, and *this* was tedious work!"

Mrs. Petersham continued to discuss her work and her life with her late husband. "Miska and I had fun working on books for children for it often meant travel with sketchbook in hand. We wandered about in Palestine for three months before we made the illustrations for our book *The Christ Child* (Macmillan, 1931). A visit to Sarasota, where the Ringling Brothers Circus made its winter quarters, gave us the idea for *Circus Baby* (Macmillan, 1950), and the hunting lodge where we ourselves spent one summer inspired *The Peppernuts* (Macmillan, 1958). Our life and work are so closely related that anyone who knows our books knows us."

In 1946 the Petershams received the Caldecott Award for *The Rooster Crows: A Book of American Rhymes and Jingles* (Macmillan, 1945). Leafing through the book one can see the detailed drawings that she speaks of — the strong featured faces, the perfect costumes, and the true-to-life settings that the Petershams portrayed. The illustration of the rhyme

> Wake up, Jacob,
> Day's a-breakin'
> Peas in the pot
> An' hoecake a-bakin'.

almost makes you feel the sleep-in-the-eyes as Jacob awakens; you can smell the coffee perking and feel the cat rubbing against Mama's leg.

Regarding the development of *The Rooster Crows,* Mrs. Petersham told me, "Our son, Miki, was a navigator in the air force during the Second World War. After listening to the disturbing 11:00 p.m. news each night, I found that I could put myself to sleep by repeating rhymes and jingles I had known as a child. This led to the idea for the book. Collecting material and making the illustrations for this volume was a protective device for us during the worries of those days. Receiving the Caldecott Award was a happy surprise and very satisfying to us."

Today her son Miki is with the Art Department of Kent University in Ohio. "I am very proud of the beautiful work he produces in ceramics and glass," she stated. "I also have two grandchildren, Mary and Michael, who are both in college!"

Mrs. Petersham lives in Woodstock, New York, in a tiny, simple house on a village street. She has a flower garden encircled by a low brick wall; one large apple tree with golden apples grows in the garden. "Actually, I have two houses. This is the one where I now live. My other house, although I no longer own it, is perhaps more real to me. It is the house and studio Miska and I built and where we lived and worked some 40 years. It is a rambling house made of stone with hand-hewn beams and casement windows, a happy storybook house standing in a pine grove. I do like the view from this present house, though. I can see the nearby mountain, and over my mountain I see stars with infinity for background, which give me faith and peace."

Describing her interests, Mrs. Petersham explained, "From the day the first seed catalog arrives until the first frost, my principal interest is my garden; I take time out for modeling clay, embroidering pictures in yarn, and sitting at my desk playing with ideas for another book for children, which as yet has not worked out to my satisfaction. I am a true branch of my homespun forefathers in many ways but am impractical and easy-going and like certain luxuries. My friends of many years are old, so I suppose I am too — in fact, I have 79 years to account for."

I asked Mrs. Petersham, "What makes a good children's book?" She answered, "For a children's book, both pictures and text must tell the story with enough drama to hold a child's attention on every page. It should not be a book to be read once and then cast aside; it should be something a child will cherish.

I feel that the format, layout, and type are also important, for unconsciously a well-designed book influences a child's taste and feeling for beauty."

Mrs. Petersham concluded our interview with some thoughts about books, children, and Miska Petersham. "Working on books for children was our joy as well as our work. We complemented each other. We both had the hope that our books would not only give pleasure to a child, but be meaningful and worthwhile."

SOME OTHER BOOKS BY THE PETERSHAMS (All Macmillan):

Box with Red Wheels (1949).
David (1958).
Joseph and His Brothers (1938, 1958).
Moses (1938, 1958).

———

Mrs. Petersham died on November 29, 1971.

Tillie S. Pine
Joseph Levine

I SUPPOSE I FIRST learned that books are created by people back in 1960 when Bank Street College of Education conducted a study in the town of Fair Lawn, New Jersey, where I was teaching. Almost immediately I became friendly with Tillie S. Pine, a short, well-tailored, erudite woman who was working with the college's staff. She was the first, real in-the-flesh author I had ever met. Since that time our friendship has ripened and mellowed.

Mrs. Pine taught for many years on the Lower East Side and in Harlem in New York City; in 1946 she joined the Bank Street College of Education Workshop. At this time she met Joseph Levine, assistant principal at Public School 68 in Manhattan and now principal of Public School 48 in the Bronx. Their professional relationship led to the preparation of a science curriculum bulletin for grades four, five, and six, which was distributed throughout the city system; the contents describe innovative approaches to teaching elementary school science, and it is still widely used today.

As a result of working with children and teachers in many parts of the city, Mrs. Pine, in consultation with Mr. Levine, created her own first book, *The Indians Knew* (McGraw-Hill, 1957), which became the first in a series applying a positive approach to early civilizations. Mrs. Pine told me, "Many children with whom we worked viewed the Indian way of life in a stereotyped fashion. This was the result of the mass media, particularly television, a new addition to most homes in the 1950's. Indians were depicted as savages who ran with tomahawks and said 'How!' " The author's approach involves extensive research through which they prove that the total environment of early civilizations were related to the forces of nature. Clear and easy science experiments are part of the books' sociological format. "We wanted children to see how we use such concepts today, without demeaning yesterdays' cultures. It is not that today's applications are better than those ancient civilizations used, it is merely that we are more advanced because our technology and scientific knowledge is so highly developed and improved," Mrs. Pine added.

In addition to the "Knew" series, the authors have collaborated on science books for young children. Titles published by Mc-Graw-Hill include *Magnets and How to Use Them* (1958), *Gravity All Around* (1963), and *Weather All Around* (1966). The unique quality of these texts is that they deal with man's contemporary environment. The authors describe the books as "action-filled" because they involve the child in the process of discovery.

Discussing their work habits, Mr. Levine commented, "We reserve one afternoon a week to work. For the past 15 years Thursday has been set aside for our writing. We meet at Tillie's apartment right after school, and we work for several hours. This is our inviolate Thursday! Of course, numerous hours are also spent in museums and libraries seeking out information needed to do our books." The team's twentieth volume is now in preparation.

"Joe and I see eye to eye on the choice of material in science," stated Mrs. Pine. "My own love for science was influenced by a high school teacher who stressed the idea that science is an integral part of everyday living. After her course, I took all the additional science courses I could!"

Mrs. Pine was born in Pultusk, Poland, a small town near Warsaw. She came to New York in 1906 with her family and has lived there ever since. She attended school in New York City and laughingly recalls going to one public school where a writers' club was forming. She was chosen to try out for it, did, and never made it! "I never forgot that incident!" she exclaimed.

Mrs. Pine is married to Nat Pine, half-owner of the Dauber & Pine Bookshop on New York's Fifth Avenue. "I met Nat in a bookstore on Second Avenue. Before I left the store, he had my address — and here I am 45 years later!" The Pines live in a midtown apartment with a dramatic view of Central Park and downtown Manhattan; summers are spent in Westport, Connecticut. Their daughter is an elementary school teacher working in Harlem. Mrs. Pine loves reading; her home is filled with books. "I have catholic tastes," she said. "I like books on science, psychology, history, and fiction and read many books in Yiddish," which she learned as a young girl. Her thinking is quite in tune with the present. "We are living in such interesting times. Youth is our only hope — even with all their hair! The young people of America, during the last generation were usually uncommitted. Today they know what they want, what they are all about, and they make themselves felt."

Mrs. Pine feels that television is one of the most important influences in a child's life today — as important as books. "Television offers an education that nothing else can match. Children absorb much information from television. They hear about technological advancements long before they are described in print, they see instant news from all parts of the world, and they witness the miracles of space travel. Unfortunately, TV is not used to its optimum potential; however, even the westerns can give children a great deal. They are more real and interesting than reading about the old West. Kids can see at a glance the mores, dress, travel, and scenery that were part of America's past. They can learn about mountain passes, wooden bridges, and creeks — things few city children today could ever even hope to see. This electronic age we're living in is great. And we must learn to grow with time."

Mr. Levine lives in Flushing, New York; his wife, Gussie, is a school secretary. The Levines have three children, Alan, an art teacher in the Spring Valley High School, Paul, a lawyer, and Susan, who works with the Department of Child Welfare in New York; they also have two grandchildren. Mr. Levine has been involved in education in New York all of his life. "I have been answering that September school bell, in one way or another, for the past 52 years," he commented. He attended the New York public schools and went to the City College of New York where he earned both his bachelor and master's degrees. For relaxation he enjoys traveling, carpentry, and spending time in his summer home in Lakeville, Connecticut.

The process of interviewing this writing team proved to be an interesting one. I learned some new facts about an old friend, Tillie S. Pine, became acquainted with her collaborator, Joseph Levine, and received a standing invitation to come back for dinner and more lively conversation.

SOME OTHER BOOKS BY MRS. PINE AND MR. LEVINE (All McGraw-Hill):

The Pilgrims Knew (1957).
Water All Around (1959).
Friction All Around (1960).
The Incas Knew (1968).
Trees All Around (1969).

Leo Politi

Good morning, Mister Swallow
Come from far away
We are glad to see you
On St. Joseph's Day.
Flitting in the sunshine
We can see you all
Building up your houses
On the Mission wall.

THESE LINES ARE from Leo Politi's (poh *lee* tee) tender story *Song of the Swallows* (Scribner, 1949), which won the 1950 Caldecott Medal. The book tells of the friendship between Juan, a little boy in the California town of Capistrano, and Julian, the old gardener and bellringer at the Mission of Capistrano, and how they welcome together the swallows' return to the Mission. Mr. Politi told me how the book developed. "The story was suggested by my editor at Scribner. When she asked if I would like to make the book, I was very enthusiastic because I like that Mission so well. The fact that the swallows return punctually every spring is to me such a sweet and poetic happening. But I have been interested in swallows ever since I was a boy in Italy, where two swallows came to nest every spring under the roof beams of my grandfather's house. I remember all the joy they

219

brought. I used to like to watch them and was always impressed by their elegance in flight."

When Mr. Politi went to the Mission of Capistrano, he learned that an old gardener named Julian had lived in the mission all his life and had recently died. This man, beloved by everyone, became one of the main characters in the book. As for Juan, he stated, "I could picture the hundreds of boys and girls like Juan who, on their way to and from school, stopped to talk with Julian and listened to the stories of flowers, birds, and of the Mission of San Juan Capistrano. Winning the Caldecott Award for this book, sort of gave me assurance that I was doing the right things for children. I felt very grateful and fortunate. It was like a stimulant to better my work, which I believe is the primary goal of life."

Mr. Politi's first book, written 11 years prior to *Song of the Swallows,* was *Little Pancho* (Viking, 1938); it was a very small book about a little Mexican boy, his dog, Coco, and their adventures in a Central American jungle. Many books followed, but his favorite remains *Pedro, the Angel of Olvera Street* (Scribner, 1946), a story about the famous Mexican Christmas celebration on Olvera Street in Los Angeles. The book was inspired by the writer-editor Alice Dalgliesh (*dal* gleesh). "*Pedro* is my favorite book, "because I put in more work on it than any of the books I have done. It was the result of many years of drawing on Olvera Street."

Mr. Politi lived and worked there when he first returned to America from Italy. "When I first saw this colorful Mexican street, I thought it would be a perfect place to work, study, and sketch and so I settled there. The street was different then," he added, "colorful, quaint. It is very commercial now and has lost the charm of its earlier days."

Inspiration for his varied books comes from different circumstances. "You may make a book because you want to preserve trees, parkland, and nature. You may make a book like *Pedro, the Angel of Olvera Street* because of the charming celebration

220

there at Christmas time or because you admire the culture of a people. Through a little story about a girl such as *Juanita* (Scribner, 1948), you try to bring forth the beauty of a culture and the characteristics of Mexicans."

From SONG OF THE SWALLOWS by Leo Politi, copyright 1949 by Charles Scribner's Sons. Permission of Charles Scribner's Sons.

Mr. Politi was born in Fresno, California, on November 21, 1908. His family took him to Italy at the age of seven. The story *Little Leo* (Scribner, 1951) was based on this trip and the years he spent growing up in Milan. He studied art for six years at the University of Art and Decorations in Monza, a town near Milan. "I had no training in writing, and naturally I find writing more difficult to do than illustrating," he said.

He and his wife are currently living in a large house in Los Angeles, California. He likes gardening and enjoys building fountains, ponds, and walks around the house. "I love my house because it is an old one, well-built, and spacious." He has four dogs; "I wish I had four hands so that I could pat them all at once." He enjoys nature and animals and spends most of his time outdoors sketching and painting. He has always been concerned about the complex age we are living in and the stress on material things. He commented, "I feel that our involvement with materialism is quite bad, but there is a growing awakening now, especially from the youth, who seek better values. I believe there will be great changes for the better."

He has always had a great feeling for children, including his own son, daughter, and two grandsons. "I love children — all children! I think each of them is like a miracle," he exclaimed. He offers this sentiment to boys and girls: "Each of you has the capacity to become a good artist, a good architect, or a good scientist or to succeed in any other human endeavor. If you work at it, there is no limit to what you can accomplish and to the happiness the work of creation can bring to you."

SOME OTHER BOOKS BY MR. POLITI (All Scribner):

Boat for Peppe (1950).
The Mission Bell (1953).
The Butterflies Come (1957).

Mariana Prieto

MARIANA PRIETO (pree *ay* toh) is a lively five feet, one inch tall, 98 pounds, brunette with "one green eye and one hazel!" She stated, "I am jittery, nuts, unpredictable, easily crushed, and easily elated by silly, simple, kind treatment. I like good conversation. I have a few dear friends who have stuck with me through the years, and I need their reassurance. I like meeting people, people of all kinds, big and little, of all ages, walks of life, colors, and races. I like trying to find out what makes them tick. I like to travel and have extensively. I collect objects and artifacts from my travels to Mexico, Yucatan, Cozumel, Jamaica, The Bahamas, Puerto Rico, and Cuba. I like exotic handmade jewelry and clothes and collect them. Friends are always giving me far-out gifts. 'If it's crazy, Mariana will love it,' they say. And I do!"

Mrs. Prieto was born in Cincinnati, Ohio. Her family moved to Cuba when she was only six months old. This was the first of many moves. "It was hectic moving back and forth from Cuba to the United States. I was yanked in and out of schools, constantly being shifted back and forth between divorced parents. I spoke Spanish before I learned English," she reminisced.

She was educated in Cuban schools and later attended the University of Miami and the University of Florida, taking

223

courses in creative writing. She then taught creative writing at the University of Miami and did radio broadcasts. "I did a children's radio program, which led me into studying what boys and girls enjoyed. I liked the sincerity and simplicity of their thinking patterns."

Her first book for children, *The Wise Rooster* (John Day, 1962), was a result of a Mexican trip." She stated, "I was enchanted with the roosters and donkeys one meets everywhere in the villages. This plus my interest in folklore led me to the book." Mrs. Prieto's book is unique because it is a bi-lingual picture book. Each illustration is accompanied by both English and Spanish texts, side by side. The book also contains vocabularies in English and Spanish, giving both phonetic pronunciations and informational notes concerning words and customs of Latin American peoples.

Continuing in this style, she wrote *Ah Ucu and Itzo* (John Day, 1964), a tale of a Mayan boy in Yucatan and his pet mouse, and *A Kite for Carlos* (John Day, 1966), which is set in the Spanish-speaking community of Ybor City in Tampa, Florida. This book deals with immigrants' problems through three generations. Her books have been used in countless ways with all types of children. In an article that appeared in *The Horn Book* magazine (April, 1968), she wrote:

> When my small Ohio cousins were reading *Alice in Wonderland* and singing about Humpty Dumpty, I was reading *El Libro de los Animales* by Saturnino Calleja of Spain and singing "Que Llueva." . . .

> I cannot help but feel that because of my early childhood, I instinctively turned to writing dual-language children's books. I endeavor to do books that will appeal equally to the Spanish-speaking child and the English-speaking child. Because I lived in both worlds, I have tried to bring to my stories the advantages of both. I trust that through these books my readers understand each other better and capture something of the magic and cadence of Spanish, and the practicality and charm of English.

Ideas for her books come from incidents, happenings, travel, research, and study. "All of my books come from basic experiences. Each comes from my heart and says something. *Tomato Boy* (John Day, 1967), a story of Florida migrant workers, was written because I really have a tomato boy who comes to my door each week selling tomatoes. I became interested in the problems of migrant workers and wanted to put them into book form," she said. And she did!

"I have no writing schedule. I jot down ideas wherever I am. I make basic sketches and see my stories in illustrated forms, striving for many word pictures. I try for high interest material, simply written. I do endless rewriting and reworking and much research. I child-test and teacher-test all my material and accept the suggestions, criticism, and advice of boys and girls. Librarians have also helped me endlessly."

Mrs. Prieto and her husband live in a small house with blue shutters "to keep away the evil spirits." They have a large yard and trees where her pet lizard and squirrels live. There are also many birds who come to her feeders and bird bath. The Prietos have a married daughter who attends the University of Miami. Besides writing books for young children, she continues to teach creative writing in the adult education program of Miami Senior High School. She offers some advice to teachers — young and old — who must come to grips with the many problems of bi-lingual children in our schools: "Have patience and don't talk down to children. Try for emotional understanding and not 'just word-talk.' Speak with your heart as well as your voice."

Mariana Prieto is filled with warmth and understanding and has truly channeled her writing and her knowledge of the Latin American culture into worthwhile and needed books for children.

SOME OTHER BOOKS BY MRS. PRIETO:

Wise Rooster; on Gallo Sabio (John Day, 1962).
Johnny Lost (John Day, 1968).
When the Monkeys Wore Sombreros (Harvey House, 1969).

Ellen Raskin

ELLEN RASKIN FEELS she can sum up her entire childhood and her writing career in the one short paragraph she provided for me: "I was born and grew up in Milwaukee, Wisconsin. My father, Sol Raskin, was a pharmacist; my mother, Margaret, a housewife. I have one sister two years younger than I. I was a child of the Depression. I was very bright in school, had few friends, was an avid reader, and a dreamer (see *Nothing Ever Happens on my Block,* Atheneum, 1966). I had to wear glasses and thought I was ugly (see *Spectacles,* Atheneum, 1968). We lived in a four-room apartment frequently visited by my mother's large family (see *Ghost in a Four-Room Apartment,* Atheneum, 1969). I played the piano from the age of four and loved it (see *Songs of Innocence,* Doubleday, 1966)."

But Ellen Raskin is wrong! She is far too important to sum up in one short paragraph. She is fast becoming one of the country's top illustrators of children's books. Her career is flourishing and it should, for she has worked hard and diligently at developing her style. Several of her books have been included in the American Institute of Graphic Arts' Annual Book Show; *Spectacles* was selected as one of the best illustrated books of 1968 by the *New York Times,* and *The Paper Zoo* (Macmillan, 1968), a book of poems selected and arranged by Renée Karol Weiss and illustrated by Miss Raskin, was included in the *New York Times'* list of "Outstanding Books."

"*Spectacles* is about *me*," she stated. "I am very nearsighted, and I live with a pair of reading glasses, a pair of working glasses with bifocals and prisms, a pair of prescription sun glasses, and an everyday pair of glasses with black rims. I don't mind wearing glasses except when it's very warm and they slip down my nose!" The book tells how the world is seen by a myopic little girl who needs glasses very badly. The mare in the parlor is actually her baby sitter; the giant pygmy nuthatch on her front lawn is her good friend Chester. The drawings are clever and highly stylized.

Over cocktails at the elegant Charles Restaurant in New York's Greenwich Village, she told me that she was just about to acquire a new pair of glasses and that she had to write *Spectacles* for all the little poor-seers all over the country.

Miss Raskin also talked about her writing and illustrating. "My writing training came from reading a great deal. I studied art at the University of Wisconsin and had worked ten years as a commercial illustrator. Writing comes much easier for me than illustrating, for writing is just ideas; after a character has been delineated, all that's necessary is the name. In illustration, after the idea comes consistency in drawing. The same characters have to appear page after page, and tons of research has to be done for every book."

Prior to moving into book illustrating, she designed book jackets. "Did I design book jackets!" she exclaimed, "book jacket after book jacket! When I reached number 1,000, I became disgusted and decided to stop. I also did advertising and magazine illustrations. But I longed to work in a more permanent form — that is, books — and especially to interpret my own ideas for a change, instead of others. Why children's books? For three reasons: They have pictures, children are able to learn and be impressed, and because I'm still a child!"

Her first book was *Nothing Ever Happens on My Block*. "You won't believe this," she said, "but it started with the doorbell ringing and a water-falling-on-the-head incident that actually happened to some children on our block when my daughter was young. Once I started to do the story, the rest just came." Commenting on her work habits she remarked, "First I write the story. Then I dummy up the book with illustrations. Next I eliminate most of the story, which by now is in pictures, and re-

From SPECTACLES by Ellen Raskin, © 1968 by Ellen Raskin.
Permission of Atheneum Publishers.

write what's left. I then begin the finished art. My work day usually extends from 10:00 to 5:00 with one-half hour for lunch and again from 8:00 to 11:00 p.m. at night. When I'm in the middle of a book, I'm a hypochondriac; other times I'm no madder than anyone else."

Miss Raskin lives in a large apartment in a new building in Greenwich Village. Her husband ("a most marvelous man"), is Dennis Flanagan, editor of *Scientific American* magazine. She has one daughter who is a junior at the University of Michigan in Ann Arbor.

Over a fluffy mushroom omelette, we discussed Miss Raskin's pleasures in life. She stated, "I'm rather social, though most of all

I prefer staying home or going to a sporting event or a Gilbert and Sullivan opera with my husband. I like music. I play the piano and harpsichord, but I only perform privately. I love sports and travel, and I love Spain. And I adore the bullfights!"

Bullfights was the magic word, for we both share an enthusiasm for the sport. We talked at length about the fights held in Madrid and Mexico. She knows all the terms and many of the fighters' names, and she bubbles about the beauty and pageantry of the sport. "Dennis and I even watch it on Sundays on UHF-TV. The Mexican fights are televised, and we love watching them. I sit with my white handkerchief and wait for a good play and wave it and shout 'Ole! Ole!'"

Over coffee we chatted about her favorite possessions, which include a drawing by Whistler, a Chinese fresco, and her collections of rare books, which include volumes by William Blake, John Milton, Henry James, and Joseph Conrad. I enjoyed meeting Ellen Raskin. I enjoyed her modesty, and I enjoyed how genuinely thrilled she was over her many recent and well-earned successes. And I enjoyed her twinkling eyes — even though they were seen through my spectacles and her spectacles!

SOME OTHER BOOKS BY MISS RASKIN:

Silly Songs and Sad (T. Y. Crowell, 1967).
Nancy Larrick, ed., *Piping Down the Valleys Wild* (Delacorte, 1968).

Margret and H. A. Rey

IF YOU DON'T KNOW who or what Curious George is, it is apparent that you've never worked with young boys and girls; and if you don't know about Curious George, find out immediately and join the laugh-in with millions of children the world over.

Curious George is one who gets in and out of trouble wherever he goes or whatever he does. When *Curious George Flies a Kite* (1958), he flies into the air on the kite's string; when *Curious George Rides a Bike* (1952), he lands in a traveling circus, nearly chokes an ostrich, and rescues a runaway bear; when *Curious George Goes to the Hospital* (1966) to have a piece of a jigsaw puzzle he swallowed removed, he has everyone laughing hysterically. In short, Curious George is an ingenious little monkey created by Margret and H. A. Rey.

I asked Mr. Rey if there really *was* a George. He answered, "No, Virginia, there is no *real* George, unfortunately. But I have always been fond of monkeys, since my early childhood days. What child isn't? We once had two little marmosets in Brazil, but, sad to say, they died when we went by ship from Rio to London in 1936. It was winter in the northern hemisphere, and they caught cold; although my wife had knitted tiny sweaters for them, they pulled their pullovers off!"

Both Margret and H. A. Rey were born in Hamburg, Germany. "H. A. lived close to the famous Hagenbeck Zoo and, as a child, spent much of his free time there. That's where he learned to imitate animal voices. He is proudest of his lion roar, and once he roared for 3,000 children in the Atlanta Civic Auditorium, thus making headlines in the *Atlanta Constitution* for the first and last time," laughed Mrs. Rey.

Mr. Rey recalled, "My family was rather stable and conservative, a pre-World War I middle-class, 'nice' family. Growing up, I found school easy and sometimes a trifle boring but was what you would call a good student. I learned without much effort, including Latin and Greek grammar and mathematics."

In 1900, at the age of two, Mr. Rey started drawing, mostly horses, and continued to draw the rest of his life. Mrs. Rey studied at the Bauhaus in Dessau, the Academy of Art in Duesseldorf, and an art school in Berlin. The Reys met in Hamburg shortly before Mr. Rey decided to leave Germany; the German postwar inflation had become so catastrophic that he could hardly survive. In 1932 he went to Rio de Janeiro, Brazil, and became an executive in a relative's firm. His job was to sell bathtubs up and down the Amazon River! In 1935 Mrs. Rey showed up in Rio, having left Germany because the Hitler regime was assuming power. That year they were married, honeymooned in Paris, and stayed there for four years. It was here that they created their first book for children. Mrs. Rey reminisced: "It came about by accident. H. A. had done a few humorous drawings of a giraffe for a Paris periodical. An editor at Gallimard, the French publishing house, saw them and called us up to ask whether we could not make a children's book out of them. We did! This became our first book, *Cecily G. and the Nine Monkeys*. One of the nine, incidentally, was George!

"Ever since we have done mostly children's books, and it seems to agree with us. H. A. is still surprised at being paid for what he likes to do best and would do anyhow."

In 1940, a few hours before the Nazis entered Paris, the

Reys left the city on bicycles with nothing but warm coats and several manuscripts, *Curious George* among them. They rode to the French-Spanish border and caught a train to Lisbon. "After a brief interlude in Rio de Janeiro, our migrations came to an end one clear, crisp October morning in 1940 when we saw the Statue of Liberty rise above the harbor of New York and we landed in the U.S.A.," stated Mrs. Rey. They settled in New York's Greenwich Village and before a week was over *Curious George* found a home at Houghton Mifflin Company, where he has been published ever since.

The Reys spent 23 years in Greenwich Village; then moved to Cambridge, Massachusetts, in 1963, where they still live. Their time is divided between Massachusetts and their cottage-studio in the woods of New Hampshire.

Regarding their collaboration Mr. Rey commented, "The share of my wife's work varies. Basically I illustrate and Margret writes. She is a superb editor and critic of my artwork. *Curious George Flies a Kite* was her story, and it goes under her name as the author; the cover says 'with pictures by H. A. Rey.' On *Curious George Goes to the Hospital,* we share the title evenly; *Curious George Learns the Alphabet* (1963) was my brain child. Margret worked on the book but not enough to justify her appearance on the title page!"

Mr. Rey's interest in astronomy ("star-gazing, that is") led to the publication of two books on astronomy, one for children, *Find the Constellations* (1954), and one for older readers, *The Stars: A New Way to See Them* (1952). Both, have "created a revolution in practical star recognition." They have been revised and kept up to date since their first printings.

Commenting on the success of their books, Mr. Rey said, "I believe I know what children like. I know what *I* liked as a child, and I don't do any book that I, as a child, *wouldn't* have liked. Maybe it's a case of retarded development or infantilism, not rare among artists. I sometimes feel I still have to grow up, although I am 70.

"It never fails that when we have a question-and-answer period after a chalk-talk at a school, one kid is sure to ask, 'How come you draw so good?' The adult answer is 'It's a gift I was born with!' I know how fortunate I am, and I'd envy myself if I didn't have such a gift."

I asked if any more *Curious George* books would be coming out in the near future. Mr. Rey answered, "I don't know. Maybe. I am collecting material as I always have, but it takes a long time, years, till there's enough suitable stuff for a book. Gags alone won't do. One has to have a *good* story."

Although the Reys do not have children of their own, their publisher says that they have millions of children. The publisher is right — and the children they have range from the very young to the very old, like you and like me!

SOME OTHER BOOKS BY THE REYS (All Houghton):

Curious George Takes a Job (1947).
Billy's Picture (1948).
See the Circus (1956).
Curious George Gets a Medal (1957).

Feodor Rojankovsky

FEODOR ROJANKOVSKY'S (*fee* oh dawr roh jan *koff* skee) photograph shows him with only a portion of the books he has authored; the total number comes close to 100!

This prolific illustrator has led an interesting life. He was born on December 24, 1891, in Mitava, Russia, on the shores of the Baltic Sea, where his father was the headmaster of a boys' high school. A year later, the family moved to Reval, now Tallinn; his childhood was divided between Tallinn and St. Petersburg, now Leningrad. "My world was limited first to the apartment of the school's headmaster, and then to the yard surrounded by stunted trees and school buildings with their noisy and gay inhabitants. As soon as the bell rang at noon, I would reach up to the window, like Pavlov's dog, from where I could already hear the noise and hubbub of boys running through the yard at such speed that the eye could not follow them. They ran after each other, they ran in zig-zags, jumping, falling, leaping, and jumping again. My ears would ring from their shouts, but I could not move away from that window. When the bell rang again, this mass of boys, all dressed the same way in dark jackets with silver buttons, crowded near the main entrance and disappeared into the building."

In the late afternoons, when all the boys had gone home, he would wander through the halls, in and out of classrooms, inspecting, searching, exploring — a private world of his own. "It was a pleasure when the boys went home," he commented. "I did not hear the noise coming from the hallway anymore; everything became quiet. The watchmen cleaned the classroom, fed the stoves with odorous birch wood, and filled up the kerosene lamps, which at that time lighted the old school building."

Mr. Rojankovsky's two older brothers were considered talented students at school. "My two brothers played in the school band and practiced at home. They gave me their instruments to try, but in spite of my efforts, no music came out of them; the horn would just hiss a little. I achieved about the same result when I tried to imitate my brothers in drawing and painting. They both were considered gifted painters at school."

Mr. Rojankovsky feels that three great events influenced his becoming an artist and literary figure. Firstly, his father read to the family very often. "Among my father's books there were two that I could look at forever. They were the *Bible* and *Paradise Lost* by Milton, with pictures by Doré." A second event was when his father took him to a small zoo where he saw "the most marvelous creatures on earth;" and a third event was his receiving a set of colored pencils. "The zoo became the favorite subject of my pictures, but the colored pencils were used up before my elephant looked like an elephant," he laughed.

After the death of his father, when he was five years old, his family moved about, finally settling in St. Petersburg. "It was in St. Petersburg that my interest in books grew and developed," he commented. "On my last Christmas in St. Petersburg, I received *Robinson Crusoe* by Daniel Defoe. The book was in a Russian translation, and it impressed me very deeply. It was the first book that I started illustrating. My sister and I drew illustrations to match the text. I was eight or nine years old at the time and remember that we felt the island and the house of

Robinson Crusoe were not well-enough represented in Granville's illustrations. I remember how I tried to 'enrich' it!"

Mr. Rojankovsky returned to Reval and went through high school there. In 1912 he entered the Moscow Academy of Fine Arts. "I was happy to be in the town where the Stanislavsky theatre was born, where Chekhov lived, and where Tolstoy often visited: Serov, Vroubel, Korovine lived in Moscow, also. Two of them were teaching in the Fine Arts Academy. Here I met the great poet Maiakovsky, a pupil of our school. At that time he had not printed any books yet and was just forming the Futurist Group. Maiakovsky called me the 'Frenchman' because of my paintings on a given subject. I was at the time under the influence of Gauguin, Matisse, and Marquet."

From 1914–1917 Mr. Rojankovsky served as an officer in the Russian army. During this period he was wounded and painted war subjects from memory while recuperating. These sketches became his first published works. He recalled, "In 1919 I was mobilized by the White Army and soon my military service was ended behind barbed wire in Poland." After he left Poland, he went to Berlin where he illustrated two children's books and finally went to Paris. "In Paris, I met my first American publishers, Miss Esther Averill and Lila Stanley who were organizers of the Domino Press. I did *Daniel Boone* (1931) for them."

Illustrations for many children's books followed. On a trip to London, shortly after the publication of *Daniel Boone,* Mr. Rojankovsky was offered a commission to do 20 drawings of Mother Goose, a character of whom he had never heard! He accepted the commission, did the drawings, and was startled to find that they were being used to adorn the outer wrappings of toilet paper; the pictures had also been made into a book that was given as a premium by the manufacturer!

Prior to the Nazi conquest of Paris, he fled to the south of France. After the German occupation in 1941, he came to the United States. In 1956 he won the Caldecott Award for John

Langstaff's *Frog Went A-Courtin'* (Harcourt, 1955), a rendering of an old Scottish ballad telling of the wedding of Frog and Miss Mousie.

Today Mr. Rojankovsky lives in Bronxville, New York, with his wife. Their daughter, Tanya, is a student at Oxford University in England. One of the things Mr. Rojankovsky enjoys most in life is "nature which surrounds us, rich or poor, sometimes menacing, sometimes caressing." And he enjoys youth today. He commented, "I have lived a long time but feel young, so I am for the young, by the young, and to the young!"

Regarding children's books, he exclaimed, "A good children's book is one that has a good text full of action but not sophisticated, one that tells the child the truth like a tale, and a tale like the truth! Today there are too many children's books. I would diminish their quantity and bring up their quality."

Feodor Rojankovsky has contributed greatly to the field of children's literature, bringing to them his love of nature, his love of children, and his love of books.

SOME OTHER BOOKS BY MR. ROJANKOVSKY:

The Tall Book of Mother Goose (Harper, 1942).
John Langstaff. *Over in the Meadow* (Harcourt, 1957).

Mr. Rojankovsky died on October 12, 1970.

Miroslav Sasek

JANET SCHULMAN, MACMILLAN's Marketing Manager, called
me to say, "Guess who's in New York City? Miroslav Sasek!
(*meer* oh slahf *sah sek*) He'll be here for a few weeks before
returning to Munich, Germany!"

I immediately, telephoned the Roger Williams Hotel in midtown Manhattan and made an appointment to see him. When I
arrived, Mr. Sasek was waiting for me in the lobby. "Would
you like to see some pictures of Washington, D. C.?" he asked
with his European accent. "Come up to the room!"

The first thing one notices about Mr. Sasek is his European
manner. Despite his age, he is thin, well-tailored, and as bubbly
as a glass of the best French champagne. Born in Prague, Czechoslovakia, he was forced to leave that country when the Commu-
nists seized power after World War II. He became a resident of
Paris, France. "I'm at home in Paris," he stated, "I love it! I
live in Munich now because my wife's work is there."

It is no wonder that *This Is Paris* (1959) was the first of his
series of charming, pictorial oversize books (all published by
Macmillan). In them he records impressions of the great cities
of the world with his keen eye and his gay sense of humor and
satire. "I originally wanted to do a series of three books — Paris,

Rome, and London. I never thought it would go on and on."

His travels have been worldwide. To prepare a book in his series Mr. Sasek explained, "I come to a place like New York, for example, that I have never visited before in my life. I begin by going to see the things I've heard about or read about — the monuments, the landmarks, and particular places of interest. One thing leads to another until the book is completed. All I really do is run from my hotel to someplace and then back to the hotel!"

Mr. Sasek showed me how he works. He roughly sketches what he sees on a small white pad, adding detail after detail until he has a finished picture. All over the sketches he jots down notes on the colors of buses, the letters in signs, costumes of the people, and even fire hydrants; the notes may be written in French, German, or Czechoslovakian, whichever language first comes into his mind. "Detail is very important to children," he commented. "If I paint 53 windows instead of 54 in a building, a deluge of letters pours in upon me! Children today know everything — the world is so much smaller. I remember returning home to Munich after finishing *This Is Cape Kennedy* (1964). My son looked at my sketchbooks and without a word from me he mentioned that this is the Apollo rocket and this is the launching pad and this is . . . I could not believe it! Sometimes I cannot believe the children of today. When I was a youngster, no one traveled. And this is why the most simple detail is most important."

After a sketch is completed to his satisfaction, Mr. Sasek goes to his hotel room and begins to draw, rarely waiting more than an hour or two before beginning the final picture that will appear in his finished book. Besides writing the text and doing the illustrations, he completely designs and prepares the layout for his books. When he is finished, the book is ready to go to press, with few or no changes necessary.

Mr. Sasek had just finished *This Is Washington, D. C.,* (1969). The book was carefully resting on a table — big and beautiful, fun and exciting. Unfortunately, he chose a poor time to visit our nation's capital, for while working there the looting and rioting that followed the assassination of Dr. Martin Luther King, Jr. occurred, and then came the Poor People's Campaign and the assassination of Robert F. Kennedy. "It was like a continuing nightmare," he said. "It was worse than Berlin in 1945! The riots were especially terrible to witness. One day while I was sketching the grave site of John F. Kennedy, the guards told me that I would have to leave; moments later trucks and crewmen appeared to dig the grave of Robert F. Kennedy. I could not believe these tragedies, one after the other."

Of all the books he has done in the "This Is" series, his three favorites remain *This Is Edinburgh* (1961), *This Is Venice* (1961), and *This Is Hong Kong* (1965). He told me, "I loved working on *This Is Edinburgh,* though I hated the weather there. In the middle of summer, it was cold and rainy. You needed a hot-water bottle in bed with you. Working conditions were good though because the nights are very short in Edinburgh. I worked from 4:00 a.m. to midnight and finished the book in two months.

"I loved Venice because Venice is so beautiful! And I loved Hong Kong because of Hong Kong. Hong Kong was a hard book to do because of the language problem. It took me hours and hours to draw the characters of the alphabet. I tried to use a camera, but it didn't work. Sometimes I could have screamed! Three times, ten times, twelve times over it took me to perfect one picture!"

As Mr. Sasek speaks, he paces around the room. He never sits down; he never stops moving. His anecdotes come at you like sheets off a printing press. "Doing *This Is Texas* (1967) I had to travel 3,000 miles by bus to see all I had to see! When I did *This Is Israel* (1962), people laughed at me for hours the way I painted the signs. They couldn't understand how I did them left to right when they both read and write their letters right to left!"

He travels with only a handful of materials — tubes of oil, paint brushes, and varied art supplies. His luggage amounts to only two suitcases wherever he goes.

From THIS IS ISRAEL by Miroslav Sasek, © 1962 by Miroslav Sasek. Permission of The
Macmillan Co. and W. H. Allen & Co., Ltd.

Mr. Sasek lives in an apartment in Munich with his wife and 14-year-old son, Dusan Pedro. Munich is not strange territory for the author-illustrator. He worked there for six years as a speaker on Radio Free Europe, and in 1960 he published *This Is Munich.*

"When I return home," remarked Mr. Sasek, "I'll unwind by picking mushrooms in the woods." Perhaps while he's there, he'll think of another place to visit and off he'll go on another journey. Mr. Sasek's books have given children around the globe the opportunity to do armchair traveling with a minimum amount of reading and a lot of delightful looking; the texts have been translated into at least ten different languages. "This Is" books are Miroslav Sasek's creations, and many more cities await the touch of his imaginative pen and brush.

SOME OTHER BOOKS BY MR. SASEK (All Macmillan):

This Is Ireland (1961).
This Is Greece (1966).
This Is the United Nations (1968).

Ann Herbert Scott

WILLIAM TAUSSIG SCOTT commented that his wife, Ann, is a cheerful person but that she thinks of herself as having strong ups and downs and a sort of roller coaster personality. She is a tall, slim woman with fly-away light brown hair, who frequently whistles as she walks down the street; she scuffs in the leaves, sloshes through puddles, stops to smell the sage in the air, and constantly forgets to turn off the heat under the tea kettle. She stated, "The combination of intense wide-ranging interests and fairly low levels of organization makes me often a little breathless. Most days I could use a few extra hours and most weeks a few extra days."

Mr. and Mrs. Scott, their son, Peter, and a recently adopted daughter, Katherine, live in a small, gray, flat-topped house in a neighborhood of nearly identical small, flat-topped houses on the edge of Reno, Nevada. Their living room window looks out on a pasture where horses graze; in the middle-distance is the sky-line of downtown Reno with its casinos and office buildings; beyond are the Sierra Nevada mountains, which are magnificently snow-capped through most of the year. Of life in Reno Mrs. Scott said, "Living on the edge of the city, we are more aware of the fine climate than the neon world of slot machines and roulette tables. We see the little wild mustang colt in the pasture behind our house every day, the inside of the casinos only rarely."

The Scotts moved to Nevada in 1961 when the University of Nevada launched a PhD program in physics. Mr. Scott, a physicist, joined the faculty to help with its direction.

Ann Herbert Scott's first book, *Big Cowboy Western* (Lothrop, 1965), developed from the years she spent working in a housing project in New Haven, Connecticut. "When I worked in New Haven in the 1950's, I was appalled by the lack of children's books picturing either urban neighborhoods or dark-skinned families. I initiated and directed LINK, a program designed 'to give inner-city children between the ages of eight and twelve the chance to become friends with a caring adult and, through an ongoing relationship, to widen their horizons and raise their aspirations.' I dreamed that someday I would write true-to-life stories that would be set in the housing project where I worked, stories in which my New Haven friends could find themselves. However, it was not until I had moved to Nevada that *Big Cowboy Western* evolved.

"This was the first children's story I had written since childhood. Like most of what I have written since, it began as a gift from a child. It was a result of the memories of years I had spent working in New Haven — an old produce peddler and his horse, a lonely, little boy in a cowboy hat sitting by himself on a bench, an irrepressible youngster who called himself Big Cowboy Western, and several families with many children where the mothers worked and there were no fathers at home.

"I have written all my life — mostly committee reports, minutes, grant requests, and doggerel for family birthdays. However, a few years ago I began looking for something worth doing that would be both income-producing and transportable since my husband's summer research takes us to different parts of the country. I decided that what I would most enjoy doing would be writing for young children and thought I would have a try at it.

"I believe the pull toward children's writing comes from something childlike within me. I've always enjoyed being around little children and wherever we've lived — farm, city, housing development — there have been a few small children who have been among my closest friends. The sense of delight and wonder little children bring to the here and now seems to awaken something deep in me. In contrast to writing for adults, which is often dreary and difficult for me, writing for children is often fun; it springs up unexpectedly in familiar places with some of the same spontaneous independence as forgotten daffodils in a leaf-covered bed."

Describing her work habits, Mrs. Scott noted, "In general I work over material for some time, usually simplifying and re-simplifying, often cutting out favorite phrases because they are not necessary to the thrust of the story. When there is something I am unsure about, six-year-old children's ideas about monsters, for example, I do a lot of talking with children. Otherwise I work from memory and imagination. I always *see* picture books as I write them; the sense of the graphics helps shape the development of the manuscript.

"*Sam* (McGraw-Hill, 1967), a story of a boy too little to do anything, was a notable exception. It came as I was scrubbing out the bathtub after a visit from a particularly experimental young neighbor. I wrote it in a few minutes, made some minor changes the next day, and sent it off."

Besides writing books for young children, Mrs. Scott has been a teacher of freshman English, is very much involved with the Society of Friends (Quakers), and has completed a nonfiction book for young adults, *Census, U.S.A.* (Seabury, 1968), which took nearly three years to complete. "This book started innocently enough when I took a job as a census taker on the Pyramid Lake Indian Reservation and stumbled into an almost completely neglected area of our national life," she remarked.

For leisure Mrs. Scott enjoys painting — both pictures and houses — dancing, talking with friends, poking around in the garden, cooking, and eating — especially rare beef and hot fudge sundaes. She loves to go exploring in untrammeled places such as lonely stretches of mountain or desert or, best of all, isolated ocean beaches. "One of my greatest pleasures right now is to watch and work with my two-year old, Peter, who is an admirer of stars and milkweed and all things beautiful. My husband and I often carry him in a backpack when we go snowshoeing or climbing in the Sierras. And sometimes we just sit by the window and watch birds at the feeder or the sun going down." Besides Peter, she has four stepchildren, Jennifer, Christopher, Stephanie, and Melanie, whose ages range from 18 to 23.

"Peace and social justice are important matters to both my husband and me, and we are often up to our ears in mailing lists, mimeographed materials, and the other paper work of social action." In a home that spills over with books, papers, and pictures, Mrs. Scott continues her efforts to better America through honest portrayals of previously forgotten boys and girls throughout our country.

SOME OTHER BOOKS BY MRS. SCOTT (All Lothrop):

Let's Catch a Monster (1967).
Not Just One (1968).

Millicent E. Selsam

NOT BEING SCIENCE-ORIENTED as a young teacher, I was always delighted to find a new book by Millicent E. Selsam. Her books are always simply written, easy to understand, and filled with beautiful prose and scientific facts; they make one want to delve further into the areas she has explored. Her work itself best exemplifies the interest she provokes in her readers:

> The forest is like a tall building. The trees rise like posts holding up a roof of leaves. Inside this forest building are many plant and animal tenants living on different floors. Each floor has its own special climate — light or dark, damp or dry, warm or cool. And each floor has its own special tenants.
>
> *See Through the Forest* (Harper, 1956)

Whether she is writing about the jungle, plants, or the human body, all of her texts are fascinating.

Mrs. Selsam was born and raised in Brooklyn, New York; she was the youngest of eight children. She attended schools in New York and graduated from Columbia University. "I taught for ten years in the high schools of New York City," she stated. "I got tired of teaching but still enjoyed the idea of communicating with young people regarding science." Her first book for children,

247

Egg to Chick (International Publishers), was published in 1946. "I did this book because I was fascinated with embryology," she told me. From that date on Mrs. Selsam has become known as one of the top science writers for young children. She is thoroughly captivated by science. "I have certain childlike qualities. I love to investigate everything and get great pleasure from growing plants indoors and out. I have always loved to know the *why* of everything. Science is dynamic and exciting, and it has changed the world."

The author enumerated the qualities of a good science book for young children in an article, "Writing About Science," which appeared in *The Library Quarterly* (January 1967). One of these qualities is:

> A good science book leads to an appreciation of the methods of science. Scientists find the answers to their questions by observing and experimenting. Children are excellent observers, and if they are given a chance to look at things themselves, they will begin to appreciate the kind of patience and effort that goes into careful observation. Science books should encourage this habit of careful observation. A good book on the seashore should move the reader to go out and examine for himself the wonderful life at the edge of the sea. A good astronomy book should turn the reader's eye to the sky and make him want to buy a small telescope. A good nature book should stimulate a young person to hear, see, smell, and taste things — to use all of his senses to observe.

To prepare *Questions and Answers About Ants* (Four Winds, 1967), she thoroughly researched the field and also spent a full year observing an ant colony that she gathered at Fire Island. "Beatrice Schenk de Regniers suggested the book. Once I started to observe ants, I simply had to follow through. They are fascinating insects and much is still to be learned about them. I spend a lot of time with children in my cottage at Fire Island. I've gotten several ideas from contacts with them." The dedication to

Questions and Answers About Ants reads, "For Billy Schilit who helped collect ants."

Her books have been translated from English into Dutch, Swedish, Danish, German, Urdu, Arabic, Japanese, Greek, Italian, and several African languages. The Selsams live in an urban renewal area of Manhattan. In her living room, she has flowers and plants that grow with the use of fluorescent lights. She loves the ocean, swimming, plants, dancing, children, and other people. She also enjoys painting, cutting bottles with a special hot wire that transforms wine bottles into glasses, vases, and other useful articles, polishing beach stones, and following the latest news in the field of science.

SOME OTHER BOOKS BY MRS. SELSAM:

Play with Vines (Morrow, 1951).
You and the World Around You (Doubleday, 1963).
Animals as Parents (Morrow, 1965).
Hidden Animals (Harper, 1969).

Maurice Sendak

IMMEDIATELY UPON ENTERING Maurice Sendak's duplex brownstone on the west side of New York's Greenwich Village, one is greeted by row after row of books. Mr. Sendak is a prodigious collector of first editions and illustrated books of different periods, and he buys such volumes wherever and whenever he can. He spends many afternoons browsing through book stores and chatting with store owners about old and rare volumes.

As he led me down a flight of stairs to the kitchen on the lower level of the house, Mr. Sendak explained that this is where he "does most of his living." Around the huge room are many antiques — a collection of blue-plate tiles, a tin tray he designed and painted, and a grouping of simple seashells. A wide fireplace with a brick oven acts as a showplace for many of these treasures. After passing through the kitchen and down a narrow hallway, one enters Mr. Sendak's studio — the place where Max and the wild things, Little Bear, and Mr. Rabbit were created. The studio is small, dark, and neatly cluttered. Books are everywhere, including collectors' items such as the works of Randolph Caldecott, George Cruikshank, George MacDonald, and, of course, volume after volume of books written and/or illustrated by Mr. Sendak. Pictures, clippings, and toys, both old and new, adorn the walls. Toy pigs (his favorites), lions (his second favorites), dogs, other animals, and a Buck Rogers space gun are among the many toys on view.

Over a studio couch hangs a Winslow Homer print; on another wall is a painting by Samuel Palmers. Mr. Sendak remarked that these two artists, plus Randolph Caldecott, Wilhelm Busch, and M. Boutet de Monvel, have greatly influenced him.

He was born in Brooklyn, New York, on June 10, 1928, the youngest of three children. His parents, Philip and Sarah Sendak, had come to the United States before World War I from Jewish *shtetls* (small towns or villages) outside Warsaw. Mr. Sendak warmly recalled his father telling long stories based on his own childhood. His sister, Natalie, gave him his first book. "I can still remember the smell and the feel of the book's binding."

His love of books led naturally into his present career as an author-illustrator. "I had always wanted to be an artist," he said. "My brother Jack and I were always making books together. Jack would write, I would illustrate, and our mother would proudly show the finished products to all the neighbors. We did about 12 books together, and we loved it!" Today Jack Sendak writes books for older children.

Mr. Sendak's first children's book, entitled *Good Shabbis, Everybody* (1950), was published by the United Synagogue Commission on Jewish Education when he was 22 years old. After attending the Art Students League in New York City for two years, he worked for a short time as a display artist at F.A.O. Schwarz, the famous toy store on New York's Fifth Avenue.

In 1951 he illustrated Marcel Ayme's *The Wonderful Farm* (Harper). This was the first of approximately 70 books he has helped create. One year later he became widely known in the field of children's literature for his droll illustrations in *A Hole Is to Dig* (Harper) by Ruth Krauss, a book that has become a modern classic. Offers by the score poured in from other publishing houses, and he soon was illustrating other books by Ruth Krauss as well as by Beatrice Schenk de Regniers, Meindert De Jong, and Randall Jarrell. In 1962 he created "The Nutshell Library" (Harper), which Brian W. Alderson, an editor and

From HIGGLETY PIGGLETY POP! OR THERE MUST BE MORE TO LIFE by Maurice Sendak, © 1967 by Maurice Sendak. Permission of Harper & Row, Publishers.

lecturer from London, feels "ought to be distributed free to everyone taking out a birth certificate."

Nominated five times for the Caldecott Medal, Mr. Sendak received it in 1964 for *Where the Wild Things Are* (Harper, 1963). Mr. Sendak explained, "This book is an example of how I felt as a child. It is a child's level of seeing things. Adults find the book fearful; however, they misinterpret childhood. Children find the book silly, fun to read, and fun to look at. This, I feel, shows the gulf between childhood and adulthood."

A reviewer for the *Cleveland Press* thought the same way when he wrote, "Boys and girls may have to shield their parents from this book. Parents are very easily scared."

Where the Wild Things Are has been translated into German, Norwegian, French, Afrikaans, Dutch, Finnish, and Japanese. It was released in England in 1967 and was criticized there as it was in the United States. "Generally in the northern countries there has been no adverse comment," explained Mr. Sendak. "I believe this is because of the heritage of Grimm and the natural acceptance of fairy tales. Wild thing themes are not unusual in these countries."

The book marked a decisive stage in his development and remains an important one to him today. In 1969 it was published in a high-quality paperback edition by Scholastic Book Services. Mr. Sendak would agree to its transformation only if the book were done exactly as it was in the hardcover edition, with the same trim size, color, and type.

After *Where the Wild Things Are,* he illustrated *Hector Protector and As I Went Over the Water* (Harper, 1965), two Mother Goose rhymes with variations. "*Hector Protector* is truly my personal favorite. It has in it my feeling for the dance and my love of music; it captures all of me. It was a keystone book in my life and is one of the most meaningful to me. It was a difficult book to do. I took a simple four line verse that is of no great consequence, then I had to expand and enlarge it, make variations on a theme, and make it my own. Many people think I actually wrote the text. Hector is my kind of kid. He's Max in *Where the Wild Things Are* and he's *Pierre,* one of the four books in "The Nutshell Library." Children identify with him, particularly boys. It's a funny, funny book, one of the funniest of all the nonsense rhymes. I get more fan mail on it than I do on *The Wild Things.* As a matter of fact, *Hector Protector* came out of *The Wild Things* and led into *Higglety Pigglety Pop!* (Harper, 1967).

Higglety Pigglety Pop! subtitled *Or There Must Be More to Life,* is a fantasy inspired by Jennie, Mr. Sendak's pet Sealyham terrier who recently died. Jennie appears in many of his works.

I asked Mr. Sendak about his work habits. He replied, "When I write, I write sporadically, and I write everything in my head. My philosophy is, anything I forget should have been excluded. I don't write anything down as I go along, but when I begin, I write steadily until I am finished. Illustrating is quite different; it is more routine, a process that comes to me naturally."

Mr. Sendak showed me several of the sketches he was preparing for *A Kiss for Little Bear* (Harper, 1968), a book in the series beginning with *Little Bear* (Harper, 1957), written by Else Holmelund Minarik. The detailed illustrations were beguiling, filled with love, humor, and tenderness. "When I did the first Little Bear book, I wanted Mother Bear to be an image of warmth and strength — nothing less than motherhood itself. So I dressed her in a Victorian costume because those voluminous skirts, the voluminous sleeves, and her voluminous figure all made for the strong and comforting tenderness I wanted her to exude. And when Little Bear sits in her lap, I had her envelop him. The folds of her skirt would surround him. There couldn't be a safer place in all the world than in Mother Bear's lap."

I noticed that in the drawings for this latest book, Little Bear had become a little bigger and somewhat chubbier. "That's life!" mused Mr. Sendak.

Mr. Sendak speaks softly and quickly at times becoming quite intense. Often he seems shy, yet other times he is outgoing and self-assured. He is short, has dark brown hair, haunting green eyes, and resembles the child characters he has created in his works — characters who will live on for generation after generation. His books will long be studied, discussed, and argued about. But most of all they will be enjoyed by millions of youngsters!

When I left his house, I made a mental note that someday soon I would add a small pig to Maurice Sendak's wonderful toy menagerie; it will become an inhabitant of the creative household that has produced bears, dogs, cats, lions, wild things — and hundreds of hours of pleasure for readers old and young.

SOME OTHER BOOKS BY MR. SENDAK (All Harper):

Ruth Krauss. *A Very Special House* (1953).
Meindert De Jong. *The Wheel on the School* (1954).
Beatrice Schenk de Regniers. *What Can You Do with a Shoe?* (1955).
Janice May Udry. *The Moon Jumpers* (1959).
———. *Let's Be Enemies* (1961).
Charlotte Zolotow. *Mr. Rabbit and the Lovely Present* (1962).

Dr. Seuss (Theodor S. Geisel)

IN A "REMODELED and augmented derelict observation tower" standing on top of a mountain next to the Pacific Ocean lives a man who describes himself thus: "Before: A man with black hair and a long nose; Now: A man with gray hair and a long nose." This man is not a wizard or a sorcerer, but he does create fantastical creatures like sneetches, oobleks, grinches, and gacks and he does have curious pseudonyms — Dr. Seuss and Theo. LeSieg, (Geisel spelled backwards.) His real name, of course, is Theodor Seuss Geisel (soos *geye* z'l). If there are any adults who have never heard of this author-illustrator, they can ask any youngster who he is, for during the past 30 years, the words "Dr. Seuss" have become household words, words that are a part of most children's vocabularies. His name has also appeared in the lyrics of popular rock song, "Little Green Apples!"

Dr. Seuss was born in Springfield, Massachusetts, in 1904. He went through the Springfield public schools and in 1925 received a bachelor of arts degree from Dartmouth College. Thirty-one years later Dartmouth awarded him an honorary doctorate of humane letters. Dr. Seuss began writing books for children by sheer accident. "I had no lofty reason whatsoever. In the fall of 1936, while aboard the S. S. *Kungsholm* on a long rainy crossing of the Atlantic, I amused myself by putting words to the rhythm of the ship's engine. The words turned out to be *And to Think That I Saw It on Mulberry Street* (Vanguard Press, 1937). Once ashore, I drew pictures to go with it. The book was my first one; it was rejected by 29 publishers before Vanguard Press accepted it. The reason most given for rejection of the manuscript was that the book was unlike other children's books on the market; hence, its chance in the marketplace was slim!"

Other Seuss books followed in rapid succession, and soon characters such as Bartholomew Cubbins, Thidwick, the Big Hearted Moose, and Horton, the elephant who hatches an elephant-bird began to appear. "*Horton Hatches the Egg* (Random House, 1940) is the favorite of my books," he stated, "probably for the selfish reason that it was the easiest to write, and I had the most fun doing it. I was doodling around with drawings, the way I like to do, and a sketch of an elephant on some transparent paper happened to fall on top of a sketch of a tree. After a short while, it was obvious to me that Horton was sitting in the tree hatching an egg!" When the first Lewis Carroll Shelf Award was established by the University of Wisconsin School of Education in 1958, *Horton Hatches the Egg* was among the books selected as worthy to sit on the shelf with *Alice in Wonderland*.

Commenting on his work habits, Dr. Seuss told me, "I have no set pattern of working. Sometimes a doodled sketch contains a character I think is worth developing; sometimes a doodled couplet of verse suggests a dramatic situation. When I get a character who appeals to me, like Horton, I introduce him to another character and see what happens. When two characters get into conflict, the plot takes care of itself. I never try out ideas on children. This, I feel, can be a terrible trap. Kids react too often to the *method* of presentation. You can charm them with a very bad story if you present it with proper salesmanship. Conversely, a good story fails if awkwardly presented. Some of the worst children's books ever published have been pre-tested with glowing results on captive audiences of kids."

Dr. Seuss never received any formal training in art or in writing. "I did have the usual amount of college courses in 'creative writing,' but when I began to write for children, I had to unlearn everything that I had been taught." In 1957 Dr. Seuss created the now-classic *The Cat in the Hat* (Random House), a book that was termed a "Beginner Book." The text was written with a controlled, limited vocabulary for the specific needs of children who are learning to read. "I remember thinking that I might be able to dash *The Cat in the Hat* off in two or three weeks. Was I mistaken! It ended up taking well over a year! To produce a 60-page book, I may easily write 1,000 pages before I'm satisfied. The most important thing about me, I feel, is that I work like hell — write, rewrite, reject, re-reject, and polish incessantly."

On January 29, 1968, the R. R. Bowker Company of New York published a list of the top 15 best sellers in the children's book field from 1895–1965. Numbers nine and fourteen on the list are *The Cat in the Hat* and *The Cat in the Hat Comes Back* (Random House, 1958), with total sales of 1,588,972 and 1,148,669 copies respectively. I asked Dr. Seuss how this makes him feel. "Scared!" he replied. "Every time I start a new book, that cat squints at me and says, 'Seuss, I bet you can't top me!'"

Besides the famous author-illustrator that we know, Dr. Seuss is president and editor in chief of the Random House "Beginner Books" series, is a painter, and has produced several Academy Award winning motion pictures, including *Design for Death,* (Best Documentary Feature, 1947), a history of the Japanese people written in collaboration with his late wife, Helen, and *Gerald McBoing-Boing* (Best Animated Cartoon, 1951). He loves to travel everywhere and enjoys gardening and swimming. He has done commercial art for magazines, newspapers, television, and has animated cartoons for the Ford Motor Company. He originated the "Quick, Henry, the Flit" comic strip advertisements while working with Standard Oil of New Jersey.

Dr. Seuss loves children but has never had any. "You have 'em!" he stated. "I'll amuse 'em!" And, oh, how he does! Whether the children are in Japan, Germany, Israel, or in the United States of America, they are all hooked on, and familiar with, such catchy verses as:

> "Young man," laughed the farmer,
> "You're sort of a fool!
> You'll *never* catch fish
> In McElligot's Pool!"
> —from *McElligot's Pool* (Random House, 1947).

As a last question I asked Dr. Seuss, "What is rhyme?"

"Rhyme?" he answered, "A rhyme is something without which I would probably be in the dry-cleaning business!"

And that's Dr. Seuss — and his name rhymes with floose!

SOME OTHER BOOKS BY DR. SEUSS (All Random House):

If I Ran the Zoo (1950).
Yertle the Turtle, and Other Stories (1950).
How the Grinch Stole Christmas (1957).
The Dr. Seuss ABC Book (1963).
The Foot Book (1968).

Symeon Shimin

IT WAS A NIPPY January day when I visited Symeon Shimin (*sim* ee un *shih* min). The stairway leading to his fifth-floor walk-up apartment-studio in New York's Greenwich Village showed evidence of the ghost of Christmas past; shimmering tinsel and pine needles were scattered here and there. Mr. Shimin greeted me warmly. Entering the apartment, one is overwhelmed by enormous canvasses, paints, and various other materials that Mr. Shimin uses to execute his work.

Mr. Shimin never intended to be an artist. He was born in Astrakhan, Russia, a town on the Caspian Sea, on November 1, 1902; he came to the United States with his family at the age of nine. "I always wanted to be a musician," he declared. "I never drew as a child. I never thought about drawing. I didn't know what *a painter* meant nor what *painting* meant. Then one day — the next day or the next week of my childhood, it seems — I drew. And I have never stopped drawing!" While in his early teens, he did free-lance advertising work, making just enough money to live on. At 20, he fought a serious bout with tuberculosis, which limited him to working an hour or so a day. "In that little time each day, I was able to earn my keep doing artwork," he commented. Following his illness, Mr. Shimin went to Europe, where he spent a year and a half studying the work of El Greco, Cezanne, and Picasso in museums and art galleries. This served as the basis for his entire art training. "I am self-taught in art, that is, except for a meaningless year spent studying at a school in New York City!"

Returning to the United States, Mr. Shimin found himself in the beginnings of the Depression. "In the late 30's a national competition was held for artists under Franklin Delano Roosevelt's Administration. Mr. Roosevelt had set up a Public Buildings Administration wherein five per cent of government building costs were to go into the arts. I planned to enter the competition and do a mural for the United States Department of Justice Building. I worked on several ideas, but the day before the final sketches were due in Washington, I decided to do something entirely different. I phoned Washington and asked if the committee would accept a drawing delivered in person rather than by mail. When they told me that they would, I went to work, finished a sketch, boarded a train in the middle of the night to D. C., and slipped it under a door! One week later I found out that I was the winner in the competition." The execution of the mural sparked several museum exhibitions of Mr. Shimin's work. He has since had several successful one-man shows.

Mr. Shimin began illustrating books for young children with the encouragement of his friends, Herman and Nina Schneider, the well-known writing team of nonfiction books. "The Schneiders asked me to illustrate a revised edition of their book, *How Big Is Big?* (Scott, 1950). I gave in, did it, and that was the start of it all!" he exclaimed. Mr. Shimin has also created illustrations for such notable books as Aileen Fisher's narrative poem, *Listen, Rabbit* (T. Y. Crowell, 1964), and Joseph Krumgold's Newbery Award winner, *Onion John* (T. Y. Crowell, 1959). His favorites are *One Small Blue Bead* by Byrd Baylor Schweitzer (Macmillan, 1965) and *Dance in a Desert* by Madeleine L'Engle (Farrar, Strauss & Giroux, 1969).

Commenting on his work habits, Mr. Shimin told me, "I don't work steadily at book illustration. I illustrate for a time and then

stop to devote myself to painting. At the moment I want to finish up my commitments and go to Europe to live for several years. In doing book illustrations, I always use live models since I am a figurative artist. I do dozens of drawings from each sketch, working and reworking until I am satisfied — until I feel the illustrations are perfect. I work in watercolor; recently I've been illustrating in acrylics. I like to allow about six weeks to do a book. I absolutely hate deadlines! I'm a night person and can go through night and day as long as I have about eight hours sleep once in awhile. I just finished a 40-hour stretch, straight through. Art means everything to me. It is my life. It is me!"

Mr. Shimin and I discussed the field of art. He stated, "I like all kinds of art if it is done with conviction. As far as I'm concerned, a great deal of what is being done today is Madison Avenue's version of the cow painters of the 1900's! I feel that one can explore a new area of art without exploiting it."

The doorbell rang, and in walked Mr. Shimin's daughter, Tonia. She is 26 years old, involved in the world of dance, and has a radiant personality. She kissed her father, said hello to me, and disappeared into the kitchen to prepare a snack. Mr. Shimin and I continued talking. The subject turned to today's times. "I'm with the youth of today. We are in a difficult period but an exciting period, one of tremendous change. I am 66 years old, and I'm so happy to be alive now," he commented. Overhearing this, Tonia laughed and peeped into the room as if to say, "He's not putting you on. He is *with* the young — he *is* young!"

Mr. Shimin has another daughter, Toby, 8. The family lives in a huge, sparsely furnished, railroad-type apartment. Mr. Shimin is an exciting man to talk with and to listen to. Leaving his apartment, I noticed several drawings done by Toby taped to the wall in the hallway. The drawings were childlike, the type any child might draw in school, but they were placed proudly on the wall, just a few feet away from a reproduction of the dynamic mural Mr. Shimin did for the United States Department of Justice. Upon departure, Mr. Shimin gave me a copy of *One Small Blue Bead*. Once home I read the inscription: "In remembrance of a lovely afternoon of talk. Good luck. Symeon."

SOME OTHER BOOKS BY MR. SHIMIN:

Gladys Yessayan Cretan. *All Except Sammy* (Little, Brown, 1966).
Ann Herbert Scott. *Sam* (McGraw-Hill, 1967).
Byrd Baylor Schweitzer. *The Man Who Talked to a Tree*. (Dutton, 1968).

Uri Shulevitz

"ONE MONDAY MORNING" (Scribner, 1967) was the second book to which Uri Shulevitz (*oo* ree *shul* eh vitz) contributed both text and pictures; it is full of the magic of a child's fantasy. The story begins on a rainy Monday morning when a king, queen, and little prince come to visit a little boy in a tenement building but he is not at home. I felt as if I were reliving the story as I climbed the staircase to Mr. Shulevitz's apartment in New York's Greenwich Village. It *was* a Monday morning, and it *was* raining, but fortunately Mr. Shulevitz *was* home.

This was a particularly exciting time to visit the author-illustrator, for the American Library Association had just pronounced him winner of the 1969 Caldecott Medal for his pictures in *The Fool of the World and the Flying Ship* (Farrar, 1968), a Russian tale retold by Arthur Ransome (1884–1967). Mr. Shulevitz had selected this tale from Ransome's *Old Peter's Russian Tales* (1916); *The Fool of the World and the Flying Ship* is a 48-page book with many, many illustrations. The dummy, done in black line drawings, took Mr. Shulevitz over six months to prepare; adding the color took two more months. He worked at a feverish pace to meet a deadline that would allow publication in November 1968.

From ONE MONDAY MORNING by Uri Shulevitz, © 1967 by Uri Shulevitz. Permission of Charles Scribner's Sons.

Mr. Shulevitz was born on February 27, 1935, in Warsaw, Poland. Because of World War II, he and his family were forced to join the stream of refugees who fled through Europe. His journey took him from country to country and finally to Paris, France. Here, at the age of 12, he won first prize in a drawing competition held among all the grammar schools in his district. "I always drew," he told me. "Drawing has always been with me. The encouragement of my parents, who were both artistically talented, probably contributed to my early interest in drawing."

Eventually Mr. Shulevitz settled in Israel. At 18, he was the youngest member to participate in a drawing exhibition at the Museum of Tel Aviv. He attended the Teachers Institute and studied at the Art Institute in Tel Aviv during the evenings. His formal training concentrated on painting. Later he joined the kibbutz Ein Geddi, located near the Dead Sea. "After a long

264

trip by the dry, stark, and hot shores of the Dead Sea, Ein Geddi unfolds like a Chinese scroll, which is quite a surprise, with its waterfall and rich vegetation," he said. For over a year he lived at Ein Geddi, where he designed a Passover Haggadah containing the narrative of the Exodus read at Seder during Passover. This was his first self-taught attempt at graphics. He managed to combine part of his military service with art, working as art director of a magazine for teenage boys and girls.

In 1959 Mr. Shulevitz came to New York, where he studied painting at the Brooklyn Museum Art School. Since that time he has visited Israel twice, but he now makes his home in New York. He became a United States citizen several years ago and intends to stay here. "I like it here and appreciate very much the possibilities the United States has offered me."

While in this country he worked several years for a small publishing house specializing in Hebrew children's books. Wanting to work on his own, he decided to make up a portfolio and take it to publishing houses. He went to Harper and Row, but the editor, Ursula Nordstrom, was in Europe. Susan Carr Hirschman (now at Macmillan) looked at his work and liked it. When Miss Nordstrom returned and looked at his portfolio, she too liked it. "Both Ursula and Susan suggested that I write a book of my own. I did not consider myself a writer but I tried anyway." After many trials, his first book, *The Moon in My Room,* was published (Harper, 1963). Mr. Shulevitz remarked, "Writing, I came to realize, has less to do with language than one thinks. First one has to have something to say. This may come in pictures or in sounds, depending on one's inclinations, and not necessarily in words."

A common thread runs through all three of the author's own books: *The Moon in My Room, One Monday Morning,* and *Rain Rain Rivers* (Farrar, 1969); all depict a child "traveling" outside his room without ever really leaving it. "I have 'traveled' myself in books," he stated, "from total fantasy in *The Moon in My Room,* to a confrontation between fantasy and reality in

One Monday Morning, to a total reality in *Rain Rain Rivers.* It was a long trip!"

The artwork in Mr. Shulevitz's books is quite varied. His interest in calligraphy and Oriental art led him to use a Japanese brush on rice paper for *The Silkspinners* (Scribner, 1967) by Jean Russell Larson. Other books are done in pen and ink, sometimes with the addition of wash, and in *The Fool of the World and the Flying Ship,* he used full-color drawings for the first time.

When he is not at work on his books, Mr. Shulevitz studies *tai-chi-chuan,* a form of Chinese calisthenics, which is also called shadow-boxing. He demonstrated some of the movements for me, explaining that this method improves the internal organs and is a non-compulsive form of body exercise. He studies *tai-chi-chuan* and Chinese calligraphy in Chinatown under the guidance of Professor Cheng.

He has two cats, Fuzzball and Bianca. Other interests include the movies (in collaboration with Tom Spain, he has made a film from his book *One Monday Morning*), the theatre, museums, and New York City. "I am tired and bored by the overstatements in the arts that life is miserable. Most of the time one finds proof for one's preconceived ideas. I am interested in looking for what is left that is worthwhile."

In just six years Uri Shulevitz has illustrated over 14 books, has been cited by the Society of Illustrators and the American Institute of Graphic Arts, and has won the coveted Caldecott Medal. Despite this acclaim, he is a quiet, modest young man who is totally absorbed in work that he loves.

SOME OTHER BOOKS BY MR. SHULEVITZ:

H. R. Hays and Daniel Hays. *Charley Sang a Song* (Harper, 1964).
Jack Sendak. *The Second Witch* (Harper, 1965).
The Brothers Grimm. *The Twelve Dancing Princesses* (Scribner, 1966).
Jan Wahl. *Runaway Jonah* (Macmillan, 1968).

Marc Simont

MARC SIMONT (see *mahnt*) forgot about me! I had to telephone him from a candy store just around the corner from the tree-lined block where he lives in New York's Greenwich Village.

"Oh, my God! Being a creature of habit," the voice on the other end of the telephone exclaimed, "I came to my studio in the East 30's. Stay there! I'll hop on my bicycle and be down in the Village in a few minutes."

It was a beautiful spring morning so I didn't mind waiting on the stoop of his apartment house. It wasn't long before a trim, tapered, well-tanned man in his fifties came coasting down the street perched on his two-wheeler. The bicycle stint wasn't so surprising after we had talked, for I learned that Mr. Simont is an avid sports fan. "I am a nut about sports, but I have a different philosophy than most people have about games. I'm not a *team* man. I like to go to games to watch the whole event. It's the movement that fascinates me. I don't shout rah-rah-rah for a particular color uniform. The color merely differentiates one team from the other."

Mr. Simont and his wife, a teacher of brain-damaged children, spend their summers in Cornwall, Connecticut. "In Cornwall I stimulated great interest in soccer. It's great for me to play there because the men, women, and children see I'm an old man, and I don't get pushed around," he chuckled. "Sports should be fun — like skipping stones across a pond or throwing apples at a tree. The competition is, and should be, the least part of sports."

Mr. Simont was born in Paris, France, in 1915. He attended school there, in Barcelona, and in New York. His family kept on the move, going from France to Spain to the United States and finally back to Paris. As a result, he attended many schools; although fluent in French, English, Spanish, and Catalonian, he was a poor student and never finished high school. He did study art, however, at the Academie Julian, then with Andre Lohte, and at the Academie Ranson where he learned fresco painting. In the late 1930's he returned to the United States and took jobs wherever he could find them. He did portrait painting, illustrations for various advertising firms, and finally he broke into the picture-book trade, doing illustrations for books by such notables as James Thurber, Ruth Krauss, and Meindert DeJong. In 1956 he illustrated Janice May Udry's *A Tree Is Nice* (Harper), which brought him the Caldecott Award. The colorful illustrations show adults, children, and animals enjoying the pleasures that trees can bring.

"I believe that if I like the drawings I do, children will like them also," he commented. "The child in me must make contact with other children. I may miss it by ten miles, but if I am going to hit, it's because of the child in me. Actually, with my work I don't know if I'm pleased until it's over." Besides illustrating books for children, Mr. Simont has done work for the magazine *Sports Illustrated*.

Marc Simont enumerated his likes: "I'm content with very little in life. I like my house in the country. I like my work. I like the city, knowing that if I have a car downstairs, I can drive to the country. I like friends, people. I don't smoke cigarettes, but I like a good cigar. I like wine. I'm crazy about skiing. There's no competition in skiing. It's a great feeling to just slide down mountains and feel the coldness and the purifying quality of cold air. It's an addiction I could get hooked on! My 21-year-old son, Doc (nicknamed for his initials *M*ark *D*alton), now in the U. S. Navy, is a superb skier. He shares my love of the sport."

"Poetry and trees are for sissies," remarked a third-grader when I showed him Mr. Simont's illustrations in *A Tree Is Nice* and *Every Time I Climb a Tree* by David McCord (Little Brown, 1967). After telling him about the author-illustrator's sports interests, he remarked, "Well if he likes sports so much, his books can't be that bad! He's gotta be a fairly nice guy!"

And how right he was. Marc Simont's books *are* nice and he *is* a nice guy!

SOME OTHER BOOKS BY MR. SIMONT:

Ruth Krauss. *The Happy Day* (Harper, 1949).
———. *The Backward Day* (Harper, 1950).
James Thurber. *The Thirteen Clocks* (Simon and Schuster, 1951).
———. *The Wonderful "O"* (Simon and Schuster, 1957).
How Come Elephants? (Harper, 1965).
Janet Chenery. *Wolfie* (Harper, 1969).

Louis Slobodkin

SOMEONE TOLD ME that Louis Slobodkin (sloh *bod* kin) was
born in a foreign land, yet I learned from him that he was born
in Albany, New York! Someone told me that he lived in Europe,
but he doesn't; he and his wife live on the tenth floor of an old
apartment house right on Broadway in New York City. "Actually, we live about seven months a year in a house and studio
that I built on Fire Island. We spend a couple of months a year
in New York, and three or four months a year we usually travel
to a warmer climate," he declared.

Someone told me that Mr. Slobodkin was a good friend of
the late James Thurber. Mr. Slobodkin won the 1944 Caldecott
Award for Mr. Thurber's story *Many Moons* (Harcourt,
1943), a tale of a ten-year-old princess who wanted the moon.
"I had no relationship to James Thurber," he said. "Our collaboration was handled entirely by the publishers, and I was not
allowed to push any of the words around in his manuscript as
I usually do when I collaborate on a book. I remember the
shock that shook the publishing house when I wanted to change
one word in Mr. Thurber's manuscript; I wanted to say, 'The
moon is made of *blue* cheese' instead of *'green* cheese.' My
reason was that in printing the book there was no provision for

yellow ink on that particular page. I only had red and blue. Anyone knows you need yellow and blue to make green!"

Winning the Caldecott Award changed his life. Up to that time Mr. Slobodkin had divided his time among a variety of arts. He attended the Beaux Arts Institute of Design in New York where he studied sculpture; he became quite well-known in this country as a sculptor. "I have three panels in sandstone in North Adams, Massachusetts, two ten-ton granite eagles in Allentown, Pennsylvania, cast iron panels on the Madison Square Post Office in New York City, an aluminum figure in the Postmaster General's office in Washington, D. C., and some other work stuck around in public buildings here and there. And I also have a lot of work in private collections. I might have devoted myself even more to sculpture and less to books if I had not won the Caldecott. For the past 15 years I've worked mainly on books."

Mr. Slobodkin entered the field of children's literature quite accidentally. He explained, "Eleanor Estes, who knew me as a sculptor, asked me to illustrate her first book, *The Moffats* (Harcourt, 1941). Thus, I became an illustrator. I began to write my own stories a few years later because I wanted to draw the pictures for them. The first book I wrote and illustrated was *Magic Michael* (Macmillan, 1944), inspired by my son, Michael, who was then four years old. I wrote the text in my sculpture studio one Sunday afternoon just for fun. Michael teaches language in the New York high schools. My younger son, Larry, is now a full professor of ecology at the University of Stony Brook.

"My stories are usually inspired by children. My sons and my three almost grown-up grandchildren have given me ideas unwittingly. My working habits are bad. I work continually when I am developing an idea or carrying through the mechanics of designing a book. Then I can go for long periods when I do nothing. I rework my drawings until I get approximately the effect I am hunting for. I found out long ago that it's difficult to get children to give you an honest opinion of the work in progress. They are so kind and sympathetic that they will say the work is *bad* if that's what you want them to say or *good* if they feel that is the response you want."

Since 1945 Mr. Slobodkin has written approximately 44 books, collaborated on 20, and illustrated and designed about 17 for which "I receive no royalties!" His books range in level from pre-kindergarten to adult. He is a good cook, likes people, particularly very young people, enjoys travel, and usually likes what he sees. "I used to belong to a lot of art societies; I don't any more. I like a number of dogs that I've met and enjoy watching the birds on our Island. I do not indulge in any sports. I like to play Scrabble." Mr. Slobodkin stands 5 feet 8 inches tall. "I am inclined toward plumpness. I have always had to diet to keep my weight down." He has brown hair, going white, blue eyes, and a whitish beard. "I have to wear glasses continually because I'm near-sighted." (With over 80 books to his credit, it is no wonder!)

Someone told me that Louis Slobodkin is a fun man to know. Thank goodness someone tells the truth about Louis Slobodkin!

SOME OTHER BOOKS BY MR. SLOBODKIN:

Eleanor Estes. *Rufus M.* (Harcourt, 1943).
――――. *The Hundred Dresses* (Harcourt, 1944).
First Book of Drawing (Watts, 1958).
The Three-Seated Space Ship (Macmillan, 1962).
Colette and the Princess (Dutton, 1965).
Round Trip Space Ship (Macmillan, 1968).

Ruth A. Sonneborn

RUTH A. SONNEBORN was born in New York City. "I grew up in a brownstone on West 70th Street, just off Central Park. My father was in politics. He was once Borough President of Manhattan, President of the New York State Senate, and a Congressman for a brief time. He was out a great deal at public dinners. Mother was a homebody; in those days women were not on the scene politically. I had one sister just a year older and two younger brothers. My grandparents and an unmarried aunt lived with us. We were quite an ingrown family, Jewish but unreligious. I went to the Ethical Culture private school. Although I did well in school, I was always in revolt there and seemed to enjoy defying authority for its own sake. I learned to read before school, only because of my competitive feelings with my sister. I read a great deal," she reminisced.

I first met Mrs. Sonneborn when I attended Bank Street College as a student. She worked as director of the Bank Street Bookstore, and we often exchanged thoughts about books for children. Through the years I have come to know her well and have grown to appreciate her warm personality and sincere interest in children and the books they grow up on. Her first book was *Question and Answer Book of Everyday Science* (Random

273

House, 1961). "This book was commissioned," she stated. "I had submitted a story that spelled out a child's outdoor experiences, one that raised and answered questions. Random House considered taking it, then decided to launch a question-and-answer book series. They asked me to do one of the books in the series."

Mrs. Sonneborn's more recent books, *The Lollipop Party* (Viking, 1967) and *Seven in a Bed* (Viking, 1968), are totally different from her earlier work. Both texts deal with the Spanish-American and his adjustment to life on the mainland. "Certainly my recent ideas that led to books stem from my Bank Street Bookstore life. I kept hearing from teachers of young children the kinds of themes they felt were missing from published works. I felt sympathetic to their needs and I felt personal involvement. I believed I might be able to write books for minority children. I chose a few themes and built stories around them. I did *The Lollipop Party* because I wanted to write a story about a child left alone for the first time. This is a universal experience or, if not, a universal fear. There is both fear and excitement in anticipating a first time alone, so I put Tomas into the situation and turned the experience into a positive one. This story could just as well have been done in a middle-class or even upper-class milieu, but I chose the Puerto Rican home because Puerto Rican children have too few opportunities of seeing themselves pictured in books. Also, the experience of being left alone is likely to happen sooner to children of poorer families."

She continued, *"Seven in a Bed* combines a serious theme with humor. I hope it will give the many children who have no beds to themselves a chance to identify more easily with this story. Most picture books reveal one child in his separate bed. I also like the warm family and the suggestions of a stern father. But I think perhaps the reason I like the story best is because I think the illustrations and the text are so completely in tune. For that I have to thank Don Freeman. He is a dear!"

Mrs. Sonneborn has long been a member of the Bank Street Writers Laboratory, a group that has produced some extraordinary talent. Her interest in urban life and the problems of disadvantaged groups stem from her being a city person. "I really care about the life and the people in the city," she declared. "Today one is constantly being bombarded by stories, scenes, and reports of the problems of city crowds and city miseries. There are city joys too, you know!"

Mrs. Sonneborn lives in a federal house built in 1828 on quiet Barrow Street in Greenwich Village, a residential street of small houses. "I like the simplicity of the period of architecture. My simple modern furniture, I think, looks well in it." She has one married daughter and two grandchildren. "My son, John, went to the Bank Street School at the age of two, and this is when I became interested in the life of young children and particularly in the school scene. Ever since that day I have spent much time volunteering in the schools my children attended. At present, in my old age, I mostly enjoy people and books and being outdoors in the country. I visit my grandchildren often, and we walk in the woods, collect wild flowers, and such things," she laughed.

She *says* she's *old,* but she's as spry as can be. She continues to work part-time at Bank Street College, continues to do work in private schools, and still manages to write books for the urban youngster — books that are desperately needed to enrich lives and provide good self-images.

OTHER BOOKS BY MRS. SONNEBORN:

Question and Answer Book of Space (Random House, 1965).
Friday Is Papa Night (Viking, 1970).

Peter Spier

"DO YOU KNOW WHAT HAPPENED to me after I finished my second Mother Goose book?" asked Peter Spier in his attractive Dutch accent. "I had to go out and buy a pair of glasses!" The book he was referring to was *To Market! To Market!* (Doubleday, 1968), the second in the series entitled "The Mother Goose Library," which the illustrator conceived. If you have seen any of these books, you'll know why Mr. Spier needed glasses. The drawings are meticulously designed, consisting of hundreds of minute details executed in full color.

"I take my work seriously," he stated. "An illustrator is like a writer; they both have a certain arsenal at their disposal — memory, imagination, and feeling. An illustrator must extend this arsenal to draw trees as trees are seen in life — high trees and low trees. He must make the people in his books come to life as well as the stores and the stones; the unimportant details become quite important if you are going to be exact — and you must!"

Mr. Spier designs his books from beginning to end. "First I visit the locale where the book takes place. I call this my journalistic quest. For example, to do *London Bridge Is Falling Down!* (Doubleday, 1967), I went to England to gather material. I can't make things come alive from photographs, travel posters, or from looking at *National Geographic* magazines. I must become a part of the location I am to draw!"

London Bridge Is Falling Down! was heralded by book critics and was awarded the Boston *Globe-Horn Book* prize for the best illustrations of the year; *To Market! To Market!* was chosen as runner-up for the award. To begin a book, Mr. Spier first creates accurate pencil drawings. He then does ink sketches and finally watercolors. A book takes him approximately four months to create, working steadily about 16 hours a day. His working habits are exact — long hours at the drawing board and hard work until a book is completed. "To finish *Hurrah, We're Outward Bound!* (Doubleday, 1968), I worked most of Christmas Day and on New Year's Eve," he recalled.

Mr. Spier was born in Amsterdam, Holland, and came to the United States in 1952 after World War II. After traveling through the country, he settled in New York City, the heart of the publishing world. He was always interested in publishing; in Holland he had been a writer and editor of a newspaper and grew up surrounded by the artwork of his father, a famous figure in the Netherlands. His first book for children was *The Cow Who Fell in the Canal* (Doubleday, 1957) by Phyllis Krasilovsky. The story is set in the Dutch countryside with which he is so familiar. His second book, *The Fox Went Out on a Chilly Night* (Doubleday, 1961), was runner-up for the Caldecott Award in 1962.

Mr. Spier lives in Port Washington, Long Island, during the winter months and in Shoreham, Long Island, in summer. His family consists of his wife, Kathryn, and their two tow-headed children, Kathryn, 7, and Thomas, 8. In his spare time, when he can leave his drawing board, he creates ship models. He also enjoys sailing and fishing.

"I have always been interested in *producing* books," he remarked. "I feel that books for children should be childlike not

From HURRAH, WE'RE OUTWARD BOUND by Peter Spier, © 1968 by Peter Spier. Permission of Doubleday & Co., Inc. and World's Work Ltd.

childish. If you look at the books Randolph Caldecott illustrated, or those books that A. A. Milne and Kenneth Grahame created, you can quickly learn that to talk down — or to draw down — to a child is senseless. Children are good judges of quality. A good children's book should appeal equally to parents."

Peter Spier's greatest pleasure in life is books and the making of books. He summed his feelings up beautifully by stating: "I look at little Kathryn and Thomas, and I think of all the wonderful adventures and experiences that are in store for them through books. They will meet friends I never met and go places I've never been. And you know what? I secretly envy them!"

Kathryn and Thomas interrupted our conversation at this point. They had just returned from swimming. Thomas eagerly

278

took me by the hand to show me his pet gerbils. Kathryn, not wanting to be outdone, took me into her room to show me her pet turtle. Unfortunately, the pressure of my own work prevented me from sharing the sizzling steaks Mrs. Spier had begun to prepare and I returned to New York City regretting I had no more time to spend with the delightful, book-loving Spier family.

OTHER BOOKS BY MR. SPIER (All Doubleday):

And So My Garden Grows (1969).
Of Dikes and Windmills (1969).

Ellen Tarry

ELLEN TARRY AND I laughed at the new title just bestowed on her — Deputy Assistant to the Regional Administrator for Equal Opportunity, Department of Housing and Urban Development, Region I. "That is quite a mouthful, isn't it?" she asked. "Actually my job is to implement equal opportunities for all minority group families in all aspects of the programs developed by the Department."

It is rather impossible to adequately describe Miss Tarry or her many lives. I first met her at an authors' afternoon held in Harlem. It was a joyous occasion for me because the previous Sunday my review of her latest book, *Young Jim: The Story of James Weldon Johnson* (Dodd, Mead, 1967), a book for teenage readers, had appeared in the *New York Times*. Miss Tarry is a delightful woman whose face lights up as she speaks.

The oldest of three girls, she was born and raised in Birmingham, Alabama. She told me how she became an author of juvenile books. "A seventh-grade teacher, Miss Elizabeth Townes, told my classmates that I would one day be a great writer, and I never stoped believing her. Lucy Sprague Mitchell of Bank Street College included me in her first Writers' Workshop, and it was there that my first books for children were born. *Janie*

Belle (Garden City Press, 1940) was my first book; it was a foundling story based on fact. When I heard the details of the case, I remembered how I had often wondered if I had been adopted. I decided it was a situation with which children would identify, especially as there is a strong note of security in the end. *Janie Belle* remains my favorite book because it has more pattern and rhythm than anything else I ever wrote."

One of Miss Tarry's best known works for young readers is *My Dog Rinty* (Viking, 1946), a book she collaborated on with Marie Hall Ets. It was one of the earliest juvenile books to portray the black child in an urban setting. "Marie and I started work on the idea of the book in the summer of 1944 and finished it after my daughter was born that November. The book was dedicated to her; she is the baby who gets the bath in the story. (Miss Tarry's daughter, Elizabeth, is now a teacher in the New York City public schools.) The late May Massee, editor at Viking, brought Marie and me together, and out of this literary association has grown a lasting friendship. Marie had been concerned over the fact that she had never seen a book about black city children. She had observed boys and girls at a community center on the South Side of Chicago but did not know Harlem, the symbol of Negro communities throughout America. It was my privilege to give her an understanding of my community and secure the cooperation of its people in our project."

A second book Miss Tarry authored for young children was *Hezekiah Horton* (Viking, 1942). "Many teachers from the deep South have told me that their students had never seen brown or black faces in a storybook before *Hezekiah Horton* and *My Dog Rinty*. By the same token, I have known white teachers who used these two early books to introduce their students to Negro life."

Miss Tarry is actively involved in civil rights movements. "Civil rights struggles have influenced my books. I am more determined than ever to continue writing about children who are children, regardless of color or creed. A note that forms the basis for all my writing is my creed — the hope that one day all God's children will walk through the open door of opportunity in dignity." This creed is summed up in the closing paragraph of *The Third Door* (McKay, 1955), her autobiography written for adult readers.

Ellen Tarry lives in an apartment on the fringes of Harlem. She is busy, active, and concerned with the problems facing today's America; she loves her work and her writing life, and she loves her new title, even though it is quite a long one!

ANOTHER BOOK BY MISS TARRY:

The Runaway Elephant (Viking, 1950).

Blanche Jennings Thompson

> You must have a silver penny to get into Fairyland. But
> silver pennies are hard to find and it isn't everyone who
> knows where to look for them, even if he has the time; so
> it is for such people . . . that this volume is prepared.

THESE ARE THE OPENING lines of Blanche Jennings Thompson's
classic anthology of verse for children, *Silver Pennies* (Macmillan), published in 1925. It was the author's first book and appeared at the time the "poetry renaissance" was at its height in
America and England. Everyone seemed to be reading poetry
then; almost everyone was writing it too.

Miss Thompson was born "a long, long time ago" in Geneseo,
New York, where she spent her childhood. At 19, she began
teaching 93 first-graders in Rochester, New York. "Half of
them came in the morning, half in the afternoon. They all
learned to read, and they learned poetry by the yard," she recalled. In 1925, having acquired a bachelor's degree, Miss
Thompson worked at the city's normal school preparing young
people to teach. It was during this time that she conducted
several experiments in teaching contemporary poetry. A Macmillan salesman who heard about her work reported back to the
New York office. Thus, she was commissioned to compile *Silver*

Pennies. "The book was first issued in a school edition, which accounts for the short introductions intended as a teaching aid. Critics are sometimes understandably irked by them, but parents and teachers still find them helpful. It remains my favorite book; after all, a book that lasted 40 years and has brought hundreds of letters from children, parents, and teachers does endear itself to the author.

"Because *Silver Pennies* turned out to be such a success, Macmillan kept me busy for several years, chiefly on anthologies." Acceptance as an author led to several religious books and work on textbooks for Harcourt, Brace. This confirmed her belief that "if your first book is a success, you don't have to do any marketing thereafter. Of course, you do have to have ideas, but the world is full of ideas." Miss Thompson's anthology of religious poetry, *With Harp and Lute* (out of print), was illustrated by Kate Seredy, the writer-illustrator who won the 1938 Newbery Award for *The White Stag* (Viking, 1937). "Kate was just getting started. She was commissioned to do the illustrations for *With Harp and Lute.* With some of the drawings in her portfolio, she went to see May Massee, at Viking Press. Miss Massee said to Kate, 'Why don't you write a book of your own?' Kate Seredy went home and wrote her internationally famous book *The Good Master* (Viking, 1935)."

In 1938 *More Silver Pennies* (Macmillan) was published. Commenting on the development of her anthologies, Miss Thompson stated, "In compiling anthologies, collecting the material can take many years for one has to locate the owners of the copyrights, sign unintelligible request forms in triplicate, and track down elusive authors of maverick magazine poems. Just one poem may require as many as half a dozen letters. The publisher needs months to find a suitable illustrator, calculate costs, decide upon format, and attend to all the meticulous editorial details incidental to publishing of a book."

Miss Thompson continued her teaching career while writing. "I was a teacher for 50 years, teaching at every level from first year to the university. In 1948 I left the public school system and became a lecturer at the University of Rochester. I worked there until a taxi accident put an end to my teaching." For the past 38 years, Miss Thompson has lived in one room on the eleventh floor of a residential hotel in Rochester. "Although I am 81 years old now, I still enjoy talking and playing finger games or cards with young children. I like to read and discuss poetry with children of all ages. I enjoy ballet and music — my tastes are reprehensibly square — and for diversion, I like to play on a flute recorder and a little African kalimba, a reed instument like a tiny harp. I always wear blue. I am single — and completely without frustrations," she said.

When *Silver Pennies* was published in Braille, Miss Thompson determined to learn Braille herself. In 1948 she received a Braille certificate and since has transcribed many books, including her own, so that blind children can read them.

On July 16, 1968, Miss Thompson autographed my well-worn copy of *Silver Pennies*. I treasure this small volume for many reasons, but mainly because she helped me find a silver penny a long, long time ago.

ANOTHER BOOK BY MISS THOMPSON:

All the Silver Pennies (Macmillan, 1967).

Alvin Tresselt

ALVIN TRESSELT (*treh* selt) and I met for lunch at the intimate
Side Door Cafe on Manhattan's East Side. It is a place where
he frequently eats as it is just around the corner from Parents'
Magazine Press where he serves as editor of the company's
juvenile division.

Mr. Tresselt is an attractive man. He wears well-tapered
clothes and sprouts a recently developed, sculptured beard. "I
was at a meeting in Bologna, Italy, recently," he chuckled, "and
I returned to New York via London on a Thursday and didn't
have to go into the office until the following Monday. When I
went into the bathroom to shave on Monday morning, I looked
at myself, looked at the beard, and said, 'I'm not going to let you
go to waste!' "

Mr. Tresselt's home is in Redding, Connecticut, about a two-
hour ride from mid-Manhattan. "I take the New Haven
Railroad into work each morning — me and the *New York
Times*. I read the paper to Port Chester, then go to sleep until I
reach the city. I've spent about a year's time just traveling on
that train!" he stated. His wife, Blossom Budney, also an author
of children's books, is currently a college student. "Blossom decided to begin college, did, and now loves it. She is going to

make a lifetime career out of going to college!" The Tresselts have two daughters, Ellen Victoria and India Rachael.

Mr. Tresselt was born in Passaic, New Jersey, on September 30, 1916, across the street from an industrial factory. His childhood was divided between the city, from September through June, and a farm during the summers. Memories of the farm were pleasant ones and inspired many of his books for children. He was always curious about nature and its phenomena and enjoyed the sights, sounds, tastes, and smells of country life.

"In school, from kindergarten through twelfth grade, I always had teachers from New England. I loved their accents and dreamed that one day I would go to New England to live," he declared. He did go to New England but not too deep into it. From 1946–1952 he worked in a defense plant in Connecticut. During this period he met Leonard Weisgard at a party, and they became close friends and housemates. Mr. Weisgard was friendly with the late Margaret Wise Brown, and the three of them became somewhat of a triumvirate in the field of children's literature. "It was Margaret and Lenny who stimulated me to put down on paper my love of nature," Mr. Tresselt declared. "I wrote *Rain Drop Splash* (Lothrop, 1946), and Lenny illustrated it."

The following year Mr. Weisgard won the Caldecott Award for *The Little Island* (Doubleday, 1946), written by Golden MacDonald — the pen name of Margaret Wise Brown. *Rain Drop Splash* was runner-up for the award that same year.

Mr. Tresselt spoke fondly of Margaret Wise Brown. "She was fun, filled with life, totally unpedictable. She had a passion for fur; her whole apartment was done in fur — fur rugs, fur pillows, she even had fur doorknobs!" (One of Miss Brown's successful books, *Little Fur Family* (Harper, 1946), was even bound in fur!)

In 1947 Mr. Tresselt wrote *White Snow, Bright Snow* (Lothrop), a beautiful book illustrated by Roger Duvoisin, which tells of adults' discomforts in a snowstorm compared with children's elation when snow finally comes. It won the Caldecott Award in 1948. In the early 1950's, Mr. Tresselt worked in New York's B. Altmans & Co., a Fifth Avenue department store, as an interior designer. Because of the success of his books, he was offered the position of editor of a new magazine, *Humpty Dumpty,* which was to be published by Parents' Magazine Press. He took the job and served as editor for 12 years. He continued to write books for young children, including the popular *Wake Up, City* (Lothrop, 1957), *Wake Up, Farm* (Lothrop, 1955), and *Hide and Seek Fog* (Lothrop, 1965), all illustrated by his friend Roger Duvoisin.

Currently he is editor of the Parents' Magazine Press juvenile line and is still busy producing books for young boys and girls — others as well as his own.

SOME OTHER BOOKS BY MR. TRESSELT:

Sun Up (Lothrop, 1949).
A Thousand Lights and Fireflies (Parents, 1965).
The Legend of the Willow Plate (coauthored with Nancy Cleaver, Parents, 1968).
It's Time Now (Lothrop, 1969).

Brinton Turkle

I ARRIVED AT THE apartment of Arthur Bell, former publicity director at Viking Press, just in time to join the pizza party being held in honor of the publication of Brinton Turkle's *The Fiddler of High Lonesome* (Viking, 1968). Many people from the book world were there, carefully juggling the mozzarella cheese between lively conversation. Mr. Turkle was sprouting a new short-styled beard, and he looked quite arty sitting on the floor in the center of the room. He was quietly beaming over the enthusiasm generated by his new book, quietly, because Mr. Turkle is a quiet, modest man.

Like many illustrators of children's books, Mr. Turkle has been drawing pictures for as long as he can remember. He was born and spent most of his childhood in Alliance, Ohio. "I was always drawing," he told me. "Unfortunately, none of my school teachers appreciated it. If only one elementary school teacher had egged me on, I think I would have acquired art skills much earlier than I did. In senior high school, I used to sit in a history class and copy pictures of people such as Marie Antoinette and Napoleon. The teacher of this class encouraged me to draw, and I did. I learned more about history that year than I ever did before!"

Mr. Turkle's first ambitions were directed toward a theatrical career; however, the insecurity inherent in the theatre eliminated this possibility for him. He worked in advertising in Chicago for a man who collected odd items for various trade magazines for the milling, paper, and meat packing industries. After several years, he left Chicago because of the tensions of the city. He married, and he and his wife moved to Santa Fe, New Mexico, where he lived for ten years. There he put his knowledge of the theatre to work. He directed plays, acted in them, and even designed sets. His interest in the theatre also included work with marionettes, an art he had become skillful in during high school.

He enjoys music, plays the piano, and he loves good food. "I don't like New York City," he stated. "I can't stand the tempo, the pace, the impersonal nature of the city, or the dirt here. I can't even stand the weather." He noted that in Santa Fe "the neighbors' doors are always open; a hand of friendship is always out."

The first book he illustrated was an adult book about a narcotics agent. "After that I worked on college texts, gradually coming down through the grades to picture books," he laughed. One ambition was to write and illustrate three of his own books so that he could dedicae them to each of his three children — Jonathan, Matilda, and Haynes — an aim that was finally fulfilled in 1968. *Obadiah, the Bold* (Viking, 1965) was dedicated to Jonathan; *The Magic of Millicent Musgrave* (Viking, 1967) to Matilda; and *The Fiddler of High Lonesome* to Haynes.

George Woods, children's book editor of the *New York Times* stated in a review of *The Fiddler of High Lonesome* that "the book is like a deep draught of mountain dew." This might very well sum up Brinton Turkle, for like his books, he is a man as fresh as mountain dew and as homespun as the lovely characters he creates with his magic pen.

SOME OTHER BOOKS BY MR. TURKLE:

Eve Merriam. *The Story of Ben Franklin* (Scholastic Book Services, 1965).

Bettye Hill Braucher. *Belinda and Me* (Viking, 1966).

Ann McGovern. *If You Grew Up with Abraham Lincoln* (Four Winds Press, 1966).

Thy Friend, Obadiah (Viking, 1969).

The Sky Dog (Viking, 1969).

Tamara Kitt. *Jake* (Abelard-Schuman, 1969).

May Garelick. *Just Suppose* (Scholastic Book Services, 1969).

From THE FIDDLER OF HIGH LONESOME by Brinton Turkle, © 1968 by Brinton Turkle. All rights reserved. Permission of The Viking Press, Inc.

Janice May Udry

JANICE MAY UDRY's (*yoo* dri) first book was published in 1956. The title, *A Tree Is Nice* (Harper), is a well-known one among teachers, librarians, parents, and, of course, children. Probably one of the greatest testimonials a book can receive is to be well-worn by boys and girls. I was leafing through a well used copy recently in New York's Donnell Library, when a girl of about seven years old came over to me, looked at me, looked at the book, and asked: "Can you read it?"

"Yes, I can," I answered.

"I read that book, too," she said. "I can read it. Want me to read it to you?"

I naturally responded with an affirmative, and this pretty little miss read *A Tree Is Nice* to me! Upon finishing the book she remarked, "That's my favorite story!" And she dashed off to look at some other picture books on a nearby shelf.

The book, illustrated by Marc Simont, won the Caldecott Award in 1956. Mrs. Udry has never met the illustrator, but they seem to make a perfect team. In his Caldecott Award acceptance speech, Mr. Simont remarked, "In *A Tree Is Nice*, Janice May Udry had given me everything an artist could want in a picture book manuscript. The idea of *A Tree Is Nice* is so fundamental and uncluttered that when I first read it, I said to myself, 'Now, why didn't I think of that?' . . . *A Tree Is Nice* has a solid basic idea presented with simplicity and charm; all I had to do was keep pace with it."

Mrs. Udry related how the book developed. "I am so fond of trees that I wanted everybody else to love them too. I remember the plum tree where I had my swing, where I played pirate ship, and where I had birthday parties when I was a child. I've seen children playing house in the shade of an inadequate bush when there was no tree in their yard, and I thought it was too bad they must play house without a tree. I am tree conscious perhaps. At the time I wrote this book we were living in the heart of the Valencia orange country in Southern California. Even more lovely than the orange trees there are the big trees — the eucalyptus, the live oaks, the peppers, and the sycamores. The suburban tracts of new homes seem very sad to me because there are no trees. When my husband and I wanted to buy a house recently, we wouldn't even look at real estate without grown trees."

The Udrys now live in Chapel Hill, North Carolina. "The trees of Chapel Hill make it a beautiful little town. Our house is small and gray and surrounded by trees," she commented. Her husband, Richard, is a sociologist and professor at the University of North Carolina. They met while they were both students at Northwestern University in Evanston, Illinois. They have two daughters, Leslie, 13, and Susan, 7. Personal pleasures include "Our pet Harvey, a small, white, Maltese dog, and trips to the North Carolina beaches and mountains. We frequently return to California to visit. I particularly enjoy reading and looking at various kinds of artwork."

Mrs. Udry was born in Jacksonville, Illinois. "I grew up on a quiet, elm-shaded street in a small college town. I had no brothers or sisters, but there were plenty of relatives in Jacksonville." After graduating from college, she worked for a year in a Chicago nursery school. "While working at the nursery, I became interested in the wonderful books for small children that were being published. I especially admired the books of Margaret Wise Brown," she declared. She decided to try writing her own book, and the result was *A Tree Is Nice*. Three years later, *The Moon Jumpers* (Harper, 1959) was published. Illustrated by Maurice Sendak, this was a 1960 Caldecott Honor Book.

"All of my books come from remembering my own childhood and from listening to and watching my daughters grow up. I sometimes read my manuscripts to them before sending them to publishers. *The Moon Jumpers* came directly from my childhood years. I remembered the hot summer evenings in Illinois. No one had air-conditioning then, and being allowed to play outside after dark was delightful to me."

In 1961 Mrs. Udry and Mr. Sendak again collaborated, producing *Let's Be Enemies* (Harper), a tongue-in-cheek look at children's quarrels. The book was recently translated into German. Mrs. Udry recalled that her older daughter, Leslie, used to say to her, "Tell me about a mean thing." She would then oblige with stories about the meanest things she could think of — to the delight of her daughter — and out of these many-times-told tales grew the delightful collection *The Mean Mouse and Other Stories* (Harper, 1962).

Mrs. Udry recently wrote a sequel, *What Mary Jo Wanted* (Whitman, 1968), to her popular *What Mary Jo Shared* (Whitman, 1966); both books portray a young black girl in true-to-life situations.

Closing our interview, Mrs. Udry added, "Marc Simont is now preparing the illustrations for my new book, *Glenda* (Harper, 1969). This is my first book since *A Tree Is Nice* to be illustrated by him."

SOME OTHER BOOKS BY MRS. UDRY:

If You're a Bear (Whitman, 1967).
Mary Ann's Mud Day (Harper, 1967).

Tomi Ungerer

FORTY-SECOND STREET between Seventh and Eighth Avenues in New York City is a kaleidoscope of people, movie houses, book stores, pizza stands, and traffic jams. It is the epitome of New York on the move. It was on 42nd Street, high above the ground, that I met Tomi Ungerer (*toh* me *ung* ger er) in his sixteenth floor atelier. Entering his studio is somewhat like walking on the street below for the first time. Paraphernalia is all over; the room is like a fun house at a giant amusement park. A dentist's chair sits beside his desk; pictures of Lyndon Baines Johnson and Elvis Presley stand on a shelf, sharing space with books, a wooden skeleton, a toy version of King Kong madly embracing a young doll, and 101 other items here, there, and everywhere.

Mr. Ungerer is over six feet tall and dashingly handsome, with sky-blue eyes and a well-sculptured, well-trimmed beard. Born in Alsace, France, on November 28, 1931, he was the youngest of two brothers and one sister. His father, a manufacturer of astronomical clocks, passed away leaving him with little memory of a father-son relationship. When he was eight years old, war broke out between Germany and France; in the early part of the war the Alsace-Lorraine region came under Nazi occupation. Mr. Ungerer has unpleasant recollections of the war years. "I went to school in Germany, and I was brainwashed by the Germans. Naturally, because of them and their tactics, I am totally anti-German."

In 1957, at the age of 25, he came to New York City. "When I arrived here I was very sick with pleurisy and rheumatism. I remember nearly collapsing in my publisher's office," he recalled. "Ursula Nordstrom, my friend and editor, gave me a $500 advance for my first children's book, which helped me to start anew. This book was *The Mellops Go Flying* (Harper, 1957)."

Surrounded by avant-garde artwork and objects he has collected, he bubbled with conversation. "I have a houseful of antique toys — I have steam locomotives that date back to before 1900. I don't have a toy *collection*, I have a toy *museum*! I buy a great many of my toys from France. I love making kites. Kites are wonderful. I love botany, too. And speleology, archeology, mineralogy, and geology!"

Mr. Ungerer's books for children include a number of atypical, but lovable, characters — the Mellops are a family of pigs, *Emile* (Harper, 1960) is an octopus, *Crictor* (Harper, 1958) is a boa constrictor, and *Orlando, The Brave Vulture* (Harper, 1966) is a bird. Commenting on his books for children, he stated, "I do children's books for myself — for my personal enjoyment. My daughter, Phoebe, now seven, hasn't even seen some of my books. She found one in school recently and brought it home to show *me*!

"I wrote *Zeralda's Ogre* (Harper, 1967; a tale of a little girl's conquest of a terrifying child-eating ogre through the magic of gourmet cooking) in one-half hour. The artwork took me four weeks. Children's books are merely captions put on pictures! I hate children's books that are written down to a child's level. Books like these have nothing, nothing at all."

Mr. Ungerer works quickly; he can finish an entire book in one day if he sets his mind to it. Besides writing and illustrating children's books, he is a brilliant satirist. His work has appeared in many of the major adult slick magazines such as *Playboy* and

From ZERALDA'S OGRE by Tomi Ungerer, © 1967 by Tomi Ungerer. Permission of Harper & Row, Publishers.

Holiday; he has done work for Canadian Broadcasting Company, New York's newspaper *The Village Voice,* and the State of New York. He paints and sculpts and likes pastrami, coffee, the poems of e. e. cummings, many kinds of music, movies, the color black, sex, trees, and his work. He is quick and witty. He moves around like a man being shot from a cannon. He is impossible, yet delightful to be with.

Leaving his studio, the 42nd Street melee did not seem as vibrant as it had before. Prior to boarding the Eighth Avenue subway, which would whisk me back uptown, an advertisement for *The Village Voice* newspaper caught my eye. The ad showed a woman pushing a green-faced, long-bearded man in a wheelchair; above their heads was a stork descending upon them with a shouting, newborn baby. The caption proclaimed, "Expect the Unexpected!" Modestly, in the lower right-hand corner, appeared "Tomi Ungerer."

Modestly, indeed!

SOME OTHER BOOKS BY MR. UNGERER:

The Three Robbers (Atheneum, 1960).
One, Two, Where's My Shoe? (Harper, 1964).
Andre Hodeir. *Warwick's Three Bottles* (Grove, 1966).
William Cole, editor. *Oh, What Nonsense* (Viking, 1966).
———. *A Case of the Giggles* (World, 1967).
Moon Man (Harper, 1967).
Ask Me a Question (Harper, 1968).
Andre Hodeir. *Cleopatra Goes Sledding* (Grove, 1968).
William Cole. *That Pest, Jonathan* (Harper, 1970).

Sandol Stoddard Warburg

TOWARD THE END OF MAY in 1967, I sat down and wrote a letter to Sandol Stoddard Warburg:

> Dear Mrs. Warburg:
>   Several months ago I came across *The Thinking Book* (Little, Brown, 1960) on the bottom of a library shelf in Fair Lawn, New Jersey. I began to thumb through the book and just cannot tell you how I felt reading it. I brought it to the attention of Bank Street College's Communication Laboratories, and they loved it, too. It is going to be made into one of their Reading Incentive Films,* starring Sidney Poitier. . . .

On June 6, I received a lengthy reply, along with a gift, Mrs. Warburg's *I Like You* (Houghton, 1965) inscribed "I like you, Lee Hopkins!" and signed SSW. This was the beginning of a friendship that has continued.

Sandol Stoddard Warburg is a remarkable woman. Besides writing books for children, she is a housewife and mother to six children: Anthony, 18, Peter, 17, Gerald, 14, Jason, 7, and two stepchildren, Katherine, 16 and Suzanne, 11. "Being a mother

---

* This film won one of the 1969 American Film Festival awards.

of six fascinating children and a wife of one very absorbing man,
I am a cook, seamstress, painter, decorator, chauffeur, nurse,
tutor, psychiatrist, operator of a summer camp, cleaning woman,
carpenter, interpreter of dreams, plumber, hairdresser, banker,
social counselor, laundress, and, oh yes, confidant and mistress!
Other than that I have time on my hands!" she exclaimed. "When
I'm not painting the house or setting plants in the garden or giving haircuts to the kids or sewing on buttons or running down
to the drugstore to refill my tranquilizer prescription, I'm right
here pounding away at the usual machine — the typewriter."
Her husband, Frank Dollard, is the executive vice-president of
San Francisco State College.

One wonders how a woman who has such a lot to do can ever
get things done. "My work habits are terrible," she remarked.
"I don't know how I get my ideas. I know when I am going to
write a book because it makes me jittery and sick at my stomach;
then, nothing will do until I finish it. The laundry piles up, the
children eat dry cereal and hot dogs, and the garden goes to
weeds. I try my ideas out on the children sometimes, but if they
do not like them, I just get mad and go right on with what I'm
doing."

"*The Thinking Book* (her first work) developed during a
bad sinus attack in the laundromat at Buzzard's Bay, Massachusetts, in June 1958. I think I was trying to cheer myself up. *Curl
Up Small* (Houghton, 1964; a book of brief poetic dialogues)
came about while I was reading the pre-Socratic Greek philoso-
phers and trying to get the children ready for bed at the same
time. The two events sort of melded, if you see what I mean."

Mrs. Warburg also did a version of *St. George and the
Dragon* (Houghton, 1963), a book for older readers adapted
from *The Faerie Queene* by Edmund Spenser. "This one I did
because I itch for mid-century America, California particularly,
because people go around not having the least idea of their heritage, their identity, or their obligation to the human race. An

American can't know who he really is unless he makes some viable connection between himself and the mainstream of America. *St. George and the Dragon* deals with the basic image of our civilization and what's left of it. So, by putting it into a form comprehensible to the young, I hoped to perform a useful service by helping children, including my own, to know better who they are and where they're at."

About her writing she stated, "In writing, one tries to be more and more honest all the time — more and more comprehensive. This, of course, need not include the 'entertainments,' which are purely for fun, like a pinwheel letting off sparks. But in the major efforts, one gives all of oneself each time, developing a feeling of affection, even passion; a work is like the feeling a passionate woman has for her newborn baby or a passionate gardener has for his newest rose, which always seems the most perfect ever."

Mrs. Warburg was born in Birmingham, Alabama, and grew up in New Haven, Connecticut. "Family life in upper-middle class New England in the 30's was pretty constipated. I went to lousy public schools till sixth grade, then to an expensive, private school, which was also lousy," she recalled.

The Warburgs live in California in a remodeled barn located in a beautiful countryside. "We have redwoods, raccoons, deer, thousands of kids, dogs, cats, horses, and rich old ladies living in enormous houses and renting their garages illegally to artists so they can pay taxes. Me? I am vain, strong-willed, shy, witty, frank, sensual, snobbish, cranky, overly quick in all my reactions, passionately loyal to those I love, and a fearsome enemy, I trust, to those who go about doing the devil's work.

"I enjoy just about everything except scraping ice cream wrappings off the floor of my station wagon. Given my choice, I would walk on the beach south of Making, an island of Mani, Hawaii, arguing with my husband and watching the children ride on the surf. Then we would have boiled breadfruit with hollandaise sauce for dinner and fall asleep under the enormous stars."

The last page of Mrs. Warburg's delightful *I Like You* reads:

> I guess I don't know why I like you really
> Why do I like you
> I guess I just like you
> I guess I just like you
> Because I like you.

And do you know what, Sandol Stoddard Warburg? I like you, too. And so do all the boys and girls who curl up small and look at your imaginative picture books.

SOME OTHER BOOKS BY MRS. WARBURG (All Houghton):

My Very Own Special Particular Private and Personal Cat (1963).
From Ambledee to Zumbledee (1968).
Growing Time (1969).

Lynd Ward
May McNeer

LYND WARD ON LYND WARD:

Age: 63
Height: 5′6½″
Weight: 152 lbs
   I wear bifocals, have brown and gray hair, which is getting thin on top, and I have bushy eyebrows, so says my wife.

Mr. Ward and his writer-wife, May McNeer, live in a suburban area of New Jersey, just ten miles north of the George Washington Bridge. They have a tiny house, with a large studio attached to it, set back in the woods on an old lumber road.

Mr. Ward was born on June 26, 1905, in Chicago, Illinois. The son of a Methodist minister, he spent his boyhood in Illinois, Massachusetts, and New Jersey; he attended high school in Englewood, New Jersey, and graduated from Columbia University with a major in fine arts in 1926. May McNeer received a diploma at the same time, and during graduation week they were married.

"I became interested in children's books while studying at Teachers College at Columbia. I decided that books, illustrating, and graphic arts were fields that interested me most," Mr. Ward declared.

His wife's background is quite different from his. "I was brought up by my mother, a gentle artist with a twinkle in her eye, and her identical twin sister, who was given to picking up and moving suddenly on impulse and who, when she moved, took us with her. My 'mothers' were widows. My brother and I acquired a reluctant firsthand knowledge of almost every part of southern geography until whim took us back to Tampa, Florida, our home base. As a result, I was never allowed to finish a term in grammar school and have gaps in my education large enough to compete with the Grand Canyon. Yet, somehow or other, and mainly by good luck, I did arrive in the Journalism School at Columbia University," she told me.

Immediately after their marriage, the Wards sailed for Europe, where Miss McNeer worked on her first children's book while Mr. Ward studied at the National Academy at Leipzig in Germany. Returning to the United States one year later, Mr. Ward's first illustrated book, for adults, appeared; in 1929 his first book for children came out. From that date to the present Mr. Ward has illustrated more than one hundred books for both adults and children. Many were authored by his wife and several were written by his daughter, Nanda Ward Haynes. (The Wards have a second daughter, Robin Ward Savage, and they have three grandchildren.)

In 1952 Mr. Ward's *The Biggest Bear* (Houghton) was published. "The book came about naturally," he commented. "Each year since my childhood, I have spent summers at Lonely Lake in the backwoods of Canada, a remote area in Ontario. I often saw bear cubs tied up, as a sort of pet, at nearby farms." *The Biggest Bear* tells the story of young Johnny Orchard and his pet cub who grows and grows and grows; the book won the Caldecott Award in 1953. He used opaque watercolors to depict his beloved Canadian countryside.

Thirteen years later Mr. Ward created *Nic of the Woods* (Houghton, 1965), which tells the story of a cocker spaniel, Nickle, son of Dime, who becomes lost in the Canadian woods. "*Nic of the Woods* is one of my favorite books," he stated, "for it represents the transformation of experience into a book."

Regarding his work habits he said, "Most of my time is spent on illustration. I do not consider myself a writer but rather an artist whose stories sometimes need some words. *The Biggest Bear* was finished completely as a sequence of pictures. Then, a minimum of words were added to hold it together. What little I know about writing is due to living and working with a fine and sensitive writer — my wife. We have worked on many books together in which there has been an approximately equal distribution of responsibility between words and pictures. This type of collaboration would probably not be possible unless the writer and artist work closely together at all stages — planning, research, and execution."

Besides using lithography, pen and ink, oils, and gouache, Mr. Ward also works in wood engraving. "I participate in many print exhibitions," he noted. He is a member of the National Academy and also exhibits in the annual exhibitions of The Society of American Graphic Artists, of which he was president for six years. His work is included in the permanent collections of The Smithsonian Institution, The Library of Congress, and The Newark Museum.

I asked Mr. Ward about future writing-illustrating plans. He replied, "I usually have a half-dozen projects simmering on the back of the stove, and I never know which one will get cooked first." For leisure, Mr. Ward enjoys carpentry, stonework, and folk singing with the family while he accompanies them on the accordian or melodica. Miss McNeer described favorite things for me. "Our cherished possessions include a gothic bookcase from my old home in the south, an ancient wooden Indian, and books and books and books. Probably our most fascinating volume is a copy of *The Biggest Bear,* bound in real bearskin, which was sent to Lynd one Christmas by his friends at Houghton Mifflin.

This is the only book that ever aroused the enthusiasm of Mr. Scratch, our Persian alley cat. We continue to hope that the binding was not actually cut from the hide of Johnny Orchard's biggest bear!"

Some Other Books by Miss McNeer, Illustrated by Mr. Ward:

Martin Luther (Abingdon, 1953).
America's Abraham Lincoln (Houghton, 1957).
Armed with Courage (Abingdon, 1957).
America's Mark Twain (Houghton, 1962).

Leonard Weisgard

LEONARD WEISGARD, (*wise* gard) his wife Phyllis, who is a designer and filmmaker, and their three children, Abigail, Christina, and Ethan live in an old Connecticut farmhouse. This talented illustrator works in a studio facing a field where Ethan Allen, the American Revolutionary War soldier, was born. His studio is built like an old meeting house and "if you stand on your head and look up," Mr. Weisgard noted, "you can see that it resembles the hull of a sailing vessel." He enjoys the area where he lives. "There are many birds, woodchucks, cats, dogs, opossum, foxes, squirrels, horses, cows, children, some people and loads of crawling things and flying things and burrowing things and scampering things all around. There are no buses nor trains nor taxis coming through this small town, but there is an old quarry, an old mine, and lots of garnet and other stones."

Mr. Weisgard describes himself as neither fat nor thin, young nor old. "I am a mixture of many things and am mostly alarmed at how little I know!" He wonders a great deal "about this surprising world we live in. I wonder mightily about our educational process and do believe we learn far more than we ever realize from people outside of schools, from those we love, respect, and admire and sometimes a great deal from those we intensely dislike. Do we learn more standing still in one place or moving about a great deal? How do we learn? May Garelick, the author, shrewdly asked *Where Does the Butterfly Go When It Rains?* (Scott, 1961). Sometimes not knowing a specific answer can be most provocative. A child asking usually finds himself an answer before he even asks; he goes to books for answers to questions that are perennially a mystery to us. I respect and admire the potential of children more than anything else. Their intelligence and sensitiveness amaze and delight me, and they make us humans who believe we may be adult seem extremely foolish."

As a parent of three children, he remarked, "It takes courage and wisdom and adventure to be a parent and a great deal of energy! We do not like to make the same mistakes our own parents might have made, so we may make mistakes in another way. We all err as we learn. We hope we learn. It is harder as we grow larger!"

Mr. Weisgard was born in New Haven, Connecticut, and grew up in New York City, England, and Brooklyn, New York. "We left New Haven, where my father owned a grocery store, and moved to London, Manchester, Liverpool, and places my father's relatives came from in England. Returning to New York, I attended the city's public schools. A teacher in the lower grades inaugurated an art squad after school, which helped provoke my interest in drawing and painting. Another teacher excited my interest in the theatre. And always it was the excitement of growing and young friends who believed in what they were doing that encouraged me. My own parents were usually aghast at what I was doing, and my interest in modern dance puzzled all!"

Mr. Weisgard studied art at the Pratt Institute and at the New School of Social Research in New York. He worked on many of the country's top magazines including *Good Housekeeping, The New Yorker,* and *Harper's Bazaar.* He also painted murals and designed costumes and sets for the ballet. He decided to illustrate books for young children "because most books for young people were so dreadful. Even school books were outrageously bad. My friends, who felt deeply about books, art, and the state of the world, felt we could do better and that I, too, should try. Because the books that had inspired us had come in a limited way from Europe, we felt we, too, could move young people's books forward and give a needed sense of involvement between the child and books.

"My first book, *The Siamese Pussy* (1937, out of print), developed as an outlet for a wish of my own — a need to leave this world and travel to another. I was the cat in the story who traveled on the ferry from Staten Island to New York as a compromise to going to Europe; I am still enchanted by what Manhattan has to offer a young person. My art studies were of value to me, but I also learned how to illustrate books by learning to dance, living, breathing, being with children, with people, being alone, reading, writing, traveling, brooding, dreaming, beachcombing, wondering, and, mostly, listening to Margaret Wise Brown."

In 1947 the Caldecott Medal was awarded to Mr. Weisgard for *The Little Island* (Doubleday, 1946), written by Golden MacDonald, the pen name used by Margaret Wise Brown, a woman who wrote many wonderful and lasting books for children. Miss Brown and Mr. Weisgard collaborated on many books and were the creators of well-known "The Noisy Books" a classic series in the field of children's literature (originally published by Scott, now published by Harper).

Mr. Weisgard spoke fondly of his work with Miss Brown. "The Noisy Books" grew out of a real need for exciting and provocative material for the very young. "Sometimes illustrating one of Margaret's books was much like a very precious form of madness not yet clinically identified; they were indeed a challenge. Margaret was like an elephant child; she always remembered what it was like herself to be a child and still continued to grow to be larger. She had, although she denied it, an innate sense of rhythm and music and toward the end of her life wrote some fine songs and music. Her life, like some extraordinary earthworm, was segmented into many paradoxical pieces, from rabbit hunter to rabbit writer, from the sublime to the ridiculous. Work, work habits, and structure were meaningless words to her; she just poured — sometimes with keen talent, sometimes with

From SALT BOY by Mary Perrine and Leonard Weisgard. Permission of Houghton Mifflin Co.

indifference — and writing-work, in any traditional sense, was not for her."

Mr. Weisgard commented on the development of his own books, their ideas, and their styles. "Books sometimes have grown from the moment of shaving, a moment of pain, a time of listening to children, from out of a dark tunnel, a groping into the past, or a stretching into the future, from amorphic places of the blackness of despair, or the joyousness of the bursting heart. And sometimes, even from the noise of a subway train.

"I have no favorites among my books. If I did, I would then stop doing them. Different books had different reasons for their birth and conception; some pleased me more than others. Illustrating *The Secret River* (Scribner, 1955), was indeed a challenge, for here was a book telling a story about a different child, and Marjorie Kinnan Rawlings told it so well that no one realized the child was a deprived, dark-skinned girl poet."

From his words, one can see that Leonard Weisgard is a sensitive individual who lives his life, and works for the best that he can give. "I like to believe I am a human being concerned with all human beings and creatures alive on this earth." In closing, he enumerated his favorite things: "I like primitive artifacts, trade signs, wooden Indians, whirligigs, weather vanes, old furniture, and old, old, old things. I also like to travel in a small boat through rivers, meeting people, knowing trees, flowers, birds, and beasts, and having friends."

Leonard Weisgard's books have won him many, many young friends — the children he admires, believes in, and produces beautiful books for.

SOME OTHER BOOKS BY MR. WEISGARD:

Margaret Wise Brown. *The City Noisy Book* (Harper, 1939).
———. *The Country Noisy Book* (Harper, 1940).
Golden MacDonald. *The Little Lost Lamb* (Doubleday, 1945).
Mary Le Duc O'Neill. *Hailstones and Halibut Bones* (Doubleday, 1961).
Aileen Fisher. *Like Nothing at All* (T. Y. Crowell, 1962).
Doris Orgel. *On the Sand Dune* (Harper, 1968).
May Garelick. *Look at the Moon* (Scott, 1969).

Brian Wildsmith

I BOUGHT MY NIECE, Kimberly Ann, a toy kaleidoscope for Christmas. After studying the flashing designs for several minutes, she remarked, "It's pretty! Like my 1-2-3 book."

The 1-2-3 book Kim was referring to was *Brian Wildsmith's 1-2-3's* (Watts, 1965), a volume bursting with color and, like all the books he illustrates, resembling the magic and excitement of a kaleidoscope. *1-2-3's* is one of Mr. Wildsmith's favorite books. "I like it because it's a complete book for me. It is beautifully printed, and despite most of the pundits' outcries, it has more than justified itself commercially. In *1-2-3's* I have taken the basic abstract forms — the rectangle, the triangle, and the circle — and related them to numbers. The book progresses through these basic shapes; it builds up into recognizable forms to give the child an understanding of the beauty and fascination of figures and also makes him aware that the world around us is, broadly speaking, built up around basic shapes."

Mr. Wildsmith was trained as a painter at the Slade School of Fine Art, University College, London, England. "I developed a love, a great love of all kinds and all periods of art. I feel that I received a firm structural base on what art is rather than just how to do it." He became interested in illustrating books for children when he and his wife, Aurel, began to raise their own. The Wildsmiths have four children — Claire, 11, Rebecca, 10, Anne, 6, and Simon, 4. "I realized just what an appalling gulf there was between what I knew to be good and fine in painting and illustrating and the awful damage being done to children's minds via children's books. I decided to commit myself fully to doing books for boys and girls. I believe in the Jesuit saying, 'Give me a child under seven years and he is mine forever.' How often have we left all that is good and free in our culture to be brought before the child too late, when his taste had already been formed, maltreated, or warped. By attracting a child to stories in pictures, consciously or subconsciously the shapes and colors seep into his artistic digestive system, and he is aroused and stimulated by them."

"I often try out material on my children, and I observe their every reaction intently. Children are fascinated with color and form, and there is no missing a child's spontaneous outburst. I adore children's writings, paintings, and often wish I could do as well." In 1963, his book *Brian Wildsmith's ABC* (Watts, 1962), was awarded the Kate Greenaway Medal, an award given by the Library Association of England to the most distinguished illustrated book published in Great Britain.

Mr. Wildsmith was born in "a strict mining village environ in Yorkshire, England, totally without culture." He recalled, "I was the oldest of four children and had a free life with very few restrictions from my parents. I was not at all interested in art; I never even saw any. I was very interested in sports and music, being a passionate piano player and cricketer — cricket is one of the most popular sports in England and one that remains a mystery to all but Englishmen! I had decided to become a research chemist, but at the last moment some strange intuition guided me away from it. Thank God!"

The Wildsmiths recently bought a lovely new house in Dulwich, London, with a garden studio surrounded by woods and parkland. The house lies just beyond the only toll gate left in

From BRIAN WILDSMITH'S WILD ANIMALS. First American publication 1967 by
Franklin Watts, Inc. Permission of Franklin Watts, Inc.

London. His favorite possession is his Blüthner grand piano. "I
saved up my money for 12 years to buy the piano! I love having
people come to my house, and I love to travel. If I didn't have
a family, I would walk around the world. I love to play cricket
and squash, a game that combines elements of tennis and hand-
ball."

During the summers the Wildsmith family live in an apartment in Gerona, Spain, where Mr. Wildsmith does a great deal
of his illustrating. Regarding his work, he told me, "All works
of art are nothing without the elusive quality of creativity —
soul, if you wish. In the final analysis, it is the sheer quality that
matters, not whether one's painting was done by rolling a tractor
over the canvas or was laboriously painted with one strand of

hair. An artistic gift is rather like having fleas — you have to keep scratching."

Brian Wildsmith has made children all over the world happy with his books. Whether he is creating books about numbers, the alphabet, iguanas, owls, unicorns, or queens, he keeps the kids in mind; they know it when they see his finished books!

Some Other Books by Mr. Wildsmith (All published in the U.S. by Franklin Watts):

Brian Wildsmith's Mother Goose (1963).
Brian Wildsmith's Birds (1967).
Brian Wildsmith's Wild Animals (1967).
Brian Wildsmith's Illustrated Bible Stories (1969).

Fables by La Fontaine Illustrated by Mr. Wildsmith:

The Lion and the Rat (1963).
The North Wind and the Sun (1964).
The Rich Man and the Shoemaker (1965).

315

Julia and John Wilson

> As soon as Becky Brooks woke up she remembered her
> birthday party. She could still see the candles lighting up
> her birthday cake last night. She remembered the magic
> moment when her mother had turned out all the lights.
>
> "Becky," she had said, "make a wish. If you blow out all
> the candles, your wish will come true."

THESE WORDS BEGIN the modern-day fantasy, *Becky* (T. Y.
Crowell, 1966), a story of a young black girl who wants a special doll more than anything else in the world. The book was
Julia Wilson's first; it developed from very personal experiences.
Mrs. Wilson recalled, "When our first child was born, we
looked for a birth announcement, but none was appropriate. We
felt that it was most unfitting to send a card with a picture of a
white baby since our baby was black. It was as though there were
no black babies born into this world. To combat this, my husband, John, illustrated our announcement."

Julia Wilson reflected upon other events that helped shape
her writing. "All through my children's growing-up period, I
read books to them with illustrations of white people. Even the
dolls they hugged, kissed, and loved were white, unlike the reality of their own lives. They themselves were black, their own
children would probably be black, and many of the people who

316

hugged, kissed, and loved them were black. As an early child-hood teacher, I knew feelings of inadequacy among minority boys and girls were reinforced by white toys and pictures. The world of books, with few exceptions, pretended that black people didn't exist. So we did something about it. We created *Becky*!"

John Wilson added, "I was able to see this story grow, identify with it, and create images that reflect my feelings about the story. I used crayon drawings for the illustrations, trying to emphasize the sense of gesture in the figures and objects, in order to give a sense of spontaneity and movement."

Mrs. Wilson was born in Chicago and grew up in New York. "My parents are Jewish immigrants from Poland. Since my father remained an unskilled worker, we lived in poor, over-crowded, working-class neighborhoods in Brooklyn. I can remember feeling like a good, quiet, unimportant, unexciting little girl in a boring school system. We left Chicago during the Depression years. My father was unemployed. We had relatives in New York who promised to help him. My father sold fish at an out-door stand in New York for awhile and then joined the people on welfare. His feet could no longer stand the cold, bitter winters."

The Wilsons and their three children, Rebecca, 16, Roy, 13, and Erica, 3, live in a suburban community in Massachusetts. Mr. Wilson is a teacher also, an associate professor at Boston University. Besides teaching and illustrating children's books, he has exhibited artwork throughout the country. A great deal of his work is in private collections. After graduating from Tufts College, he studied at the Museum of Fine Arts in Boston, at Fernand Léger's school in Paris, and at several schools in Mexico City. He commented, "I guess I am most happy when I am completing a drawing or a painting. I like meeting, talking, exchanging ideas with, and relating to people. I enjoy sports, too, particularly swimming and playing table tennis."

Mrs. Wilson enjoys making hooked rugs and jewelry and refurbishing old furniture. She has a personal philosophy about life and the times in which we are living. "I dislike hearing a child

317

made fun of or humiliated or seeing him bored to tears in a class-room. I have worked with black and white children, both middle-class and working-class. I feel that when I respected boys and girls as individuals, allowed them to respect their style, and of-fered them support, understanding, and an exciting program, I could generally see some growth in each child. There was always some chaos, more messiness, from the rigid adult's point of view, in my program, but I am convinced that this is what children thrive on."

She continued, "I like encouraging people to do their thing. I believe that a society needs to be supportive of the people who live in it. That is, a government needs to be responsible to the needs of the people, whether they be economic, social, or psychological in nature. I hope that eventually, with the threat of atomic war-fare, the power that the wealthy and the strong use to gather more for themselves will be replaced by a collective, social power."

SOME OTHER BOOKS BY MR. WILSON:

Jean Craighead George. *Spring Comes to the Ocean* (T. Y. Crowell, 1965).
Joan M. Lexau. *Striped Ice Cream* (Lippincott, 1968).

Rose Wyler
Gerald Ames

"TELL HIM ABOUT CHRIS, the chimpanzee," Gerald Ames suggested to his wife, and Rose Wyler did. "In our book *The First People in the World* (Harper, 1958), the opening words are 'Shake hands with a chimpanzee . . .' Upon publication, the editor thought that a picture of the two of us posing with a chimpanzee would be good publicity. Well, we visited a circus out on Long Island, and it was there that we met Chris, a three-year-old chimp. We had arranged to borrow him for the day to take the publicity photos. The first bit of fun we had with him was en route to New York City. We let him pay a bridge toll. You can imagine the look on the collector's face!

"Even greater complications developed later when we were leaving our apartment building. We boarded the elevator and went down several flights, when all of a sudden it stopped. The superintendent's wife entered the car with her two small children. Both were drinking milk from a bottle. Chris, being a bottle-baby himself, reached for the bottle. At this, the woman began to shout and scream, 'Police! Police! Help! A gorilla, a gorilla!' The end result of this incident was much confusion — and a dispossess notice from the landlord!"

This husband-wife team have had a lifetime of fun and adventure together while working on their various nonfiction trade books for children of all ages. To research and complete such volumes as *Magic Secrets* (Harper, 1967) and *Spooky Tricks* (Harper, 1968), they work with youngsters in their immediate apartment building, a cooperative located in Manhattan's Washington Heights. "Our laboratory is our living room," said Mrs. Ames. "Children of all ages come in to watch me perform magic tricks; after I do them, I explain the 'secrets' to see if they can handle them. If they can, they go into our books; if not, we don't use them. The children actually collaborate with us. For *Magic Secrets* we ransacked the literature on magic to find material children could perform easily. *Spooky Tricks* came about because one youngster wanted some to perform on Halloween; a little girl asked, 'Show us some spooky tricks!' And that is how the volume came to be, including the title!"

The exciting part of the aforementioned books, and others like them that Miss Wyler and Mr. Ames have created, is that through the secrets and tricks primary-age children become acquainted with fundamental science learnings, learnings that pave the way for more advanced thinking.

Rose Wyler was born in the Bronx, New York, and grew up in Weehawken, New Jersey. "I was interested in science from the earliest time I can remember," she stated. "I always had a collection of stones, bugs, or leaves and always wanted to know more about nature. I could never find books on nature as a child, so, at 11, I decided I was going to write them." Throughout her school life she devoted most of her time to the study of nature. In her early twenties, she graduated from Teachers College at Columbia University with the distinction of being the first person ever to receive a master's degree in elementary science. Her varied accomplishments include writing for radio, television, educational films, and encyclopedias and actively working the field of science education from pre-kindergarten to the college level.

Miss Wyler and Mr. Ames, both previously married, combined their families — two boys and one girl. Their daughter, Eva

Lee Baird, coauthored *Science Teasers* (Harper, 1966) with Miss Wyler. The writing team enjoys the outdoors; they spend summers in Maine and occasional vacations on St. John in the Virgin Islands, where they live in the campgrounds and swim and snorkel. "We spend hours on end in the water interviewing fish for the Bureau of Internal Revenue," chuckled Mr. Ames.

"Tell him one more story, the one about the museum," he said, and Rose Wyler obliged. "I was standing in the Museum of Natural History Bookshop one day when an eight-year-old came to the counter to buy *The New Golden Book of Astronomy: An Introduction to the Wonders of Space* (Golden, 1965). After the child paid for the book, I couldn't help but tell him, 'You know, I wrote that book!'

"The child shrugged his shoulders and merely remarked in an unbelieving tone, 'Yeah?'

"Several minutes later the child's teacher came up to me and asked, 'Are you Rose Wyler, the author?'

" 'Yes,' I replied.

" 'Oh!' exclaimed the teacher. 'A child in my class just bought your book and told me that some crazy, little old lady said *she* wrote it!' "

The three of us laughed heartily at this anecdote. My writer friends' eyes twinkled, revealing that they both love their work and the rewards they reap from their endeavors.

SOME OTHER BOOKS BY MISS WYLER AND MR. AMES:

What Makes It Go? (McGraw-Hill, 1958).
Prove It! (Harper, 1963).
The Golden Book of Biology: An Introduction to the Wonders of Life (Golden, 1967, rev. ed.).

Taro Yashima

"JUN ATSUSHI IWAMATSU is my real name. I could not use it during World War II because of my involvement with the Office of Strategic Services. The name Taro Yashima (tar oh yah shee mah) was the symbol of homesickness to me. *Taro* means fat boy, healthy boy; *yashima* means eight islands, old Japan, and peaceful Japan," explained Mr. Yashima.

Mr. Yashima was born in the small Japanese village of Kagoshima on the southern peninsula of Kyushu. His father was a country doctor; his mother served as his father's assistant. After graduating from the village school, Mr. Yashima went to high school and then to the Imperial Art Academy in Tokyo for three years. "I was a rascal in school!" he exclaimed.

In 1939 Mr. Yashima and his artist wife, Mitsu, left their five-year-old son, Mako, and came to the United States to further study art. When war was declared against Japan, they joined the war effort on behalf of the United States. In 1945 Mr. Yashima went to Japan as an officer in the United States Army and found his son who was then 15 years old. Mako rejoined his parents in the United States.

In 1953 Mr. Yashima's first picture book, *The Village Tree* (1955), was published by Viking Press, which has continued to publish his work. "Around 1951–1952 my daughter, Momo, began to ask me for a story. I began to seek my own stories — those inside me — and I thought I could have something to tell her about as long as I existed. A small tree stood in my earliest memories of childhood, almost as if it were a symbol of my childhood. I made *The Village Tree* for our daughter." Momo is a prominent figure in many of the author-illustrator's works.

Mr. Yashima told me about his work habits. "I get a hint of an idea through an inspiration from life. Sometimes this hint is as small as a poppy seed. I set up an envelope to collect any sort of material that seems connected with this seed. I think through the meaning of these materials until they ferment by themselves. The final fermentation is helped by researching, traveling, and reworking things over and over again."

His books *Crow Boy* (1955) and *Plenty to Watch* (1954; coauthored with his wife) also stem from his recollections of childhood. *Seashore Story* (1967) was rooted in a trip back to Japan. "Visiting there after 24 years, I felt myself as the character Urashima, the sad old man in the story. Every place I went to was so changed, all except for my peninsula. This did not change as it is, and always has been, so poor. Yet there was such a beautiful younger generation in Japan, much more than I expected."

The Yashimas live in a house on a hilltop outside Los Angeles in California. The house is furnished with early American furnishings and two cats and three dogs. He stands five feet eight inches tall, weighs 160 pounds, and sports a crewcut. "I like my hair even shorter than this, but people will think I am an ex-convict! People think I am cheerful, passionate, and positive toward life and art. When I am not so, I don't show myself to them! I like resting, playing with trees and flowers in the yard, and considering myself a wounded soldier. I like landscaping around the yard, and once in awhile I kick the ball just to strengthen my body. When I was young, I was a great sportsman. I mostly played soccer."

His son, Mako, is an actor and was nominated for the Academy Award in 1967 as best supporting actor for his performance in *The Sand Pebbles.* Momo is now a student at a state college in California, majoring in English literature. Besides illustrating books for children, Mr. Yashima directs the Yashima Art Institute where he teaches fundamental techniques and methods of art instruction.

His three favorite books are the ones that were selected as runner-ups for the Caldecott Awards — *Crow Boy,* the story of Chibi, a small boy in a Japanese village who is left out of everything at school because he is different; *Umbrella* (1958), a story of Momo, a young Japanese-American in New York who wants to use her new umbrella, and *Seashore Story,* a book retelling a Japanese legend in a contemporary setting. "In these stories," he stated, "my message was stronger than others, and

From THE CROW BOY by Taro Yashima, copyright 1955 by Mitsu and Taro Yashima. Permission of The Viking Press, Inc.

I worked harder on them than ever before. And I guess, since they have been so well-accepted, that people like them better than my others."

His style varies from book to book, but his illustrations give a unique luminosity to all of the beautiful books he has created.

ANOTHER BOOK BY MR. YASHIMA:

The Youngest One (Viking, 1962).

Margaret B. Young

THROUGH DEMONSTRATIONS, from the dramatic non-violent Civil Rights March on Washington in 1963 to the riots of the summers of 1967 and 1968, the United States has finally become aware of the black person and the problems he has faced for the past hundreds of years. Just as the U.S.S.R.'s launching of Sputnik in 1957 sparked the mass production of science books for children, the civil rights movements in the 60's has stimulated the publishing of material about the cultural heritage of black people.

In 1966 *The First Book of American Negroes* (Watts), appeared. It was written by Margaret B. Young, wife of the late Whitney M. Young, Jr., executive director of the National Urban League. It was Mrs. Young's first book. "A friend who had written for Franklin Watts, Inc., told them about me. Langston Hughes had done *The First Book of Negroes* in 1952, and they had wanted him to do another, updating events since 1954 and limiting it to Negroes in America. He was quite busy and didn't get to it, so they asked me to come in and talk about it, and there I was," she recalled.

"My approach to the book was determined a great deal by children's questions and events that were taking place in the

1960's. I knew there were a number of biographies, although certainly not enough, and also a few books with a historical bent. To me, children needed books that met them right now, today, and retraced in a logical sequence events and people who helped shape events, giving them an explanation of *why*. *The First Book of American Negroes* is not so much a book about *who* and *when* but *why*. For example, why is the educational pictures for Negro children as it is? To answer a question such as this meant tracing back from slavery, to no schools, separate schools, the National Association for the Advancement of Colored People's legal suits, and the 1954 Supreme Court decision. Another common question is, why do Negro people live in segregated areas? Well, whether it is Watts, Hough, or Chicago's South Side, the story of how Harlem developed has common threads with all these areas. I tried to treat other important aspects of living in the same way."

Mrs. Young has also authored two "Picture Life Books" — *The Picture Life of Martin Luther King, Jr.* (Watts, 1968) and *The Picture Life of Ralph Bunche* (Watts, 1968). She discussed each of these books. "I have an understandable deep emotional attachment to *The Picture Life of Martin Luther King, Jr.* It came out shortly before his assassination, and I have moving letters from teachers and little children expressing their affection for him and his work. It's a very hurting thing. (The book, now in its third printing, includes the assassination of Dr. King in April, 1968.) Dr. Ralph Bunche is a long, long idol of our family, so I think I felt honored and a little awed to be able to do a book on him. Being acquainted with both men made researching them pleasurable and a bit easy, because I already knew a great deal about them and simply had to think of a way to convey my feeling of their greatness to small children. I had worked with Dr. King's sister at Spelman College and taught his brother at summer school at Atlanta University, and my husband had worked with him and his father. Dr. King's mother let me use some pictures from their family album. I chose the photographs for both the King and the Bunche books. Dr. Bunche and his United Nations office were both very helpful. His teacher from New Mexico permitted me to use a class picture when he was a young boy; U.C.L.A. sent me a picture of him as a basketball star.

"Before I begin a book, I think about the subject; I can do this while I cook dinner! Then I start reading broadly to get a feel of what's out there, research-wise. I rarely even take notes during this period. Next I make a tentative outline, which usually becomes the permanent one. I then read, taking notes on the facts and ideas I need. I write a rough draft in longhand and rewrite the rough draft in longhand. Then comes the first typewritten draft, editing, and retyping before being sent to the editor."

Mrs. Young majored in English at Kentucky State College. "I had hoped to either teach or write or both. I taught freshman composition in a college for awhile and then went to the University of Minnesota for a master's degree in educational psychology. I trained for counseling but was aware that a better understanding of people would be useful if I ever went into writing. When the children were small and we were living in college communities, to keep busy and affluent, I used to type theses for students. I received a pretty good supply because word went around that not only would I type them, but I also couldn't resist the temptation to edit and sometimes advise! Even while I attended Aurora High School in Aurora, Illinois, I leaned toward the newspaper and yearbook staffs."

She speaks of herself as being "critical but in a truth-seeking way. I sometimes bend over backwards trying to be objective and examining all sides of a question. I don't like generalizing about races, religions, or classes of people. I like good conversation based on thoughts rather than emotions. I have a sense of humor but a rather dry one. I like punny types of jokes."

Mrs. Young loves the theatre; however, her busy life does not allow her to go too often. Mrs. Young also loves music of all kinds. They have a beagle, "a sweet, sort of stupid dog. It is my daughter's pet but somehow my responsibility."

Commenting on her own childhood years, she told me, "I had four sisters. While growing up I was old enough to remember something of the Depression years. Though we were poor for 'things,' our family did have the riches of a mother and a father who were strong on discipline and homework. I always liked to read. I skipped a grade in school, so I was younger than most of my class. In addition, I was physically small so I couldn't camouflage my age. Books became my friends; all kinds of books. There were some I couldn't check out from the branch library because of my age. I used to sneak in and stand among the stacks and read them there."

Mrs. Young lives in Westchester County, New York. "It's not a lavish house, just comfortable without nearly enough bookshelves." She has two daughters, Lauren, 16, a junior at New Rochelle High School, and Marcia, 22, who recently married and is attending the University of Iowa.

"Actually my interest and preoccupation with children developed as our children did. Naturally I read to them a lot, and we would make up stories. I also became alert to their questions, especially during the seven years we lived in Atlanta, Georgia. Shortly after our move to Georgia from Nebraska, Marcia asked, 'Why can't we eat downtown?' I asked a new Atlanta friend what she told her seven-year-old son when he asked a similar question. She replied, 'He has never eaten downtown, so he doesn't ask!'"

Mrs. Young finds children unusually stimulating and appealing. "They have so much feeling, and in them there is so much hope. That's why I like to write for them."

Margaret Young's life and work are dedicated to the hope that one day soon all children will be able to live, work, and eat together downtown.

Herbert S. Zim
Sonia Bleeker

HERBERT S. ZIM HAS to his credit approximately 80 books written for children and 20 series of books that he has edited. He has spent over 30 years teaching in the fields of science and science education and has served as a consultant on many national committees. His work has spanned the range from pre-kindergarten through the university level. "Writing is not my major occupation, however," he declared. "I have many fields of endeavor which, while related, take up a good deal more of my time."

Despite this, sales of his books have reached well past the 40 million mark and are increasing at the rate of two or three million a year. Approximately 25 of his books have been translated into foreign languages. He commented, "I think I am probably the only author of children's books who has had something translated into Navajo, the language of the largest tribe of Southwest Indians."

Dr. Zim told me, "I hardly know when I began writing. As a child I had things published in newspapers and won prizes in writing contests. Actually I've taken no courses in writing or journalism other than courses normally required during a college education. About 1940 I was doing some experimental work with sex education involving a fifth-grade class. My wife, Sonia Bleeker, asked me to write this up; it became my first book, *Mice, Men and Elephants* (Harcourt, 1942). The book essentially deals with the fundamental characteristics of mammals; these characteristics include factors of intelligence and reproduction, two areas in which young adolescents are specifically interested. It provided a core around which our developmental work was centered. Clifton Fadiman read the manuscript, first to himself and then to his own children, liked it, wrote me and said so, and immediately thereafter Harcourt published it."

Several other books were developed from Dr. Zim's experimental teaching, and nearly all of his work has been based on data derived from his *Study of the Scientific Interests and Activities of Adolescents,* which was published in 1940. *Mice, Men and Elephants* and *Codes and Secret Writing* (Morrow, 1948) have a special appeal to the author because they were developed directly with young people in school situations.

Dr. Zim commented on his work habits, "As far as actual working habits are concerned, my general pattern is to review the content area, spending considerable time in reading and re-reading background material. While doing this, I take notes and gradually organize these notes into a tentative pattern for the book. Since most of my books are written to space requirements, a process of selection, tightening, and combining is also involved to cover the material within the limitations that have been set up by publishers. Then I go to work either at the typewriter or on the dictaphone, depending on the book I am doing. I make a rough draft and rework it at least two or three times; with some books I plan the layouts and illustrations and make a rough dummy before I have the thing well at hand."

Dr. Zim did all of his study, both graduate and undergraduate, at Teachers College, Columbia University, in New York. His wife, also a writer, came to the United States from Russia as a child. Dr. Bleeker has created approximately 30 books on anthropology for children, plus other types of books and translations. "We have, until recently, had available a library of 7–8,000 books and many files of pamphlets and other research materials so that we had a good deal of printed resource material on hand. Often our research will involve visits to museums, zoos, botanic gardens, travel in different areas of this country and abroad, and interviewing people; in short, following whatever pattern is dictated by the subject at hand," Dr. Zim explained.

He was born in New York City, on July 12, 1909. During his childhood, his residence changed with the needs of his father who was a painter, sculptor, and etcher. He and his wife now live on Plantation Key, south of Key Largo in the Florida Keys, in a large, modern house that is practically in the Atlantic Ocean.

"At the time I was professor of education at the University of Illinois, I discovered that more and more administrative duties were handed my way; with this ahead, Sunnie and I thought of finding a place where we could work more on books and sever our connections with the administrative aspects of academic life. At that time the Everglades National Park was being created; since I had worked with the Fish and Wildlife Service, I wanted to go down and see the area with the hope of writing something about it. Eventually we did go down into the area, and from the Everglades, drove down to the Keys. When the time came for us to make our choice, we debated strongly between the area around Patagonia in southwestern Arizona and the Keys, choosing the latter because of the climate and because it was relatively closer to New York and publishing contacts. We've never regretted our choice, though we still like the Southwest immensely and go there as often as we can."

The Zim's house is strikingly modern, strong and simple in design. It houses the workrooms, library, and several collections about which Dr. Zim said, "Sunnie and I have been traveling for some 40 years. During our early travels we began our collection of American Indian artifacts, mainly from the West and the Southwest. Later we moved farther south into Mexico, Central America, and northern South America, extending the collections to a variety of pre-Columbia materials collected in the field and obtained from dealers." A good part of this collection has already been given to the Logan Museum of Anthropology at Beloit College, to the University of Illinois, to the Milwaukee Public Museum, and to other institutions.

"We began our collection of African materials only about five years ago. We've picked up about 20 pieces for our collection in London. Most of the African material comes from the West Coast of Africa, from such tribes as the Uruba, Dogon, Ashanti, Fahn, and others in the Congo and along the Ivory and Gold Coasts," he continued.

Other artwork in their home include paintings by people who have illustrated their books, Mexican artists, and artists in Europe and Asia. There are also many paintings and sculptures by Dr. Zim's father, who had won a number of awards.

For leisure the Zims enjoy boating and fishing. "Both of these are right at our front door. We do a good deal of gardening and planting. We have a pet macaw that receives our attention, and numerous visitors come in from all over the world to share their experiences with us." They have two sons, Aldwin, 26, and Roger, 23.

SOME OTHER BOOKS BY DR. ZIM:

How Things Grow (Morrow, 1960).
Fossils (Putnam, 1962).
Fishing (Putnam, 1965).
Sharks (Morrow, 1966).
Non-Flowering Plants (Putnam, 1967).

SOME OTHER BOOKS BY DR. BLEEKER (All Morrow):

Ashanti of Ghana (1966).
Pygmies: Africans of the Congo Forest (1968).
Ibo of Biafra (1969).

Miss Bleeker died on November 13, 1971.

Charlotte Zolotow

IF ONE WERE TO READ THE 40-plus books that Charlotte Zolotow (*zol* uh tou; rhymes with "how") has written over the past 24 years, one would have an almost-complete course in the development and psychology of the very young child. Mrs. Zolotow, who never formally taught children and did not major in education in her college career, states "I have always been interested in writing and in children. Jean Piaget was one of my favorite reading people. Writing came quite naturally to me. I can recall winning a silver pencil in grade three for a composition I wrote. Actually, all I could do was write," she laughed. "I couldn't add or subtract, nor could I remember names and dates!"

Mrs. Zolotow was born in Norfolk, Virginia; her family settled in New York City while she was still a young girl. She attended the New York City public schools and went on to study literature at the University of Wisconsin. At the University she met her husband-writer, Maurice Zolotow. "While in college I wrote many stories; however, the stories were *about* children, not *for* them. After our marriage I worked at several jobs. It was not until I began working at Harper and Row that I started to write books for children. I was an assistant to Ursula Nordstrom, the editor of juvenile books. It was she who encouraged me to expand an idea I had about being in a park for 24 hours. I wrote her a memo on the idea, later expanded it, and I had my first book, *The Park Book* (Harper, 1944). It was illustrated by H. A. Rey.

"I left Harper to raise a family. I managed to continue to write despite pots boiling over, poodles barking, Maurice working in the attic, and my two children running underfoot."

Maurice Zolotow is known for his writings on theatrical personalities such as Alfred Lunt, Lynn Fontanne, and the late Marilyn Monroe. Mrs. Zolotow told me an anecdote about her son that occurred when he was in the seventh grade. "When Stephen's teacher heard his last name, she remarked something to the effect, 'Oh, your mother does those charming books for little children.'

" 'Yes,' replied Stephen, 'she does. But my *father* writes about Marilyn Monroe!' "

Mrs. Zolotow's books grow from both her own distinct memories of childhood and from watching her own children grow up. *Do You Know What I'll Do?* (Harper, 1958), is her favorite book; *Big Brother* (Harper, 1960) and *If It Weren't for You* (Harper, 1966) keenly depict sibling rivalry and sibling relationships; *The Storm Book* (Harper, 1952) developed from a visit by a young friend.

"A young friend of Stephen's was visiting us in New York when a very bad storm broke out," she related. The child was petrified. I held her in my lap, comforted her, and whispered things such as, 'Look how pretty it is,' and 'It will be over very soon.' I loved storms as a child. I guess I wasn't smart enough to be afraid of them!" *The Storm Book* simply describes the storm from the stillness before it comes to the beautiful rainbow it produces when it has gone. The text, illustrated by Margaret Bloy Graham, was runner-up for the Caldecott Medal in 1953. *Mr. Rabbit and the Lovely Present* (Harper, 1962), illustrated by Maurice Sendak, was a runner-up for the Caldecott Award in 1963.

Regarding children, Mrs. Zolotow commented, "I don't think that adults take children seriously; they don't take their humor seriously; they don't respect children enough. It's something we must do. One of the reasons I love my work here at Harper so much is that I am, and adore being, involved with young talent."

The Zolotows live in Hastings-on-Hudson, New York, in a 60-year-old house. "The house is not old enough to be an antique but old enough to need many repairs," she laughed. She loves to garden and has her own herb garden where she grows dill and parsley, a vegetable garden, and a garden that sprouts flowering plants. "It's hard for me to choose between growing vegetables and growing flowers. I love them both. I love anything that grows." She also likes to cook. She hates the city: "There are no flowers and no trees!"

Mrs. Zolotow returned to Harper's junior books' department several years ago; she is currently a senior editor. Her office reflects her love of gardening. Here and there is a vibrant red rose, a sprig of leaves, and flowering plants. They all add a lovely background to this truly great author who has given us so much to be thankful for in the field of literature for the very young child.

SOME OTHER BOOKS BY MRS. ZOLOTOW:

The Sleeping Book (Lothrop, 1958).
The Bunny Who Found Easter (Parnassus, 1959).
The White Marble (Abelard, 1963).
The Quarreling Book (Harper, 1963).
My Friend John (Harper, 1968).
The Hating Book (Harper, 1969).

Appendix

338

The Newbery Medal is named in honor of John Newbery, an 18th century bookseller and publisher. The Medal is presented annually by a committee of the Children's Service Division of the American Library Association to "the author of the most distinguished contribution to American literature for children." These books are primarily for older children. The list below cites the year the book received the award, the title, the author and publisher.

Note: * denotes the author is included in this volume; ** denotes that the author is mentioned.

1922   *The Story of Mankind*. Hendrik Van Loon. Boni & Liveright.**
1923   *The Voyages of Doctor Dolittle*. Hugh Lofting. Lippincott.
1924   *The Dark Frigate*. Charles Boardman Hawes. Little, Brown.
1925   *Tales from the Silver Lands*. Charles J. Finger. Doubleday.
1926   *Shen of the Sea*. Arthur Bowie Chrisman. Dutton.
1927   *Smoky, the Cowhorse*. Will James. Scribner.
1928   *Gay Neck*. Dhan Gopal Mukerji. Dutton.
1929   *Trumpeter of Krakow*. Eric P. Kelly. Macmillan.
1930   *Hitty, Her First Hundred Years*. Rachel Field. Macmillan.
1931   *The Cat Who Went to Heaven*. Elizabeth Coatsworth. Macmillan.
1932   *Waterless Mountain*. Laura Adams Armer. McKay.
1933   *Yung Fu of the Upper Yangtze*. Elizabeth Foreman. Holt.
1934   *Invincible Louisa*. Corneila Meigs. Little, Brown.
1935   *Dobry*. Monica Shannon. Viking.
1936   *Caddie Woodlawn*. Carol Ryrie Brink. Macmillan.
1937   *Roller Skates*. Ruth Sawyer. Viking.**
1938   *The White Stag*. Kate Seredy. Viking.**
1939   *Thimble Summer*. Elizabeth Enright. Holt.
1940   *Daniel Boone*. James H. Daugherty. Viking.*
1941   *Call It Courage*. Armstrong Sperry. Macmillan.
1942   *The Matchlock Gun*. Walter D. Edmonds. Dodd, Mead.
1943   *Adam of the Road*. Elizabeth Janet Gray. Viking.
1944   *Johnny Tremain*. Esther Forbes. Houghton.
1945   *Rabbit Hill*. Robert Lawson. Viking.**
1946   *Strawberry Girl*. Lois Lenski. Lippincott.*
1947   *Miss Hickory*. Carolyn Sherwin Bailey. Viking.
1948   *The Twenty-One Balloons*. William Pene du Bois. Viking.
1949   *King of the Wind*. Marguerite Henry. Rand McNally.

THE LEWIS CARROLL SHELF AWARD

This annual award was established in 1958 by the University of Wisconsin School of Education and cooperaitng state organizations "to select those books worthy enough to sit on the shelf with *Alice in Wonderland.*" Publishers select those books they feel should receive the award. These are then submitted to a committee of five representative librarians, teachers, parents, and writers. A unanimous vote from this committee is necessary to qualify for the award. The list below cites only those books that are by authors and/or illustrators in this volume.

Note: * denotes that the author or illustrator is included in this volume; ** denotes that the author or illustrator is mentioned.

1958   *Little House in the Big Woods.* Laura Ingalls Wilder.
Harper, 1932, 1953.**

Horton Hatches the Egg. Dr. Seuss. Random House, 1940.*
1959   *The Five Chinese Brothers.* Claire Huchet Bishop. Coward-
McCann, 1938.*

The Courage of Sarah Noble. Alice Dalgliesh. Scribner's, 1954.**

The White Stag. Kate Seredy. Viking, 1937.**
1960   *Curious George Takes a Job.* H. A. Rey. Houghton Mifflin, 1947.*

Onion John. Joseph Krumgold. Crowell, 1959.**
1961   *And to Think That I Saw It on Mulberry Street.* Dr. Seuss.
Vanguard, 1937.*

Ben and Me. Robert Lawson. Little-Brown, 1939.**

The Moffats. Eleanor Estes. Harcourt, 1941.**
1962   *Inch by Inch.* Leo Lionni. Obolensky, 1960.*
1963   *The Griffin and the Minor Canon.* Maurice Sendak. Holt, 1963.*

Rabbit Hill. Robert Lawson. Viking, 1945.**

The Wheel on the School. Meindert De Jong. Harper, 1954.**
1964   *Roller Skates.* Ruth Sawyer. Viking, 1936.**

Where the Wild Things Are. Maurice Sendak. Harper, 1963.*
1965   *A Wrinkle in Time.* Madeleine L'Engle. Farrar, 1962.**
1966   *Once a Mouse.* Marcia Brown. Scribner, 1961.*

1968   *Drummer Hoff.* Barbara Emberly. Prentice-Hall, 1967.*

The Fiddler of High Lonesome. Brinton Turkle. Viking, 1968.*
1969   *Little Toot.* Hardie Gramatky. Putnam, 1939.*

THE KATE GREENAWAY MEDAL

This award was established by the Library Association of England
in 1955 for the most distinguished illustrated book published in Great
Britain. The award was withheld the first year and awarded for the
first time in 1957 for a book published in 1956. American publishers are
given in parentheses. Those listed below are included in this volume:

1963   *Brian Wildsmith's ABC.* Brian Wildsmith. (Franklin Watts)
International.
1967   *The Mother Goose Treasury.* Raymond Briggs. (Coward-Mc-
Cann). Lund, Humphries.

Index: Names and Titles

Editor's Note: The names indexed are those of deceased writers and illustrators, book people who were not interviewed but are mentioned, editors of publishers' departments of children's books, and interviewees who are cited in interviews other than their own (refer to the contents for all full interviews). Book and series titles are those about which some fact is given; titles merely listed within or at the end of the interviews are not indexed.

346

347